Constitutionalism and Religion

ELGAR MONOGRAPHS IN CONSTITUTIONAL AND ADMINISTRATIVE LAW

Series Editors: Rosalind Dixon, *University of New South Wales, Australia,* Susan Rose-Ackerman, *Yale University* and Mark Tushnet, *Harvard University, USA*

Constitutions are a country's most important legal document, laying the foundation not just for politics, but for all other areas of law. They allocate power among different levels and branches of government, record and promote a society's shared values, and protect the rights of citizens. Countries around the world are adopting written constitutions, though what defines a constitution is evolving to include a variety of sources beyond canonical texts, such as political conventions, statutes, judicial decisions and administrative law norms.

This cosmopolitan monograph series provides a forum for the best and most original scholarship in constitutional and administrative law, with each book offering an international, comparative or multi-jurisdictional approach to this complex and fascinating field of research.

Titles in the series include:

Political Technology and the Erosion of the Rule of Law
Normalizing the State of Exception
Günter Frankenberg

Constitutional Sunsets and Experimental Legislation
A Comparative Perspective
Sofia Ranchordás

Constitutionalism and Religion
Francois Venter

The Arab Spring
An Essay on Revolution and Constitutionalism
Antoni Abat i Ninet and Mark Tushnet

American Judicial Power
The State Court Perspective
Michael L. Buenger and Paul J. De Muniz

Citizen Journalists
Newer Media, Republican Moments and the Constitution
Ian Cram

Constitutionalism and Religion

Francois Venter

Potchefstroom Campus, North-West University, South Africa

ELGAR MONOGRAPHS IN CONSTITUTIONAL AND
ADMINISTRATIVE LAW

Edward Elgar
PUBLISHING

Cheltenham, UK • Northampton, MA, USA

© Francois Venter 2015

All rights reserved. No part of this publication may be reproduced, stored in a retrieval system or transmitted in any form or by any means, electronic, mechanical or photocopying, recording, or otherwise without the prior permission of the publisher.

Published by
Edward Elgar Publishing Limited
The Lypiatts
15 Lansdown Road
Cheltenham
Glos GL50 2JA
UK

Edward Elgar Publishing, Inc.
William Pratt House
9 Dewey Court
Northampton
Massachusetts 01060
USA

A catalogue record for this book
is available from the British Library

Library of Congress Control Number: 2015943013

This book is available electronically in the Elgaronline
Law subject collection
DOI 10.4337/9781785361623

ISBN 978 1 78536 161 6 (cased)
ISBN 978 1 78536 162 3 (eBook)

Typeset by Columns Design XML Ltd, Reading
Printed and bound in Great Britain by TJ International Ltd, Padstow

Contents

Preface	vii
Table of cases	ix
Introduction	1

PART I RELIGION, THE STATE AND CONSTITUTIONALISM

1.	The roots of a relationship: religion, the state and its power	9
	1.1 An historic tie	9
	1.2 Religion: the term	9
	1.3 Law and religion	13
	1.4 Church and state	20
	1.5 Power and justice	26
	1.6 A knot that cannot be untied	29
2.	Globalization, constitutional law and religion	31
	2.1 Globalization and constitutional law	31
	2.2 Constitutional law and constitutional comparison	34
	2.3 Effects of globalization on constitutional law	39
	2.4 Globalization and religion	45
3.	Constitutionalism	46
	3.1 Constitutionalism as standard and *tertium comparationis*	47
	3.2 The domestic meaning of 'constitutionalism'	52
	3.3 Internationalization of constitutionalism	69
	3.4 Constitutionalism and the constitutional state	76
	3.5 Constitutionalism as comparative touchstone	79

PART II RELIGION IN LAW

4.	Religion in constitutions	87
	4.1 Ubiquity of religion in constitutions	87
	4.2 Non-establishment constitutions	89
	4.3 Dubious constitutional protection of religion	92
	4.4 Historical church/state alliances	96

	4.5 Religion in the state amidst globalization	102
	4.6 Religion and constitutionalism	108
5.	Religion in international law	111
	5.1 Religion in the development of international law	111
	5.2 Religion in international law	113
	5.3 Religion in international diplomacy and political battles	122
	5.4 Religious non-state international actors	125
	5.5 Conclusion	127
6.	Travails of the judges in religious cases	129
	6.1 Introduction	129
	6.2 General functions of the state with incidental religious implications	131
	6.3 State-initiated actions having direct religious implications	159
	6.4 Governing activities initiated from religious perspectives	166
	6.5 What judges have in common in religious adjudication	175

PART III OBLIGATIONS OF THE CONSTITUTIONAL STATE IN RELIGIOUS MATTERS

7.	The weaknesses of contemporary statehood in the face of religious pluralism	181
	7.1 Current fortunes of statehood	181
	7.2 Responses to migration	199
	7.3 Secularism as the 'natural' response	202
	7.4 The return of religion	208
8.	The demands of constitutionalism regarding religion	212
	8.1 Assumptions about constitutionalism and religion	213
	8.2 Elements of constitutionalism germane to religion	214
	8.3 The need for the constitutional state to recognize the social relevance of religion	219
	8.4 Directive considerations of constitutionalism regarding religion	221
9.	A post-secular approach to religious pluralism	223
	9.1 Supplanting secularism with constitutionalism	223
	9.2 The potential weakness of constitutionalism	229
	9.3 Moving from neutrality to objectivity	237

Bibliography 241
Index 259

Preface[1]

This book emerged from the author's engagement (the nature of which is reflected in my publications listed in the Bibliography) with constitutional comparison. The explosive surge of comparative activity in the context of public (especially constitutional) law must no doubt be ascribed, at least partially, to the phenomenon often hazily referred to as 'globalization'. Markers of globalization such as the mobility of humanity across borders, hitherto unprecedented in history, have perceptible, though sometimes opaque, consequences for our understanding of the contemporary state, its powers, responsibilities and foundations. One of these consequences is the increasing prevalence of religious pluralism in the populations of most states of the 21st Century. Another indicator of globalization is the deepening penetration of constitutional language emerging from the history of the state in the 'Western' world into the global vernacular. A prominent example of this is the notion of 'constitutionalism', which is widely used as a cipher for a desirable state of affairs in any country, but whose meaning is vague, at least around its edges.

To broach, as is the present intention, the theme of an appropriate response for the constitutional state to the difficulties arising from religious pluralism without providing an outline of the meaning in which key concepts such as 'religion', 'globalization', 'constitutional comparison' and especially 'constitutionalism' are used, would be futile. Simply using homonymic constitutional terminology without clarifying one's choice of meaning (incidentally a phenomenon that occurs too often in constitutional writing) is to contribute to confusion rather than elucidation. Therefore, the earlier chapters of this book are dedicated to outline and solidify the conceptual context within which the theme is addressed in the later parts.

Formulating uncontested definitions for constitutional notions and producing unopposed solutions to legal problems will always be an

---

[1] Venter, F., 2015, *Constitutionalism and Religion*, Edward Elgar, Cheltenham, was accepted for publication following a double-blind peer review process conducted by the Publisher.

unreachable objective. However, definition and solution are essential components of the lifeblood of legal scholarship, because they create a framework for the discussion, disputation and production of answers to intractable questions. In the final chapter lines drawn from the preceding delineation of the meaning of key concepts, comparative analyses of current practice, and the interpretation of global trends regarding the state and religion, are drawn together. The result is a suggestion for the direction in which constitutional states may seek an improved approach to religious pluralism in the interests of justice. It is hoped that the suggestion merits consideration on the agenda of constitutionalism and that its discussion among readers will bring about its further refinement.

The regional or local perspective from which constitutional comparison is undertaken can determine its nature and goals. More often than not, comparatists seek to strengthen their arguments for the improvement of their home legal order by means of their description and analysis of comparative materials. Such is a legitimate approach, but not one that is followed here. The themes and questions addressed here so penetrate the realities prevalent in so many jurisdictions that the comparative perspective is not one specifically focused on the author's native environment (South Africa). Globalization has indeed caused constitutionalism and religious pluralism to be universal phenomena calling for intensive consideration and improved solutions to the problems generated thereby in all jurisdictions.

I am grateful to Edward Elgar Publishing for the professional processing of the manuscript, including its expeditious submission to rigorous prior peer review. I have benefited much from the comments of the three reviewers that were provided to me anonymously by the publisher before finally submitting the text for publication.

The research necessary for the writing of this book was made possible by the financial support generously made available by the Alexander von Humboldt Foundation, the Max Planck Society and the National Research Foundation. The opinions, findings and conclusions reflected here are however exclusively those of the author and therefore do not in any way bind or commit any of the funding institutions.

This book is dedicated to my children and grandchildren with the wish that their lives will not be blemished by secular neutrality.

Francois Venter
North-West University
Potchefstroom
March 2015

Table of cases

CANADA

Alberta v Hutterian Brethren of Wilson Colony, [2009] 2 S.C.R. 567 148
Bruker v Markovitz, [2007] 3 S.C.R. 607 148
Canadian Civil Liberties Assn. v Ontario (Minister of Education) (1990), 71 O.R.
  (2d) 341 135
Chamberlain v Surrey School District No. 36 [2002] 4 S.C.R. 710 .... 135, 138
S.L. and D.J. v Commission scolaire des Chênes and Attorney General of Quebec
  2012 SCC 7, [2012] 1 S.C.R. 235 .... 134–41, 149
Loyola High School v Quebec (Attorney General) 2015 SCC 12 139
McAteer v Attorney General of Canada 117 O.R. (3d) 353 148–9
Québec (Procureur général) c. Loyola High School 2012 QCCA 2139 139
R v Big M Drug Mart Ltd, [1985] 1 S.C.R. 295 134
R v Oakes (1986) 26 DLR (4th) 200 38
Syndicat Northcrest v Amselem, 2004 SCC 47, [2004] 2 S.C.R. 551 173–4
Zylberberg v Sudbury Board of Education (Director) (1988), 65 O.R. (2d) 641 ...134

EUROPEAN COURT OF HUMAN RIGHTS

Bayatyan v Armenia App no. 23459/03 (ECHR, Grand Chamber, 7 July
  2011) 156–7
Bukharatyan v Armenia App no. 37819/03 (ECHR, 10 January 2012) 156–7
Campbell and Cosans v the United Kingdom App no. 7511/76 (ECHR, 25 February
  1982) 15
Cha'are Shalom Ve Tsedek v France [GC] App no. 27417/95 (ECHR, 27 June
  2000) 151–2
Eweida and Others v the United Kingdom App nos 48420/10, 59842/10, 51671/10
  and 36516/10 (ECHR, 27 May 2013) 15, 162, 170
Grzelak v Poland App no. 7710/02 (ECHR, 22 November 2010) 147
Kokkinakis v Greece App. no. 14307/88 (ECHR, 25 May 1993) 95
Lautsi v Italy App. no. 30814/06 (ECHR, 3 November 2009) 147
Lautsi v Italy App. no. 30814/06 (ECHR, Grand Chamber, 18 March 2011) 147
N.A.N.S. v Sweden EUCtHR App. no. 68411/10 (ECHR, 27 June 2013) 150
Otto-Preminger-Institut v Austria EuCtHR App no. 13470/87 (ECHR, 20
  September 1994) 174
Savez Crkava 'Riječ Života' v Croatia App no. 7798/08 (ECHR, 9 March 2011)..154
Schilder v the Netherlands App no. 2158/12 (ECHR, 16 October 2012) 153
Ülke v Turkey App no. 39437/98 (ECHR, 24 April 2006) 156

FRANCE

Alsace-Lorraine Conseil Constitutionnel, Decision no. 2012-297 QPC: JO 23 of 21 February 2013...159–60
Sunday Rest Conseil Constitutionnel Decision no. 2009-588 of 6 August 2009... 165

GERMANY

BverfG, 2 BvR 1693/04, 31.5.2006..144–5, 155
BverfGE 7,198, 15.1.1958..38
BverfGE 19,206, 14.12.1965...100
BverfGE 46,73, 11.10.1977..161
BVerfGE 52,223, 16.10.1979 143
BVerfGE 93,1, 16.05.1995 145
BVerfGE 122,89, 28.10.2008 173
BVerwG 6 C 25.12, 11.9.2013...172
VerfGH 60,1 (Bayern), 15.1.2007..147

ISRAEL

Design 22 Shark Deluxe Furniture Ltd v Rosenzweig 2005(1) Isr. L. Reps. 340 [2005]...164

NEW ZEALAND

Takamore v Clarke [2012] NZSC 116 167

SOUTH AFRICA

Christian Education South Africa v Minister of Education 2000 (4) SA 757 (CC) 14, 158–9
Department of Correctional Services v Police and Prisons Civil Rights Union (POPCRU) 2013 (4) SA 176 (SCA)..155
Du Plessis v De Klerk 1996 3 SA 850 (CC) 197
Garden Cities Incorporated Association not for Gain v Northpine Islamic Society 1999 (2) SA 268 (C)..152
MEC for Education, KwaZulu-Natal v Pillay 2008 (1) SA 474 (CC)....................147
Prince v President, Cape Law Society 2002 (2) SA 794 (CC)..............................166
S v Lawrence; S v Negal; S v Solberg 1997 (4) SA 1176 (CC)..............................165
S v Makwanyane 1995 (3) SA 391 (CC) 139
Smit NO v King Goodwill Zwelithini Kabhekuzulu 2009 JDR 1361 (KZP) (Juta's unreported judgments, case no. 10237/2009)..150

Strydom v Nederduitse Gereformeerde Gemeente, Moreleta Park 2009 (4) SA 510
(EqC) 163

TANZANIA

Dibagula v Republic (Court of Appeal 24/08/2001) accessible at http://
www.interights.org/commonwealth-and-international-law-document/3079/
index.html (accessed 7 February 2014)...174

UGANDA

Sharon v Makerere University (Supreme Court, 18/08/2006) accessible at http://
www.interights.org/commonwealth-and-international-law-document/3362/
index.html (accessed 5 February 2014)...157

UNITED KINGDOM

Aston Cantlow and Wilmcote with Billsley Parochial Church Council v Wallbank
[2001] EWCA Civ 713 and [2003] UKHL 37 97
Calvin v Smith and Another (1608) 7 Co Rep 1a 38
Mandla v Dowell Lee [1983] 2 AC 548 147
R v Registrar General, Ex p Segerdal [1970] 2 QB 697...169
R (on application of Hodkin) v Registrar General of Births, Deaths and Marriages
decided on 11 December 2013, available at http://www.bailii.org/uk/cases/
UKSC/2013/77.html (accessed 29 January 2014) 13, 169

UNITED STATES

Lemon v Kurtzman 403 U.S. 602 (1971)..24–5
Lynch v Donnelly 465 U.S. 668, 691 (1984) 24
Prince v Massachusetts 321 US 158 (1944) 165...158
Marbury v Madison 5 U.S. (1Cranch) 137 (1803) 38

Introduction

The key question that is addressed in this book is how the notion 'constitutionalism' can provide the constitutional state with functional standards according to which the challenges of religious pluralism may be dealt with justly.

Why this is a relevant question is determined by various factors. In 1991 M.H.A. Reisman wrote perceptively:[1]

> Since the Iranian Revolution, a new vocabulary and a new set of demands appear to have found an enduring place in discussions about international politics and law. They have generated curiosity about and a renewed scholarly interest in religion and its potentially explosive political effect on our science-based civilization, which takes pride in cultivating the capacity for sophisticated, rational and logical thoughts and which has, in many ways replaced supernatural beliefs with scientific theories.

Since then 'our science-based civilization' has on the one hand continued on the road of an exponential progression in scientific and technological advances, while on the other hand the world has seen a concomitant escalation of religiosity, probably enhanced by religion-related conflict and by the growth of religious pluralism in the global demography.

These developments have not only attracted renewed interest in issues related to religion in the social sciences and humanities, but are also quite pronounced among natural scientists. To name but two examples: the Human Genome Project was brought to fruition under the rival leadership of both a Christian theist, Francis Collins and an atheist, Craig Venter (no relation of the author); and a well-publicized and fiery disputation in books and public media has been raging for some years between the Christian Oxford mathematician, John Lennox and the atheistic Oxford biologist, Richard Dawkins over the question whether religion should be an influence in science.

Decisions over how to teach children about evolution and religion, if religious instruction should be undertaken in public schools and if

---

[1] Reisman (1991) 107.

religious symbols and dress in the classroom or on uniforms should be allowed or prohibited, have led to hard-fought litigation in many countries.

Religious pluralism is progressively becoming a characteristic of the populations of most states; rather the norm than the exception. This is a fact with which constitutions, legislatures, governments, courts and societies have to deal in the 21st Century. Being inherently controversial and complex, the resurgence of religion as an overt motivation for social behaviour is a reality with which many in authority would prefer not to have to deal. Not surprisingly, therefore, legislative, judicial and administrative evasion of the need to take a clear stance on religious controversy is in evidence around the world. Some seek answers in state neutrality, others in subtle or express religious preferentialism.

Clearly neither avoidance nor preferentialism offers a reliable route to the achievement of justice. In a world whose human (and therefore religious) demography is in constantly accelerating flux, securing and preserving optimal fairness and justice for all must be a prime goal for the enlightened state. The question with which the world of constitutional government is therefore increasingly being confronted is whether a just approach can be developed for dealing with the challenges of religious pluralism.

Despite the endeavours of some to extricate religion from the sphere of law, the linkage is historic, evident and indisputable. Through the ages states have responded differently to the phenomenon that the governed populace is not only religious but also diverse in its religious beliefs and structures. Simultaneously some global standards for good governance and democratic constitutional structuring of the contemporary state are receiving broadening acceptance, if not always in practice, at least rhetorically. Regional, supra-national and international legal norms intended to promote religious accommodation are also growing in volume. Finding the desired balance between denial that the state has a key role to play in dealing with religious pluralism and active utilization of the law to promote a particular religion is therefore a topical challenge.

The effects of religious migration in a globalizing world, a comparative critique of the merits and shortcomings of approaches to the religious pluralism of contemporary constitutional states, some influences of supra-national and international law on the subject and suggestions regarding the obligations of the 21st Century constitutional state in these matters are addressed here. A progression from factual description to principled evaluation via normative and theoretical analysis is presented.

Religion is pervasive. Consequently not many aspects of individual or social life can be isolated from its effects. Drawing up and discussing a comprehensive catalogue of instances of situations and contexts within which the state may be challenged to deal with issues of potential religious conflict is not possible, but a review of jurisprudence goes some way towards exposing the extent of the range of issues that regularly arise in this regard. Although respect for or infringement of the right to religious freedom is a matter that inevitably comes up in such a discourse, there is much more to it: various other individual and social interests and functions of the state are involved.

The difficulties arising from religious issues are not limited either to the global North or to the South, to the first world or the third world, or to established or new democracies. Even a cursory glance at the history and current practices in many countries shows that clear-cut answers to the constitutional state's responsibilities regarding religion are not readily available, and that courts, legislatures, governments and even scholars often avoid the apparently intractable problems attending the matter.

In the Christian era of Europe, which was also the era of the emergence of the nation state, it was not only possible, but also demanded by society, that the dominant religious sentiments expressed by Christianity in its various configurations be respected, protected and supported by emperors, kings and governments. The occurrence of long-lasting and widespread wars among European Christians, frequently founded upon real or supposed religious differences, makes it clear that it was and still is difficult enough to deal with pluralism within one and the same belief system. This is currently also being demonstrated by the fierce factionalism among various Islamic sects.

In the course of history, conflict across fundamentally different systems, especially between Christianity and Islam, was exacerbated by raw struggles for territorial and political power. In short, the subjective religious partisanship of the rulers was understood to be justified. With the exception of some of the remaining Islamic theocracies, republics and kingdoms, that is no longer the case. The religious pluralism of the populations of most states in the 21st Century is such that religiously partial governance brings about injustice towards significant components of society adhering to religions that are not favoured by the state. Whereas this was not seen to be a problem in Europe in the pre-Enlightenment Christian era, contemporary demands on the constitutional state do not countenance systemic injustice and discrimination in any form. The Christian era was followed by a period of secularism, and the world has now entered into a post-secular phase – leaving the law and the state with many questions.

Questions that are addressed in this book include the following:

- What does 'religion' mean?
- What is the relationship between law and religion?
- What are the effects of globalization on constitutional law and constitutional comparison, in particular regarding religious pluralism?
- How are state sovereignty and citizenship changing and how do these changes affect religion?
- What are the elements of universalized constitutionalism?
- What are the typical forms in which constitutions deal with religion?
- How does religion impact on international law and *vice versa*?
- How do judges approach cases involving religion around the world?
- How do contemporary constitutional states respond to religious pluralism, and are established constitutional concepts such as the social contract, constituent power and the counter-majoritarian dilemma still relevant?
- What does constitutionalism demand of the constitutional state regarding religion?
- Where might the beginnings of a better solution than secular neutrality be sought?

It is hoped that the raising of these questions and the suggested responses to them will promote further debate and discussion of the urgent issues surrounding the link that is drawn here between constitutionalism and religion.

The book is divided into three parts, each consisting of three chapters. Part I deals with religion, the state and constitutionalism. Chapter 1 is intended to expose the ties between religion and the state. Chapter 2 touches on the effects of globalization on constitutional law, and constitutional comparison and its relevance to religious pluralism as an issue in constitutional law. As part of the effort to identify a conceptual space within which just responses by the state to the problems generated by religious pluralism may be sought, Chapter 3 is an endeavour to clarify the meaning of the rather elusive notion of 'constitutionalism' in order to render it useful.

Part II investigates contemporary modes in which law deals with religion. Chapter 4 focuses on constitutional approaches to religion, and Chapter 5 describes the position that religion takes in international law. Chapter 6 traverses the extensive territory covered by the jurisprudence of a range of courts in religious cases around the world. This overview of judgments, selected for their demonstrative value as indicators of the nature of law and religion issues, particularly highlights the difficulties that arise in all regions of this globalized world when law is called upon to deal with religion.

In Part III the possibility of moving towards solutions more satisfactory than the usual is explored. Chapter 7 looks critically at the inadequate responses that constitutional states make when they deal with unavoidable religious questions against the background of the growing reappearance of religion to the public square and the shortcomings of traditional constitutional thinking. Chapter 8 brings the findings on the nature of constitutionalism in Chapter 3 to bear on the reality of the demands on the state when dealing with religion, and Chapter 9 concludes with a suggestion of the direction in which solutions may be sought to the difficulties in which the contemporary constitutional state finds itself as its task to deal with religious pluralism intensifies.

PART I

Religion, the state and constitutionalism

> Each person possesses a multitude of group affiliations, some deriving from biological attributes (sex, race and family ties) and others founded on an historical base (a shared national, cultural, religious or linguistic disposition or alliance). Affiliation with a group may provoke any degree of commitment to the perceived or real interests of the group, including, at one end of the spectrum, profound indifference and, on the other, a group consciousness that might find expression in quite fanatic aspirations and radical action. The latter, rather than the former, has brought on to the agenda of sociology, the law and political science how best to accommodate the group identities represented in a political community within the laws and/or the structures of the state.[1]

The religious convictions, practices and claims of individuals and groups are highly prominent in the range of affiliations that is ineluctably on the constitutional agenda of any state. The roots of the involvement of the state with religion go deep, and it seems that no attempt to unearth them has any prospect of success. The rising prominence of the notion of constitutionalism supplies participants in the domestic and international legal discourse on the relationship of the state with religion with a promising framework within which clarity on an appropriate approach to address the contemporary challenges may be sought.

---

[1] Van der Vyver (2005) 536.

1. The roots of a relationship: religion, the state and its power

1.1 AN HISTORIC TIE

The interaction between the state and religious institutions goes back to the emergence of the state as a distinct legal or constitutional construct. The historical roots of statehood reach down at least to the classical Greek and Roman eras, but statehood as such has been coming to fruition only over the past few centuries. The European history of church and state is where the foundations of the current global discourse on the theme were laid. That is also where our current conceptions of statehood originate.[1] From the outset European Christianity inspired a distinction between governmental and religious authority, inevitably leading to competition for supremacy. Law is not barren of normative aspirations such as justice and ethics, much of which are or were originally motivated by religious convictions. The knot tying law to religion cannot be untied. But before we can consider the nature of this knot we need to clarify some terminology.

1.2 RELIGION: THE TERM

A set of terms relating to religious matters is often used in conjunction, not always without confusion. These include 'religion', 'belief', 'faith', 'cult' and 'worship', words that are essential for a discussion of this nature.

In all manifestations of human society, faith, religion and religious practices are ubiquitous. These are profoundly human characteristics and activities, distinguishing, according to the major religions, man from beast. The complexity of the human condition and of society, however,

---

[1] For example, Tierney (1996) 29–57. Tierney also describes the development of the foundations of (the only partially successful) religious tolerance among different Christian denominations and the emergence of scepticism, which opened the way for secularism as it is understood today.

renders it possible to conceive of a variable continuum containing elements such as someone's world view, views, opinions, beliefs, convictions, faith, religion, loyalty, ethics, morals, culture, modality of worship and philosophy. Where and according to which criteria each of these elements might be placed on the range is open to debate, especially for the purposes of attempting to determine how a particular individual will react when confronted with the need to take a position on a religious issue.

The complexity of the human makeup makes a conclusive stance on these matters based on pure reason impossible. The individual's point of departure in such matters, as determined by personal temperament and related factors, will decide the response. And yet the state is required to deal with these characteristics and activities of individuals and societies in a consistent manner through the employment of the instruments of the law.

A vocabulary exists for dealing with these matters, but the language is not always employed with precision, often causing notions such as belief, faith, religion and so on to be used interchangeably. Due to the limitations of language as a medium of communication, the achievement of precision regarding words potentially bearing emotive and subjective meaning is not achievable. One can hardly be dogmatic about terminological choices in this context but, for a consideration of the interaction between religion and constitutionalism, at least some internal consistency is desirable.

This point is made exhaustively by Tiedemann, for instance in the first chapter of his book on religious freedom.[2] Tiedemann points out that Cicero introduced the Latin word *religio* to indicate the precisely defined ritual practices followed in the worship of the Roman gods. Later Christian writers such as Lactantius and Augustine shifted the meaning of the word away from ritual action towards binding (*religare*) belief; in other words, the complete Christian belief system and the associated practices. In the course of the 'age of enlightenment', during the emergence of rationalism in the 17th and 18th Centuries, the notion of religion became detached from specific religious systems and rites to become a collective term indicating the whole variety of religious beliefs as a cultural phenomenon. The linguistic difficulties of giving meaning to imprecise words leads Tiedemann to distinguish between porous conversational notions on the one hand and terminology as a means of conferring precise scientific meaning on the other. He emphasizes the

---

[2] Tiedemann (2012) 1–13.

need to award meaning to a term in such a manner that it does not deviate too far from the colloquial meaning, but far enough to serve a clear purpose. Since the phrase 'freedom of religion' is a legal term employed for the purposes of regulation and adjudication, it requires a precise meaning. Tiedemann sees two possible reasons for the protection of the freedom of religion: either for the purposes of tolerance or in acknowledgement of human dignity.

John Witte, a seasoned contributor to the field, offers two approaches to the definition of religion.[3] According to him, broadly speaking, religion 'embraces all beliefs and actions that concern the ultimate origin, meaning, and purpose of life, of existence. It involves the responses of the human heart, soul, mind, conscience, intuition, and reason to revelation, to transcendent values, to fundamental questions.' Witte's narrower description is that religion embraces 'a creed, a cult, a code of conduct, and a confessional community', on each element of which description he elaborates as follows:

> A creed defines the accepted cadre of beliefs and values concerning the ultimate origin, meaning, and purpose of life. A cult defines the appropriate rituals, liturgies, and patterns of worship and devotion that give expression to those beliefs. A code of conduct defines the appropriate individual and social habits of those who profess the creed and practice the cult. A confessional community defines the group of individuals who embrace and live out this creed, cult, and code of conduct, both on their own and with fellow believers.

Witte's useful approach will be used as a guideline in what follows. We will use 'religion' in Witte's narrower sense, thus indicating a belief or convictions held by more than one person. 'Religion' therefore indicates not only the beliefs of a community or group of people sharing a personal view, but also the communal expression of their convictions in observable, external forms, often also including structures and teachings.[4]

Some additional elaboration on the terms 'faith' and 'belief' is called for. What a religious person believes can be described as that person's subjective faith. Unfortunately the conventions of everyday language are imprecise, since it happens not seldom that one hears or reads about 'a faith' when the intention is to refer to a religious system or structure. Used thus, 'a religion' and 'a faith' amount to the same idea. This usage will be avoided here in order to limit the meaning of 'faith' to personal

---

[3] Witte (2006) 100–101.

[4] Another way of describing various 'facets of religion' is presented by Gunn (2003), who, at 200–205, describes religion as belief, identity and a way of life.

belief, that is, the individual's personal convictions regarding not only his or her own place in life, but also regarding the origins, progress and future of everything within one's knowledge, experience, expectation and speculation. Despite the best efforts of those who have sought answers to these matters by the exclusive employment of human reason,[5] it stands to reason (wordplay intended) that profound personal convictions are powerfully and unintentionally influenced by one's foundational life experiences, domestic environment, parental and social teaching, and social interaction.

Seen thus, faith is built upon belief. Belief, however, does not relate only to religion. Believing something essentially means holding something to be true, such as that daylight is the factual result of the shining of the sun. Why there is a star that we call the sun and how it came into being is for most people a matter of religious belief. Put differently, those who accept creation as the unprovable origin of existence believe divine creation to be an existential truth. Although belief is therefore not reserved for religious faith, faith does depend on belief.[6]

Pamela Slotte opens her illuminating article on the interrelationship between the concepts 'religious' and 'secular' in European human rights law, in which she also attends closely to the difficulty of defining religion, as follows:[7]

> The right to freedom of religion or belief involves the protection of something that tests the limits of the scientifically 'verifiable', but nonetheless is considered imperative to human rights law because of the presumed importance to human life. It is commonly assumed that we are dealing with assertions that come across as bearers of truth, yet are not provable in the sense that they cannot be verified or falsified by reference to a supposed objective reality. In this respect, the phenomenon of religion cannot be approached from a scientific standpoint. Yet, while 'informative' value cannot be determined, the meaningfulness of faith to human beings is not considered bound up with this fact.

---

[5] One prominent modern example is that of John Rawls, who argues (*inter alia* in Rawls (1997) 799–800) that it should be possible to employ everyone's capacity for the conceptions of justice and the good to resolve political controversies rationally as citizens, regardless of people's adherence to opposing religions or 'comprehensive doctrines'.

[6] Van der Vyver (2005) 503–506 points out that many jurisdictions avoid scrutinizing the exact meaning of 'religion' due to 'the conceptual difficulties', and that in international law freedom of religion and freedom of belief are linked, but that 'not every belief ... is included in the protection afforded to religion and belief'.

[7] Slotte (2010) 231–232.

Slotte demonstrates how, in the jurisprudence of the European Court of Human Rights, the meaning of 'religion' is determined by an understanding of the 'secular'.

The tension between religion and secularism lies at the heart of the difficulties that contemporary states are experiencing when required to deal with religious pluralism. Thus for example, with reference to German constitutional law, Kathrin Groh emphasizes the need, when defining religion for legal purposes, to find a balance between the subjectively held beliefs of individuals and religious communities on the one hand and the objective responsibility of the sovereign state to serve social well-being on the other. The legal definition is concerned with convictions concerning transcendental factors beyond a person's control that steer his or her existence. According to Groh attempts to broaden the definition for legal purposes beyond the minimum requirement of transcendency by adding enquiries into the content of the belief, will clash with the human dignity content of religious freedom itself, and also with the obligations of the state to maintain neutrality in matters of religion.[8]

As will emerge in our further discussion, the notions of secularism and neutrality loom large in matters concerning constitutionalism and religion.

1.3 LAW AND RELIGION

The human condition, especially in its social context, if it is to be peaceful, is known to all to require regulation. The obvious reason for this is that social order does not come about without rules. The most visible forms in which social regulation is cast are the law and religion. Appropriate legal regulation serves, *inter alia*, the interests of a fair and just society. Religious regulation is directed, *inter alia*, at denominational structures and their functioning. Law is intended to establish order for and among citizens within the state; on the other hand religious structures

---

[8] Groh (2009) 84–87. For an exposition of the matter of the legal definition of religion in English law, see the 2013 judgment in *R (on application of Hodkin) v Registrar General of Births, Deaths and Marriages* para. 34 *et seq*. In para. 34 Lord Toulson remarked: 'There has never been a universal legal definition of religion in English law, and experience across the common law world over many years has shown the pitfalls of attempting to attach a narrowly circumscribed meaning to the word. There are several reasons for this – the different contexts in which the issue may arise, the variety of world religions, developments of new religions and religious practices, and developments in the common understanding of the concept of religion due to cultural changes in society'.

and rituals serve the purpose of guiding the faithful when giving expression to their creed.

In the early development of societies, history teaches us that governmental, legal and religious leadership often overlapped, most famously in ancient Egypt, the Inca civilization, the Roman, Japanese and Chinese Empires, and in many African kingdoms. As societies develop an increased complexity of social relationships, state and religious leadership usually separate. Citizens living in developed and diversified societies, however, do not lose their need to understand and explain the world, life and human destiny – a need usually catered for by religion.

The nature and scope of law and of religion as such are matters calling for deeper consideration but, both being regulative and simultaneously applicable, it is inevitable that there will be interfaces between them, some harmonious and others conflictual. The South African Constitutional Court described this situation as follows:[9]

> [R]eligious and secular activities are, for purposes of balancing, frequently as difficult to disentangle from a conceptual point of view as they are to separate in day to day practice. While certain aspects may clearly be said to belong to the citizen's Caesar and others to the believer's God, there is a vast area of overlap and interpenetration between the two. It is in this area that balancing becomes doubly difficult, first because of the problems of weighing considerations of faith against those of reason, and secondly because of the problems of separating out what aspects of an activity are religious and protected by the Bill of Rights and what are secular and open to regulation in the ordinary way.

The value of this *dictum* lies in the description of the interface between law and religion, but it also illustrates the predilection of the judge concerned (often shared by proponents of agnosticism and atheism) to relegate religion to the status of irrationality, as though there is little or no reason in faith. This is an obvious oversimplification. Undoubtedly believers of whichever conviction (including atheists and agnostics[10]) do

---

[9] *Christian Education South Africa v Minister of Education* 2000 para. [34] per Sachs J.

[10] Insofar as substantiation of the inclusion of non-denominational convictions in the broad category of religion might be called for, consider the wording of Article 2 of Protocol No. 1 to the *European Convention on Human Rights*, which reads as follows:

> No person shall be denied the right to education. In the exercise of any functions which it assumes in relation to education and to teaching, the State shall respect the right of parents to ensure such education and teaching in conformity with their own religious and philosophical convictions.

find the basis of their faith in an acceptance of that which cannot be proven. The route to that basis, however, always winds through reasoning, rationalization and accepted facts, be they assumed, historical or contemporary. This does not constitute a real distinction between law and religion: although legal argument is normally characterized by systematic reasoning, the foundations of legal reasoning are to be found in the acceptance of doctrinal presuppositions such as justice, fairness, dignity, equality, and so on. Subscribing to legal doctrine is therefore very similar to, and in some respects closely linked to, unprovable religious belief.

Both law and religion are dogmatic. 'Dogma' can be defined as 'a belief held unquestioningly and with undefended certainty'.[11] Both theology and law as scholarly disciplines address dogma. The present project does not allow for an elaborate navigation through the rough seas of epistemology. It will have to be sufficient here, for the purposes of challenging the idea that religion is all belief and law is all reason, to briefly consider the nature of legal dogmatics. The valuable contribution of Aulis Aarnio[12] can guide us here.

Aarnio is concerned with the legitimation of 'legal science', which is not understood to be part of the social sciences and is easily taken to be merely ideographic (dealing only with specific sets of fact) and not nomothetic (formulating general norms). He overcomes the linguistic difficulty that English is inclined to reserve the word 'science' for the physical and natural sciences by allocating the meaning of *Rechtswissenschaft* and *science du droit* to 'legal dogmatics'.[13] He then proceeds[14] to

---

In *Campbell and Cosans v the United Kingdom* (1982) the European Court of Human Rights para. 36 in effect dealt with a 'philosophical conviction' about corporal punishment of school children on the same level as a religious conviction. See also *Eweida and Others v the United Kingdom (EuCtHR)* (2013) para. 79:

> The Court recalls that, as enshrined in Article 9, freedom of thought, conscience and religion is one of the foundations of a 'democratic society' within the meaning of the Convention. In its religious dimension it is one of the most vital elements that go to make up the identity of believers and their conception of life, but it is also a precious asset for atheists, agnostics, sceptics and the unconcerned. The pluralism indissociable from a democratic society, which has been dearly won over the centuries, depends on it.

[11] For example, Blackburn (2005) 104.
[12] Aarnio (1997).
[13] Aarnio (1997) 1–2. Robert Alexy, cited by for example, Andreas Voßkuhle (2012) 111 summarizes his conception of legal dogmatics as a class of rules (*Sätzen*) that relate to the posited norms and jurisprudence, but are not identical

trace the history of the tension between natural law (originating in the theology and metaphysics of, for example, Aquinas and Suarez) and positivism and the line of rationalism running through both (e.g. Grotius and Wolff) and confronts the eventual and still perpetuating dilemma of the relationship between justness and legal certainty (predictability): 'If we consider reasonableness the only criterion of legal thinking, the difference between law and morals disappears altogether. Dispensing justice becomes dispensing justice in individual cases. Then the other essential element of law, predictability, disappears'.[15]

Justification is for Aarnio an essential element of dispensing justice, and 'a legal interpretation that is justified in a comprehensive and integrated way is in accordance with both law and justice'.[16] Legal dogmatics has the functions of interpreting (in other words, clarifying the content of) and systematizing (in other words, further analysing by abstractly theorizing) the law.[17] It is clear: only the most rigid rationalist can accept the notion that law is the product only of reasonable and rational thought, separated and distinct from considerations of morality, values founded upon belief (whether religious or ontological) and dogmatic conceptions constructed on foundational theory.

Law and religion thus share some features. Both have moral connotations, although with distinguishable implications – the one primarily temporal, the other primarily transcendental. Both are expressed in the form of norms that require obedience and are typified by procedural practices. In law, obedience is enforced by the state, whereas religious obedience is primarily a matter of individual conscience, although religious institutions also defend their integrity by enforcing conformity with prescribed norms and procedures on pain of exclusion or censure – some extremely strictly and comprehensively, and others less so.

Most religious belief systems promote positive and peace-promoting attitudes such as tolerance and love, but they also distinguish sharply between believers and non-believers (in the belief system concerned). Where adherents of different religious groupings have to share space, resources and social institutions, they tend to become exclusive and

---

to them, relate to one another, are discussed and set out by a professional and have normative content.

[14] Aarnio (1997) 7–17 – his first chapter under the title 'Reason and Authority'.
[15] Aarnio (1997) 14.
[16] Aarnio (1997) 16.
[17] Aarnio (1997) 75, 285.

competitive. Human history is strewn with examples not only of religious competition but also of religious intolerance, often resulting in bloody conflict.[18]

In circumstances of religious tension occurring within a single legal jurisdiction, the conflict becomes a legal problem: how legally to regulate religious discord in a manner which will maintain and promote tolerance and social peace without discriminating against any of the religious groupings and without stepping outside the ambit of the law is a particularly intractable problem, since those who are entrusted with the responsibility of regulating and adjudicating are human and therefore exposed to their own religious (or profound ontological) convictions.

To contribute substantively to existing accounts of the nature of both law and religion is not the present intention. What is required here is no more than pointing out some major distinctions between them relevant to the purpose of this book. Having made mention of the dogmatic nature of the law as a scientific undertaking, it is necessary to anticipate and remove possible confusion regarding this discussion. We need not here be concerned with the distinction between the two scholarly disciplines of law and theology, since we do not need to transcend the boundaries of law, which is the present field of investigation, and venture into the domain of theology. Mention of dogma is relevant, however, because the dogmatic nature of neither law nor religion is limited to legal scholarship and theology. Theological dogma obviously varies according to the religion upon which it is constructed – Roman Catholic dogma for example differs fundamentally from any of the dogmas included in Hinduism. It is important to note a parallel truth regarding legal dogmatics: different perspectives on law produce divergent dogmatic approaches. For instance, understanding law to be essentially a collection of binding injunctions resulting from sovereign prescription leads to dogmatic stances different from understanding law to be the product of principled formulation in accordance with foundational values. Considering law to be the preserve of reason in contrast to faith as the source of religion is a stance in legal dogmatics. This last mentioned dogmatic stance incidentally also supports the view that the state is secular in the sense of being isolated from religion. These are matters that will require further attention as we proceed.

Essential differences between the phenomena 'law' and 'religion' can, for our present purposes, be highlighted sufficiently by means of mentioning some of their distinguishing salient characteristics.

---

[18] See for example, Christenson (2013).

Religion belongs in human existence, both profoundly personal and public. Personal religious belief underpins communal practices. Those sharing the same religious convictions usually develop rituals, liturgies, dogmas, cults and in many cases structures or spaces as sites for communal devotion. Sincere adherence to a religion is unfailingly preceded by personal conviction. Education, social environment, culture and example certainly are compelling factors in the process of personal acceptance of a religion, but ultimately authentic religious belief depends fully on internal, unforced conviction.[19] Loss of faith essentially leads to the termination of membership of the religious community concerned, exclusion from the real or perceived privileges and benefits of such membership, and in some cases to social marginalization and ostracism.[20]

Law, on the other hand, is primarily a normative construct. It is necessarily public: the proverbial Robinson Crusoe no doubt had personal religious convictions but no need for law until Friday arrived on the scene. Law does not require personal or public subjection or belief in its content but demands obedience, not as an optional choice, but as an enforceable result. Being subject to the law does not require education or acculturation but mere presence under the jurisdiction concerned. The

---

[19] No doubt every religious community or movement has its share of insincere and half-doubting fellow travellers but no religion can retain the integrity of its following by the prohibition of apostasy: forcing an individual to believe or to disbelieve anything is not possible.

[20] This description of religion may challenge the position taken here that agnosticism and atheism are essentially religious stances, because structures and rituals do not normally characterize the proponents of agnosticism or atheism. Put differently, opposition to structured and organized religion does not constitute *a* religion but it is 'religious', as in being based upon a profound belief. A profound religious conviction does not need to be organized or institutionalized. A useful test for the religious nature of agnosticism and atheism is their rejection of (other) religious beliefs as untrue, accepting only their own perception of the truth, albeit 'anti-religious'. Consider for example the arguments presented by Webber (2009) 43:

> The fact that the freedom [of religion] finds its origin in religion does not mean that it is trapped within a particular conception of religious orthodoxy or even – this is the important point – that its moral justification is limited to self-consciously religious beliefs. ... [T]he very idea of religious freedom presupposes a willingness to recognise commitments that operate in a comparable way whether or not they conform to a preconceived idea of religion. ... After all, for the religious zealots of the Reformation era, the other's faith was not religion; it was the most profound and dangerous error.

In the current context 'non-religious' beliefs also distinguish themselves from the law in that they are human activities as opposed to normative constructs.

transgression of legal rules, when enforced, has clear consequences, generally detrimental to the transgressor, enforced by the compelling authority of the state. Nevertheless, law is not disconnected from foundational human stances: its fairness is measured in terms of conceptions of justice and its effectiveness in the absence of specific enforcement is dependent upon the acceptance of its legitimacy by the society in which it applies.

Law and religion thus occupy different areas of personal and social existence. Religion involves individual and communal activity, whereas law as a social system or structure constitutes a passive normative framework.[21] The difficulty on which we are focused here lies in the inescapable need for the law to regulate matters concerning religious activity in a manner that is fair to all under the equally unavoidable circumstance that the foundational suppositions upon which legal norms are created cannot be ignored as though they do not exist.

Mark Witten, writing in the Canadian context, compactly summarizes the typical secular response to the difficulties occurring at the interface between constitutionalism and religion:[22]

> Canadian constitutional law is not neutral, but is rather a political culture that is partisan to its own informing values. As Professor Benjamin Berger contends, Canadian constitutional law shares the political culture of liberalism, an ideology that birthed the modern democratic state and its institutions. Berger argues that law inevitably casts religion in a manner that comports with its own cultural assumptions: religion as an individual experience, religion as a private matter, and religion as an expression of autonomy. Thus, for religion to be understood, recognized, and accommodated at law, it may be forced to resonate with the judiciary's preferred construction of religion. In addition, it also follows that law's comprehension and treatment of religion is deeply influenced by liberalism's *epistemological* assumptions, which are the assumptions of *rationalism*. Rationalism presumes a way of knowing that elevates reason and considers the criterion for truth to be exclusively intellectual and deductive, as opposed to sensory, mystical, or experiential. Moreover, because the rationalist philosophy of the Enlightenment developed in reaction to religious power, its assumptions hold unique implications for law's treatment of religion.

---

[21] Law is naturally 'practised' by professional lawyers and actively created and amended by legislators, administered by bureaucrats and governments, but it is not after its manifestation dependent for its existence, as is the case with religion, on being practised.

[22] Witten (2012) 92–93.

1.4 CHURCH AND STATE

The state is the primary domain of the law, and 'the church' that of religion in its public manifestation. The word 'church', usually associated with Christianity, does not have an inclusive meaning that covers the spectrum of religions, but is nevertheless used by many to indicate the tension between law and religion in the phrase 'church and state'.[23]

The controversial Roman emperor Constantine 'the Great', founder of Constantinople, proclaimed the Edict of Milan in 313, thereby ending the Roman prosecution of Christianity and laying a foundation for religious tolerance, although such tolerance had a chequered career in the subsequent centuries. Constantine's embrace of Christianity also initiated an era of significant overlapping in Europe of the interests and powers of church and state.[24]

The issue of the division of authority between church and state was accentuated in the 5th Century when Aurelius Augustinus taught about two cities, one the city of God for the pious and the other the city of sinful man, the two cities uncomfortably coexisting until the end of time.[25] In 494 Pope Boniface laid down the notion of two powers, the one sacred (that of the Pope) and the other royal (that of the Emperor).[26] In the 11th to the 13th Centuries, during the Papal Revolution, this was developed into the two swords doctrine, separating the temporal (the state) from the spiritual (the Roman Church).[27] At the hands of Luther[28] and Calvin[29] in the 15th Century the Reformation introduced a doctrine of two kingdoms as a variation, but also a continuation of the essential idea

---

[23] The publishers of the *Journal of Church and State* (Oxford University Press) for example, describe its purpose as follows: 'The *Journal of Church and State* seeks to stimulate interest, dialogue, research, and publication in the broad area of religion and the state. *JCS* publishes constitutional, historical, philosophical, theological, and sociological studies on religion and the body politic in various countries and cultures of the world, including the United States.'

[24] See for example, Temperman (2010a) 13–17.

[25] Cf. for example, Duijnstee (1930) with a useful overview at 290–295.

[26] Cf. for example, Rommen (1935) 258–260.

[27] See for example, Rommen (1935) 255–258, 260–266.

[28] See for example, Pierard (1986), especially 193–195 and Heckel (2013) 38–42.

[29] Calvin explicitly rejects the papal claim to 'the right of both swords' in *The Institutes of the Christian Religion* Chapter 11 sections 9–16.

that people are simultaneously bound to submit to both the religious and secular authorities, each within its domain.[30]

Ending the Thirty Years War that raged devastatingly across Western Europe to a large degree between Catholics and Protestants, the Peace of Westphalia of 1648 confirmed the notions of the *ius emigrandi* (subjects of a ruler who did not share his religion had the right to emigrate peacefully), and of *cuius regio, eius religio* (first expressed in the Peace of Augsburg declared in 1555 between Catholics and Protestants in the 'Holy Roman Empire of the German Nation'), thus also serving as an historical high-water mark for the Protestant Reformation[31] and the geographical division of Europe between Roman Catholicism and Reformational Protestantism. An effect of Westphalia was also the emergence of religious freedom as the first constitutionally protected fundamental right, in that the parties agreed that citizens whose religion differed from that of their rulers should not be persecuted by the rulers.[32]

The European 17th and 18th Centuries were also the dawning era of scholarly genius, social and philosophical exploration, religious turmoil, the opening up of what the Europeans considered to be the 'new world', and the gaining of access to and domination of the riches of the regions of the globe inhabited by 'uncivilized' people. In this intellectually and politically turbulent golden age it was also not strange if lawyers like Descartes and Leibnitz blossomed into mathematicians, or for natural philosophers like Newton to spend as much – if not more – time on fervently studying the Bible as on contemplating mathematics and

---

[30] The Synod of Bern of 1532 for example, took the following position (cited and translated by Bruening (2005) 66):

The greater and more sublime is the spiritual and heavenly government ... The lesser, which belongs to the Bernese magistrates, is the earthly government. The Christian falls under the jurisdiction of both. In his conscience, which God alone judges, he belongs to the spiritual government without the intervention of any creature. But with regard to his body and temporal goods, the Christian is subject to the external sword and human administration.

[31] See for example, Christenson (2013) 740.

[32] Croxton and Tischer (2002), under the entry 'CUIUS REGIO; EIUS RELIGIO':

The Peace of Westphalia sharply limited the doctrine by setting 1624 as the 'normal year' for religious affairs: whatever religion was practiced at that time was allowed to continue, and although the ruler could change the state church, he could not interfere with the public worship of his other subjects. The Peace of Westphalia also diverged from the *cuius regio* principle because it guaranteed freedom of worship in private homes and the right of religious dissidents to emigrate.

physics as an endeavour to unravel the assumed divine code of creation.[33] It was the era of Rousseau, Hobbes, Montesquieu, de Vattel and John Locke, who urged the drawing of clear lines between 'the business of civil government from that of religion'.[34]

Natural law as the product of the assumed rational human mind became a powerful influence on the emergence of constitutionalism at this time. Thomas Hobbes more or less sealed the distinction between the spiritual and temporal, church and state, in his *Leviathan* of 1651, where he wrote:[35]

> How then can we be obliged to obey any minister of Christ, if he should command us to do anything contrary to the command of the king, or other sovereign representative of the commonwealth whereof we are members, and by whom we look to be protected? It is therefore manifest, that Christ hath not left to his ministers in this world, unless they be also endued with civil authority, any authority to command other men.

The Enlightenment of the 17th and 18th Centuries can be understood to have been the era during which the individual gained particular prominence in law, society and philosophy. Zafirovski, for example, rightly points out that what are generally assumed to be the foundational values of 21st Century constitutionalism – such as liberty, equality, justice, democracy, inclusion, human rights, dignity, well-being and happiness, humane life, civil liberties, scientific rationalism, technological and social progress and optimism, economic prosperity, free markets, secularism,

---

[33] For example, Dolnick (2011) 211.

[34] For a clear précis of this history and thinking, see Witte (2006) 212–222 and also Witte (1996) Chapter 4. Loth (2007) 1737 neatly draws the picture of the rise of modernism after the Peace of Westphalia as follows:

> scientists like Newton changed the picture of the universe beyond recognition, describing it as a clock in which every event was connected through lawlike causal generalizations. Starting with Descartes, philosophy came into the grip of three dreams: the dream of a unified science (Newton), a unified method (Descartes), and a unified language (Leibniz). This 'quest for certainty' also had its impact on social thinking. Political philosophy changed from the art of politics from Machiavelli to the picture of society as a construction sketched by the social contract philosophers (Hobbes, Rousseau, Locke).

[35] In Chapter 42 of *Leviathan* in the paragraph marked in the margin 'From the authority Christ hath left to civil princes'.

pluralism and diversity, individualism, universalism and humanism – all originated in the Enlightenment.[36]

This was the atmosphere under which the iconic Constitution of the United States was conceived, as the American Founding Fathers were putting the ideas of the Enlightenment geniuses of political philosophy into practice. The subsequent influence of the US Constitution around the globe, its interpretation and application as an exemplar of progressivism, political maturity and balanced advancement can hardly be measured in absolute terms, but it was immense up to at least the end of the 20th Century.[37] The American influence was not the only factor that steered approaches elsewhere in the world, but the manner in which American law deals with religion in the constitutional context has had a discernable worldwide echo. This is not to say that there is anything approaching consensus among Americans on this issue, but clear trend lines can be drawn, especially regarding the jurisprudence of the Supreme Court in Washington.

The constitutional pivot around which the developments in this context turn is the first phrase of the First Amendment of 1791, which states: *Congress shall make no law respecting an establishment of religion, or prohibiting the free exercise thereof.* The manner in which this 'non-establishment' and 'free exercise' clause has been interpreted over the past two centuries has varied. Since 1947, coinciding with the current era of the blooming of constitution-writing around the world, the emphasis in American law has been on strict separationism, that is, the supposed isolation of state action from religious influence.

Some Americans consider the Constitution to stand as a substitute for religion in the public domain.[38] The idea that the Constitution is the foundation of a 'civil religion' is not a recent development, however. As

---

[36] Zafirovski (2011) Chapter 1 under the heading 'Liberty, Life, and Happiness for All: The Ideals and Legacies of the Enlightenment in Modern Societies Revisited'.

[37] Temperman (2010a) 118–119 lists some 28 Constitutions adopted between 1900 and 2006 containing 'non-establishment' clauses.

[38] Davis (2011) 97 describes the American civil religion as follows:

The Pledge of Allegiance is our creed, the Constitution is our scripture, and our founding fathers are our patriarchs. We are devoted to democracy, we pray for our progress, and we are committed capitalists. Our prisons are our civil religion's purgatory, where we hope the criminal perpetrators prove penitent. We celebrate our saintly soldiers on Memorial Day, and we praise our political prophets such as Martin Luther King, Jr.

far back as 1839 John Quincy Adams dramatically stated: 'Fellow-citizens, the ark of *your* covenant is the Declaration of Independence. Your Mount Ebal, is the confederacy of separate state sovereignties, and your Mount Gerizim is the Constitution of the United States.'[39]

In 1990 Stephen Griffen wrote:[40]

> Claims that the US Constitution is a magnificent document which 'embodies the American spirit, the American Dream', are not really open to rational debate. They are expressions of quasi-religious faith and patriotic sentiment and are not advanced on the basis of argument. It is questionable whether such assertions even have the Constitution as their subject – they seem to use the Constitution as a symbol for the nation as a whole.

In 1971 the Supreme Court handed down its judgment in *Lemon v Kurtzmann*,[41] in which a test was devised for the conformity of laws with the non-establishment element of the First Amendment. This 'Lemon test' states as follows: 'First, the statute must have a secular legislative purpose; second, its principal or primary effect must be one that neither advances nor inhibits religion; finally, the statute must not foster an excessive government entanglement with religion.'

It is interesting to observe that the test is concerned with 'religion' as a phenomenon, and not 'a religion'. In effect, the Supreme Court therefore required schools that wished to receive government funding to denude their teaching completely of any religious connotations and to concentrate on 'secular' education. This result was endorsed by Justice O'Connor in 1984 when she refined the first element, 'a secular legislative purpose', with an 'endorsement test' in *Lynch v Donnelly*.[42] She proclaimed that '[t]he proper inquiry under the purpose prong of *Lemon*, ... is whether the government intends to convey a message of endorsement or disapproval of religion'.

In his review of recent Establishment Clause jurisprudence, Samuel J. Levine effectively demonstrates how erratic the judgments are, and points

---

[39] Cited House (1999) 204.
[40] Griffen (1990) 200.
[41] *Lemon v Kurtzman* 403 U.S. 602 (1971). Cf. Laycock (2010) at 103–122 (containing an excerpt from *Religion in American Law: An Encyclopedia*).
[42] *Lynch v Donnelly*, 465 U.S. 668, 691 (1984).

out[43] that 'the growing religious diversity in American society, accompanied by increasing numbers of self-identified secularists or non-believers, adds another level of complexity to an Establishment Clause analysis'.

The common meaning of 'secular' is 'wordly' or not-sacred. Thus the secularization of the state can superficially be understood to point to the process of the termination of the ecclesiastical domination of government. This would appear to be the root of the language of the US Supreme Court in its judgment in *Lemon v Kurtzman*, where the word 'secular' is employed many times without an explanation of its meaning being offered. Thus the imperative of a 'secular legislative purpose' was not explained, other than through the distinguishing of 'the secular' from 'the religious'. Etymologically the distinction, considered by the Supreme Court to be trite, is most probably founded on the two cities, two swords, two kingdoms doctrines mentioned above.

The American example, having been greatly influential, is however by no means the only model that is followed by contemporary constitutional states and in international law. Constitutions in which the American non-establishment approach is not followed make interesting reading regarding the understanding of the 'separation of church and state'. The contemporary constitutional arrangements concerning religion in various representative countries will be considered in Chapter 4. The approach of the courts in some other systems will be discussed in Chapter 6. Further attention will be given to the meaning of secularism, *inter alia*, in Chapter 7.

At least four phases in the history of 'church and state' can therefore be identified:

- A pre-differentiation phase where law and religion, 'state and church', overlap.
- The emergence of the two cities, two kingdoms, two swords doctrines.
- The establishment of the notions of secular liberalism running concurrently with the emergence of the modern state.

---

[43] Levine (2012) 778. See also McConnell (2009) 100:

For 16 words that remain completely unchanged from their adoption some 215 years ago, the Supreme Court's interpretation of the Religion Clauses of the First Amendment of the United States Constitution have shown remarkable malleability. Arguably, the court's interpretation of these Clauses has changed more often, and more dramatically, than of any other provision of the Constitution.

- The current phase of the post-liberal, post-secular confrontation by the state of the realities of religious pluralism.

1.5 POWER AND JUSTICE

The obvious reason for the importance of the state for religion is that the state is endowed with compelling power,[44] including over matters that affect the practice of religion. The manner in which this power (or authority, which is the more civilized expression) is exercised in a particular situation relates directly to the nature of the particular state and the moral considerations underlying the legal order within which the state and its structures have been conceived and are operating. To illustrate: if the authority of a state emanates exclusively from the ability of the government to impose its will on all under its jurisdiction under the threat of aggression, one has to do with a dictatorship or autocracy that is exercising its power in terms of a morality of violence; if, on the other hand, the authority of a government is motivated by an ability to persuade those under its jurisdiction to conform to its stated wishes, some form of open democracy is in place, operating on a morality of legitimacy.

No doubt a legitimate democracy is to be preferred, but even in such a case the state must have the means of enforcing its authority, if needs be, by the judicious employment of force. It is this indispensable element of compelling force that distinguishes the state from most other social institutions. The regulatory framework within which state authority is exercised is the law. Legal regulation distinguishes itself from most other forms of social regulation in that constantly behind it is the potential of enforcement by means of the application of the state's monopoly on the permitted application of its institutionalized superior might.

---

[44] Max Weber famously defined the state as follows (Weber (2010) 8): 'Staat ist diejenige menschliche Gemeinschaft, welche innerhalb eines bestimmten Gebietes – dies: das "Gebiet", gehört zum Merkmal – das *Monopol legitimer physicher Gewaltsamkeit* für sich (mit Erfolg) beansprucht.' (Freely translated: The state is that human community that successfully claims for itself the monopoly of legitimate physical empowerment, typically within a specified territory.) Although Weber's definition of a state is sometimes contested, the element of coercive power can scarcely be excluded from its definition. See for example, Hoffman (1995) Chapter 3, where he defines a state as 'an institution which claims a monopoly of legitimate force for a given territory', whereas government 'pertains to the pursuit of order within a community'.

The most profound question that needs to be answered in the process of one's grasp of the nature of the state and of the law as an abstract but real instrument in its hands by means of which its authority may be exercised legitimately concerns the source of the state's power. The answer to this question inescapably requires one to make a moral if not a religious choice. The instinctive response in established Western legal thinking to the question of where power originates is to proffer theories of liberal democracy as the foundation of the authority of the state.

Liberalism has had much to do with the development of the notion of constitutionalism (with which we deal in Chapter 3), and its current effect on jurisprudence and academic work continues to be powerful. This is demonstrated clearly by the currency of the names of liberal philosophers such as John Locke, Ronald Dworkin and John Rawls in the context of our current theme. But it has to be asked: is liberalism *an sich* a prerequisite for contemporary constitutionalism, democracy, human rights, and constitutional and international jurisprudence? For the liberal(ist) the answer will obviously be 'yes', but does that mean that liberalism must continue to dominate constitutional discourse and disqualify other approaches to constitutionalism? Is constitutionalism exclusively a liberal dogma? Is liberalism a shibboleth for those seeking admission to the global debate on constitutional balance and justice? In Chapter 7 below it is argued that this is not the case. The world of constitutionalism is labouring under the shortcomings of fictitious constitutional constructs and terminology produced over centuries by hugely influential liberal thinkers. Alternatives to these ubiquitous concepts are not readily available, but there is a global need to fill the vacuum that the shrinking credibility of classic liberal thinking is leaving behind.

Where should we then turn to find an answer to the essential question of the origins of state authority? If the answer is not to be sought in pragmatic formalism,[45] the search calls forth considerations of religious belief (even if that belief is 'secular'). Involving belief in one's understanding of the source of state authority harbours the possibility of (re-)merging 'church' and state, but such a merger is not only impossible (except, theoretically, in the case of monist theocracies such as are in evidence in the Muslim world) without injustice to other religions, but is also not required. A religious explanation of state authority does, however, generate the problem of inconsistent and even irreconcilable understandings of the sources of the authority of the state, particularly in

---

[45] Möllers (2007) seems to imply that pragmatic formalism reigns supreme in current general German constitutional thinking.

a religiously plural society: different religions have different explanations for authority, a fact that goes some way towards explaining the refuge that many take behind secularism at the cost of their religious convictions.[46]

The logic behind state secularism is that if the state, the law and authority do not need to be justified in religious terms, the blandness of secularity offers an escape to assumed harmless neutrality. This is, however, by no means a satisfactory result, because it leaves the most profound human attribute, religious belief, unrequited. On the other hand, making choices explicitly based on religious considerations is guaranteed to offend those with dissimilar convictions. That is nevertheless exactly the result also of imposing the convictions of liberalism, secularism, agnosticism or atheism on the state and its organs. To this dilemma we will return in the final chapters of this book.

Measuring whether or not the state is performing its tasks and exercising its authority as it should involves invoking standards of justice. Being slightly less profound (though by no means removed from profundity) than a view on the sources of state authority, positions taken on the nature and requirements of justice are nevertheless also determined by moral points of departure. They are committed to predetermined values, inevitably based on religious belief. Unsurprisingly there are therefore various ways in which justice may be construed.[47]

Fortunately (rendering it unnecessary here to launch into a comprehensive deliberation on justice) we have the benefit of a universally instinctive human reaction to the question of fairness and justice. This reaction is often referred to as 'reciprocity', also called 'the golden rule', and has been professed with slight variations by a wide range of religions through the ages. Ulpianus, for instance, famously coined the rule *suum cuique tribuere*.[48] An excellent treatise on this golden rule as a guide for ethical conduct was published in 1996 by Jeffrey Wattles. He expresses it in the following model with a major premise, a minor premise and a conclusion:[49]

---

[46] A particularly revealing topical example of this is the tension in Turkey between secularity and Islam.

[47] Literature through the ages dealing with the notion of justice abounds. For a compact overview see for example, Ritsert (2012) Chapter 1 and the sources cited there.

[48] See for example, Ritsert (2012) 15, where he also points out how Kant developed it into the position that it is unjust to suppress the free will of a person, and thus infringe upon his or her dignity.

[49] Wattles (1996) 165–166.

1. Treat others as you want others to treat you.
2. You want others to treat you with appropriate sympathy, respect, and so on.
3. Therefore, treat others with appropriate sympathy, respect, and so on.

Flores describes reciprocity, which was originally attributed to K'ung-fu-tzu (Confucius), as 'a principle firmly entrenched in the "Eastern" comprehension of the world that is also present in the "Western" one' and which is implicit in the notion of the rule of law, and even finds it expressed by exponents of liberalism such as Dworkin and Rawls.[50]

Citing Paul Ricoeur, Wattles describes[51] justice as being 'characterized as a social institution, as involving communication, listening to arguments, and arriving at a decision backed up by force; justice also is an idea or ideal of equitable distribution'.

Dealing fairly with religious pluralism requires this kind of justice. The success that courts have achieved while dealing with religious matters in various systems will be considered in Chapter 6.

1.6 A KNOT THAT CANNOT BE UNTIED

History, philosophy, language and morality have all been engaged in the process of interweaving the very human institutions of law and religion, and they continue to do so. Simultaneously little doubt can remain that failure to distinguish appropriately the social and personal realms within which each exists and is practised creates grave difficulties, especially in the diversified societies of the 21st Century. Where 'church and state' are not properly separated, where the state attempts to suppress religion, where religious institutions attempt to prescribe proper conduct to the

---

[50] Flores (2013) Chapter 6 *passim*. At 77 he writes:

The principle 'reciprocity' attributed to Confucius is closely related not only to several of the principles integral in our conception of the 'rule of law', such as 'isonomy', 'generality', 'constancy', 'the harm principle' – as a justified limitation to liberty – and limits to 'majority rule', but also to the classic one contained in the Greek word *isotimia* and to the modern 'equal concern and respect' advocated among others by Dworkin and Amartya Sen, following John Rawls and his 'difference principle'.

[51] Wattles (1996) 159.

government, where the state promotes one religious entity to the detriment of others in a religiously plural population, trouble, tension, confrontation, competition and dissatisfaction flourish.

Taking flight behind inaction and disinterest regarding religious matters is also a sure recipe for putting strain on the relationship between citizens (in other words, individuals who are in their existential nature religious) and the state as the bearer of compelling legal authority.

We must therefore conclude that, while law and religion represent fully distinct sets of norms, there is a link between them that cannot be broken: it is a knot that cannot be untied without negative consequences and one which is ignored or pushed aside only at the cost of a loss of legitimacy and credibility.

2. Globalization, constitutional law and religion

Where law meets religion, constitutional law as the normative framework for the allocation, regulation and limitation of public authority is innately prominent. For the purposes of gaining an understanding of the contingencies and questions that arise from this meeting, it is necessary to update the image that this discipline of law evokes in one's mind. In fact, closer scrutiny reveals a measure of urgency for a 21st Century revision of some of the tenets of constitutional law that have gone unchallenged for too long. To this we will return in Chapter 7.

The urgency for the proposed conceptual reconnaissance is emphasized by the escalation of the tempo of globalization which produces the potential for both increased uniformity and challenges to established constitutional thought. Globalization is, however, not an uncontested concept and so is the idea that globalization-induced constitutional comparison has become indispensable to the field.

This chapter therefore probes the linkages between constitutional law and globalization and the effects of constitutional comparison on constitutional thinking around the globe.

2.1 GLOBALIZATION AND CONSTITUTIONAL LAW

In the journal *Scientific American*, which is widely read around the world by scientists of many stripes, Professor John Sexton of New York made the following observations in 2012 regarding globalization:[1]

> [T]he speed and ease with which we now communicate have so accelerated the flow of ideas that the scientific enterprise is more interconnected than ever before. And while this greater connectivity has not altered the basic quest – the pursuit of knowledge and the advancement of humankind – the increased globalization of scientific research has created a more open intellectual ecosystem that draws more smart people into the conversation.

---

[1] Sexton (2012) 30.

Sexton was primarily dealing with the natural sciences but his remarks are equally true for the social sciences and humanities. The pervasive accessibility of the news media of the world, the expedited dissemination of scholarly communications in all fields of research, the worldwide judicial dialogue and the intensified international scrutiny of local occurrences – all of these cause trends, developments and schools of thought, good and bad, to take root quickly, and to be exposed to rapid change. Along with the real or perceived threats to individuals and to society that are brought about by the ever-accelerating global flow of people, money, goods and ideas, globalization also engenders heightened levels of awareness of how things work in other parts of the world. This is also true of constitutional law, despite its uniqueness in every state. Constitutional law, which is deeply grounded in centuries of history, localized culture and tradition, is however not a particularly malleable field of law. It nevertheless appears that the most evident effect of globalization on constitutional thinking is an increased acceptance around the world of the desirability of what growing numbers of citizens and institutions consider to be a good idea: constitutionalism.

Constitutional law as a discipline of legal practice, jurisprudence, research and scholarship can be an inward-looking field related to the constitutional arrangements of a particular state. This slightly myopic manifestation of the discipline is legitimate, but the single state is no longer, if ever it was, its exclusive domain. In fact, the constitutional law of any country can be understood properly only against the background of its history – and no state is, historically or currently, a constitutional island. This is particularly true of new constitutional states, but also of the influential constitutional systems of our era, all of which share historical antecedents and many of which have influenced one another in their development.[2] Furthermore, contemporary constitutional practice, be it in the form of constitutional drafting, legislation, administration or adjudication, has developed prominent comparative features. Credible

---

[2] A telling example which is not always illuminated adequately is the influence of the 18th Century constitutional law of the United States on that of revolutionary France. Very direct evidence of the American influence is to be found in the records of the French Constituent Assembly of 27 July 1789, where Champion de Cice was reported to have said the following (taken from Favoreu (1990) 39):

> This noble idea coming from another hemisphere was to be implemented here first. We participated in the events which led North America to freedom: it shows us on which principles we should rely to keep ours. The New World on which we put chains in the past is today showing us how to protect ourselves.

constitutional scholarship can hardly be undertaken without comparison. The constitutional law of every extant state is therefore continually being exposed to external developments in constitutional thinking, enhanced by the impulses of globalization.

'Globalization' can be a glib catch-all term for unhelpful and vague generalization. It is in fact used for various purposes, including mobilizing resistance against capitalism, and describing global trade, migration, politics, and so on. It can also, however, be used to a more positive purpose, namely to identify by means of comparison some global trends of a constitutional nature that are influencing the content and functioning of local constitutional law.

The term 'globalization' implies more than occurrences across the boundaries of several countries. It also has to do with more than the international involvement of various states. It is more than transnational, that is, involving diverse 'nations'. Strictly speaking it engages the whole of the 'globe', that is, planet earth and everything on it. This strict meaning is perhaps more inclusive than the more realistic reference to *most* of the world, although the strict notion represents the underlying concept. It is a matter of perspective: looking at developments and activities from a vantage point detached from the local, regional or national – from planetary space as it were – but taking account of reality on the ground.

In their thoughtful contribution to a book on globalization's development since the 19th Century, historians Löhr and Wenzlhuemer compactly define globalization as 'the process of the gradual detachment of patterns of socio-cultural interaction from geographical proximity' and they consider 'global' in this context to refer 'to the increasing number of personal or institutional connections that transcend local horizons and let actors across the entire globe interact with each other'.[3]

Looking at constitutional law comparatively is nothing new. Aristotle was a constitutional comparatist,[4] Montesquieu compared constitutions extensively,[5] and the drafting of new constitutions through the centuries would have been a strange thing in the absence of comparison. The historical examples are in fact early indications of a globalized approach to constitutional law, although the express linkage of constitutionalism and globalization is a relatively recent phenomenon.

---

[3] Löhr and Wenzlhuemer (2013), Chapter 1, 3.
[4] Cf. for example, Donahue (2006) 4.
[5] See for example, Zucca (2009).

There are credible retroactive constructions of age-old forms of globalization, especially from an economic perspective, going back to the extensive trade practices of Greece, India, China, Rome and the Vikings, among others.[6] In his recent book on the 'cosmopolitan state' Patrick Glenn acknowledges that globalization occurred in ancient times when the 'oldest instrument of globalization may well have been the wheel', and in the 19th Century the telegraph compressed the time for communication, which may not have been as glamorous as some of the current instruments, and did not have the velocity, volume and visibility of today, but nevertheless brought about globalization.[7]

The recent emergence of the notion of globalization is more pertinent to the present discussion. Factors like the maturing of communications technology, intensified economic interdependence, the accessibility of fast modes of travel, the termination of the Cold War in the late 20th Century, global climate change and the exponential growth of the world population have all contributed to and still continue to promote the notion of globalization, ensuring its extensive use in the present-day social vocabulary as a self-evident reality.[8]

The difficulties surrounding the precise definition of constitutionalism will not, for the time being,[9] divert us from a more modest consideration of the influence of global trends regarding conceptual preferences in the (internal) constitutional law of contemporary states, especially insofar as this is relevant to dealing with religious pluralism.

2.2 CONSTITUTIONAL LAW AND CONSTITUTIONAL COMPARISON

In his invited editorial for I.CON early in 2013,[10] Ran Hirschl made the point that constitutional comparison cannot usefully be approached merely from the perspective of the law. He cites American works on 'comparative constitutional law' published in the late 19th Century in which the study of politics was already accepted to be an integral component, and he then goes on to make a solid case for the incorporation of the social sciences in comparative constitutional studies. Thus

---

[6] Cf. for example, Moore and Lewis (2009b).
[7] Glenn (2013) 166.
[8] For example, Glenn (2013) 167–171.
[9] For a discussion of these, see Chapter 3.
[10] Hirschl (2013).

social scientists like Löhr and Wenzlhuemer[11] and Hardt and Negri[12] for example recognize the impact of globalization on the nation state and its sovereignty, seemingly finding it easier to deal with such matters as historical and socio-political phenomena than one would expect legal theorists to be able to do. A very good reason for this is that law, in its nature, is umbilically connected to the state. Hirschl's point is well taken, but the constitutional comparatist should not mistake the fact that the world of knowledge and science is steadily becoming more interdisciplinary in its nature to mean that law as a discipline is being subsumed into a borderless world of intermingled concepts of sociology, history, economics, politics and such. Nevertheless, and without disregarding the widening knowledge environment within which constitutional law needs to be studied, the constitutional lawyer's focus must still be on the state, however it is changing, and on legal norms, however they are being generated.

Very few contemporary states do not have consolidated, written constitutions. The *writing* and promulgation of a constitution, however cumbersome and well researched the process might be, can nevertheless not be seen as an end in itself. A constitutional text is merely the foundation upon which the substantive content of constitutional law is built. The *making* of substantive constitutional law involves political, administrative and judicial practice in response to the ever-changing realities that have to be faced in the course of practical governance. It is therefore useful to distinguish between constitution-*writing* and constitution-*making*, reserving the concept of the writing of a constitution for the development of an actual constitutional text, while using the expression 'constitution-making' to refer to the more comprehensive process of the planning for, negotiating (where required) and discussion of a proposed new constitutional dispensation *and* the subsequent authoritative interpretation, application, analysis, discussion, adjudication and critique of the constitutional text. Whereas the writing of a constitution in this sense usually occurs infrequently in any given state, and often only at unusual historical junctures, followed by more or less frequent adaptations of the text by an entity endowed with amending competence, 'constitution-making' as shorthand for the making of constitutional law is a never-ending process whereby dynamic life is given to an otherwise abstractly documented set of norms.

---

[11] Löhr and Wenzlhuemer (2013) 6–10.
[12] Hardt and Negri (2000) *passim*.

Although a constitutional document may reflect even the most advanced universal thinking on matters constitutional, the subsequent progression of giving life to the document (the constitution-making process) can in our era not be isolated or saved from the influences emanating from the ever-increasing substance of global constitutional trends. Legal and social factors, originating from diverse sources around the globe that influence the meaning and understanding of a constitution, are numerous, they have a powerful impact on constitutional law, and they seem to increase constantly in their effect. This ever-growing influence on domestic constitution-making is accelerated further by the free-flowing global interaction among jurisdictions at various levels, including the judicial, scholarly, political and economic communities. To this can be added the influence and the rising pervasiveness of international law. These influences can either be beneficial or detrimental and are usually a mixed bag of benefits and drawbacks.[13]

One may legitimately ask if the flourishing of constitutional comparison is really new. After all, comparison in public law is much older than the consciousness of its method.[14] Comparison indeed has been strongly in evidence through all of the waves of constitution-writing since the 18th Century, but the institutionalization of the comparison of constitutional law in the form of the founding of scholarly associations and university chairs attending to it is not much older than 60 years.[15]

The archetypal Constitution of the United States of America was drafted by the Constitutional Convention in 1787 on the foundations of the foregoing confederal documents, the existing constitutions of the 13 states, and under the influence of the philosophies of European authors such as John Locke and Hugo de Groot. There can be no doubt that these and other writers of the era strongly influenced the thinking of the American 'Fathers of the Constitution'. The compliment was returned across the Atlantic in that the practical implementation of continental thinking in revolutionary America inspired the French Constituent Assembly of 1789 to make the French the first European constitution-writing nation, thereby initiating modern continental constitutionalism.[16]

As early as the 19th Century both the US and French Constitutions strongly influenced the constitution-writing of South American countries

---

[13] It will be argued in the following chapters that one of the negative side-effects of globalized constitutionalism is the idea that secular neutrality offers a solution to the challenges presented by religious pluralism.
[14] Wieser (2005) 9.
[15] Wieser (2005) 9–14. See also Zweigert and Kötz (1998), Chapter 4.
[16] See n. 2 above.

such as Mexico and Argentina. In the era of colonialism the constitutional notions of the colonial powers, especially Britain and France, were adopted in many parts of the world, though frequently in adapted forms.[17] After World War II the USA as the primary victor emerging from the war was, in addition to its constitution-writing role in Japan, a significant presence behind the work of the *Parlamentarischer Rat* which formulated the German *Grundgesetz* of 1949, the latter subsequently itself becoming an influential example in other parts of the world, especially but not exclusively in post-Soviet Eastern Europe. After the war the scene was also set for the acceleration of the process of decolonization, not only in the underdeveloped parts of Africa but also for instance in the British 'dominions' of India, Canada and South Africa, causing a rash of new constitutions to be produced. The most recent wave of constitution-making was of course generated by the fall of the USSR, which saw the Soviet 'empire' in Eastern and Central Europe disintegrate into multiple sovereign states and also led to the release of the logistical and ideological grip of communism on the third world.

Following constitutional examples from other parts of the world is therefore nothing new, but constitution-writing has become more than a comparative exercise in which examples from elsewhere are selected, as it were, 'off the shelf', to be introduced in one's own system, with larger or smaller adaptations to the local conditions.[18] A universal language of constitutionalism has been established, a glossary of constitutional principles and values is at hand, and a catalogue of constitutional structures is constantly and casually referenced by constitution-makers. Constitutional lawyers have developed a common vernacular enabling them to speak with one another against the background of a wide spectrum of jurisdictions. Gone are the days when a Dicey could be forgiven for

---

[17] See for example, Franck and Thiruvengadam (2003) 500–504 for a compact overview.

[18] Cf. Harding and Leyland (2007) 327:

Constitutions are no longer taken from the peg, but are tailored with some precision and consideration of global experience as well as local needs and practicalities. The constitution-making process has also been considerably democratised, which opens up both the careful consideration of diverse solutions and the accommodation of different views. The comparative dimension is now so ingrained that it is hard to imagine any constitution-building effort without it.

presenting the French *droit administrativ* negatively for the purposes of developing his own peculiarly English conception of the Rule of Law.[19]

In most Western states the role of the judiciary in constitution-making is particularly prominent. This statement needs no more proof than the mentioning of a constitutional *locus classicus* in the various jurisdictions, such as *Calvin's Case* of 1608,[20] by which British colonial constitutional law was steered across the world for three centuries; the United States Supreme Court's *Marbury v Madison* of 1803,[21] today still the point of departure for a discussion on judicial review and the so-called counter-majoritarian dilemma; the German *Bundesverfassungsgericht*'s judgment in the Lüth-case of 1958,[22] whereby it was settled that the fundamental rights provisions of the *Grundgesetz* of 1949 embodied not only the defensive rights of the individual but also an objective order of values applicable to all reaches of the law; the Canadian *R v Oakes*[23] of 1986, in which the interpretative approach to the Charter of Rights of 1982 was

---

[19] Cf. the celebrated Dicey (1885), Chapter XII and Sir Ivor Jennings' introductory comment in Jennings (1938) 99–104:

> So long as the view of Dicey prevailed that there was in England no such thing as administrative law, English students of public law were trying to do exercises in a strait waistcoat. If the common law were codified it would probably be found that two-thirds of English law – in bulk and not necessarily in importance – was administrative law. The result of the predominance of the Dicey school was that most of the modern law was being ignored by the academic lawyers, and the result of the growing acceptance of the fact (obvious to anyone who even glances through an American or continental book) that Dicey took one small part of French administrative law and ignored the rest has been to give a great impetus to the study of the problems involved in the growth of State activities.

[20] *Calvin v Smith and Another* (1608) 7 Co Rep 1a.

[21] *Marbury v Madison* 5 U.S. (1Cranch) 137 (1803).

[22] BverfGE 7,198, 15.1.1958, 205: 'Ebenso richtig ist aber, daß das Grundgesetz, das keine wertneutrale Ordnung sein will ... , in seinem Grundrechtsabschnitt auch eine objektive Wertordnung aufgerichtet hat und daß gerade hierin eine prinzipielle Verstärkung der Geltungskraft des Grundrechte zum Ausdruck kommt. Diese Wertsystem, das seinen Mittelpunkt in der innerhalb der sozialen Gemeinschaft sich frei entfaltenden menschlichen Persönlichkeit und ihrer Würde findet, muß als verfassungsrechtliche Grundentscheidung für alle Bereiche des Rechts gelten.'

[23] (1986) 26 DLR (4th) 200.

laid down; and the South African Constitutional Court's *S v Makwanyane*,[24] in which each of the 11 justices delivered a judgment declaring the death penalty unconstitutional while effusively citing foreign authorities.

Which post-constitution-*writing* force will be most influential in the constitution-*making* process following the adoption of a new constitution may vary from one case to another. An example of the unpredictability of the constitution-making process is that of the Japanese Constitution of 1947. The constitutional text has not been amended since its adoption, and the judiciary has performed an important though subdued role in its further development as provided for by the Constitution. One may therefore be forgiven for expecting the emergence of a constitutional law created in the image of the West, and yet, through practice and usage, the meaning of this document written more than six decades ago by General MacArthur's US military lawyers has been thoroughly 'Japanized' without losing its core importance.[25]

The Japanese and similar examples cause one to doubt that globalized one-size-fits-all value-laden conceptions such as state secularism are helpful for the solution of questions regarding local religious diversity.

2.3 EFFECTS OF GLOBALIZATION ON CONSTITUTIONAL LAW

One of the effects of globalization on constitutional law is that state authorities (including the courts) are often called upon to deal with issues widely known also to be cropping up elsewhere in the world. Approaches to and the resolutions of these issues vary, but many of those responsible for dealing with them take glances, some unguarded and others furtive, at the work of their peers abroad. For students of constitutional law the comparative study of the different approaches is a captivating enterprise. The effects of globalization on citizenship and statehood, considered below in section 7.1, exemplify this.

Although it cannot be a focal point for the purposes of the present discussion, it is unavoidable in the interests of perspective that notice should also be taken of the constitutionalization of international law before consideration is given to the 'internationalization' of constitutional law.

---

[24] 1995 (3) SA 391 (CC).
[25] Cf. Venter (2000) 60–63, 133–135, 214–215.

2.3.1 The Constitutionalization of International Law

The stock reply to the question of how one distinguishes between international law and (domestic) constitutional law is that international law is concerned with the legal regulation of the relationships between the subjects in this field, which are states, whereas constitutional law is the jurisdiction-specific field of law regulating the allocation, distribution and exercise by the state and its organs of government authority over the citizens of the country concerned.[26] In principle this distinction is still valid, but its solidity is constantly being watered down. No longer are sovereign states the only subjects active in international legal relations, and international norms increasingly penetrate the municipal law of sovereign states without necessarily being sanctioned or transformed by national authorities constitutionally endowed with state authority. Because of the ever-expanding globalization of the law, national constitution-making, particularly in the sense of the post-promulgation development of a constitutional order, cannot be isolated from these tendencies.

In 2002, observing the rising importance of constitutionalism, which was accompanied however by an increasing criticism of the conventional wisdoms of constitutional law, Neil Walker construed the notion of 'constitutional pluralism' as opposed to 'constitutional monism'. This he explained with reference to the European Union (without, however, limiting his general analysis to the EU), as follows:[27]

> Constitutional monism merely grants a label to the defining assumption of constitutionalism in the Westphalian age ... namely the idea that the sole centres or units of constitutional authorities are states. Constitutional pluralism, by contrast, recognises that the European order inaugurated by the Treaty of Rome has developed beyond the traditional confines of inter-*national* law and now makes its own independent constitutional claims, and that these claims exist alongside the continuing claims of states. The relationship between the orders, that is to say, is now horizontal rather than vertical – heterarchical rather than hierarchical.

Similarly Sophie van Bijsterveld, emphasizing the 'inevitable pull towards internationalisation and the scale and intensity of the internationalisation of policy and law which we are witnessing',[28] remarks:[29]

---

[26] For a concise rendering of the historical background of this distinction, see for example, Glenn (2013) 157–158.
[27] Walker (2002) 337.
[28] Van Bijsterveld (2002) 30.

Regardless of the extent to which the state may diminish in importance, it will no longer retain its position as the predominant *locus* for the organisation of public decision-making. The role and function of the national state is undergoing a metamorphosis and leading to confusion with regard to what is to be regarded as 'public' or not. It is becoming more difficult to distinguish the state from other institutions and organisations. It is precisely in this sense that the state is losing its 'state-ness.' The core characteristics of the state are at stake.

An excellent analysis of the debate on the constitutionalization of international law opens with the following remarks:[30]

> In recent years, the concept of world constitutionalism has become remarkably popular among international legal scholars. While fifteen years ago, endorsing it was considered a somewhat extravagant position – associated with delusional, rather than progressive thinking – there is currently much fervent support for the concept. To refer to 'constitutional structures' in international law or even to the 'international constitution' or the 'constitution of international law' has become commonplace in legal doctrine.

However, the authors go on to describe and contrast the various and remarkably diffuse approaches to this matter, and suggest that, because of 'world constitutionalism' being an abstract notion which has strong constitutive but weak regulatory effects, it should be referred to as a 'legitimization institution'. They seek to find the foundations for world constitutionalism in the identification of humanity's common goals and shared identity. Interestingly this seems to imply that foundational views of 'good' principles and values, if sufficiently widespread, will enhance the constitutionalization of international law.

In similar vein Anne Peters argues for the realization of the potential of global constitutionalism as a means of introducing remedies for the legitimacy shortcomings of international law, but also for national constitutionalist deficits brought about by globalization and as a tool for interpreting international law.[31]

The gist of the doctrinal battle over constitutionalism, concerning governance in the global context, has been captured by Daniel Halberstam[32] as three streams of thought, ranging from local constitutionalism (said to be propounded by 'new sovereigntists'), global constitutionalism

---

[29] Van Bijsterveld (2002) 22.
[30] Diggelmann and Altwicker (2008) 623.
[31] Peters (2009).
[32] 'Local, Global and Plural Constitutionalism: Europe Meets the World' Chapter 4, and the other contributions in De Búrca and Weiler (2012).

(pursuing a cosmopolitan ideal) and pluralist constitutionalism (based on a non-hierarchical diversity of sites of public authority, competing for but reciprocally respecting each other's authority).[33]

An interesting twist to the notion of the constitutionalization of international law was revealed by Anthea Roberts in an analysis of the trend to find and interpret international law norms by means of the comparison of judgments of various national courts.[34] She found that it has become possible in this context to speak of 'comparative international law', although not without acknowledging difficulties such as differences in the manner in which courts 'domesticate' international law and the existence of the same methodological stumbling blocks that are prevalent in comparative law in general.

2.3.2 The Internationalization of Constitutional Law

If one considers the escalating tendency of the incursion of the global market (as perhaps the primary driver of globalization) on the freedom of choice of the contemporary state's policy-making competencies in many fields, the constitutional affirmations of national sovereignty further tend to lose credibility under the onslaught of globalization. The state, however, along with its sovereignty is far from becoming redundant, since its existence and authority continue to be fundamental premises upon which the law and its authority are construed. What does need to be reconsidered is how the meaning of these concepts is changing (see section 7.1 below).

It has become a constant occupation of constitutional comparatists to investigate how international trends affect domestic constitutional law and constitution-making. After all, if it is true that such a basic constitutional premise as state sovereignty is being challenged on the strength of developments within the global community, the question arises spontaneously whether a legitimate national constitution can still be written or developed without accounting for characteristics of constitutional law that have gained global currency, or without acknowledging the effects of some norms of international law.[35]

Despite the fact that the application of a constitution is limited almost exclusively to the territorial jurisdiction of the state concerned, and that it

---

[33] See also Krisch (2010).
[34] Roberts (2011).
[35] Backer (2007–2008) 13 thinks not: 'States increasingly looked to international standards of legitimate state organization in drafting their constitutions.'

is at least theoretically impermissible[36] for an external authority to impose a constitution on a sovereign state, all constitution-writing and constitution-making is, and has increasingly become, wide open to active global scrutiny. Characteristic of globalization, access especially by electronic means to the immense store of published comparative materials has very few limits. This is true of scholarly materials and court judgments, as well as draft and adopted constitutional and legislative texts, sometimes translated from languages known less widely into ones more generally understood, and of instruments of international law. With such accessibility come significant pressures of influence in the form of what might be called a global *communis opinio* of acceptability. This seems to result in the knowledge of those involved in constitution-making, be they advisors, legislators, judges or scholars, that the work that they are doing is in the global public domain. One indication hereof is that contemporary constitutions, even of countries that patently do not have the characteristics of globally recognized constitutionalism, due for example to their express socialist[37] or Islamic[38] underpinnings, are often also clothed at least partially in constitutionalist language.

The fact that constitution-making is open to unrestricted scrutiny nevertheless does not cause constitution-makers to reach the same conclusions or to resolve issues in the same or even similar ways. It does, however, mean that role-players are almost compelled to compare the approaches to and resolution of issues with which they are confronted with what is being done in the rest of the world.

Citing the work of David Law, Hirschl[39] refers to the 'brisk traffic in constitutional ideas' leading to 'generic constitutional law'. He argues that constitutional law around the world has similar theoretical concerns, uses similar analytical methods and follows similar doctrines due to

---

[36] Leaving aside external diplomatic, economic and political pressure, processes (now mostly historical) of decolonization and the usurped privileges of a victor over the vanquished in war, all being exceptions really proving the rule.

[37] Article 1(1) of the Chinese Constitution of 2004 for example, provides: 'The People's Republic of China is a socialist state under the people's democratic dictatorship led by the working class and based on the alliance of workers and peasants', while in article 33(3) it is provided that 'The State respects and preserves human rights.'

[38] Article 2 of the Constitution of Bahrain of 2002 provides: 'The religion of the State is Islam. The Islamic Shari'a is a principal source for legislation', while article 18 states that 'People are equal in human dignity, and citizens are equal before the law in public rights and duties. There shall be no discrimination among them on the basis of sex, origin, language, religion or creed.'

[39] Hirschl (2013).

'interlocking relationships of history and sovereignty, adjudicative methodology, the broad normative appeal of various rights, and the tensions underlying judicial review itself'.[40]

When the term 'globalization' is attached to a description of the internationalizing trends in constitutional law, there is a danger of overemphasizing its effects and ending up with notions of universalization and homogenization, a world society under a world government. Rather, Isabella Löhr and Roland Wenzlhuemer suggest that the term 'globalization' should be used to indicate 'the process of the gradual detachment of patterns of socio-cultural interaction from geographical proximity'.[41]

The indisputable effect of globalization on constitutional law is that national constitutional isolationism can no longer be maintained, if ever it could. On the other hand, the national constitutional order of a state is still designed to apply primarily where the authority of the state concerned can be exercised most comprehensively, which is normally understood – or at least has been since the 17th Century – to be within its territorial boundaries.[42] Patrick Glenn, however, argues cogently that 'factual globalization' brings about the overrunning of boundaries by information affecting not only state territory but also and to a greater extent the concept of the state as such.[43] Philipp Kiiver[44] captures the challenge of internationalization to constitutional exclusivity as follows:

> The starting points of the Enlightenment-inspired development of domestic constitutional standards – separation of powers, government *sub lege*, rule by many with the consent of the governed, guaranteed civil and political rights, and so forth – are fundamentally different from the basic principles applying to the international realm: sovereign equality of states, the ability of governments to commit their state (and their citizens) and non-intervention in internal affairs. Strict adherence to purely domestic constitutional standards in the face of internationalisation is often neither feasible nor desirable.

Regardless of the reality that conventional constitutional law is constantly being subjected to influences and strains from various directions, the globalized world still has far to go – and it appears to be unlikely to

---

[40] Law (2004–2005) 659.
[41] Löhr and Wenzlhuemer (2013) 3.
[42] Glenn (2013) 83–85 links the emergence of state boundaries with the development of map-making and Ulrich Huber's coining of the phrase 'conflict of laws' in the 1670s.
[43] Glenn (2013) 170–171.
[44] Kiiver (2010) 112.

happen in the foreseeable future – before it ceases to be in need of constitutions, constitutional law and constitutionalism. That 'national' constitutional law has, however, been opened widely to external influences is clear, and it is beyond contestation that the unchaining of constitutional interpretation from territorial constraints will continue.

2.4 GLOBALIZATION AND RELIGION

One of the most recognizable phenomena that characterizes globalization is the mobility of the world's population.[45] Inevitably, the movement of people across boundaries brings with it the pluralization of religion in the destination states. The internationalization of constitutional law entails heightened levels of constitutional comparison and a concomitant absorption of constitutional concepts in constitutional orders around the globe. This transfer, migration, transplantation or reception (whichever designation may be appropriate or preferred in particular cases) is carried by constitutional language whereby ideas such as fundamental rights (including freedom of religion), constitutional review (including the adjudication of religious disputes) and constitutionalism (which is incompatible with injustice) are infused into the global constitutional discourse. Thus the difficulties faced by state authorities when they are confronted with contesting demands emanating from a pluralistic citizenry are increasingly described using similar language. Religious pluralism therefore represents constitutional challenges that are sprouting in the fertile soil of globalization.

---

[45] For some statistics in this regard, see section 7.1.2 below.

3. Constitutionalism

History has proven that lasting and sustainable societal, national and international peace is an unattainable ideal. The level of peace in the world is constantly fluctuating. The more consolidated a citizenry is, the more it will tend to feel threatened by the loss of its uniqueness by the commixture of other identities within its ranks or by threats of external domination. Globalization is diluting the uniqueness of the citizenries of most states, although there is hardly any contemporary instance of such dilution that has caused the former 'national' identity to be subsumed or replaced by cosmopolitanism.

Constitutional and legal orders are strong indicators of the character of a citizenry, especially where democracy underpins the system. Due to the absorption by many societies of 'other' religious mentalities and structures, the legal orders of such societies are challenged to find ways to keep the religious peace by means of balanced justice. In most constitutional states it is no longer possible to allow the law to be guided, expressly or by implication, by some predominant religious stance. This has led to the increased popularity of the idea that secular neutrality provides a solution. It seems that, in the absence of credible alternatives, many are reconciled to state secularism.

Such a 'solution', however, cannot but have the effect of disguising religious prejudice, a point to which we shall return below. Nevertheless, the state as the primary institution endowed with the power required to preserve societal peace between divergent religious components in society continues to be obliged to find solutions to preserve peace within its religiously plural citizenry. What should the standards be against which the success of the state's actions for the preservation of religious peace should be tested? The notion of constitutionalism needs to be interrogated, since it may offer itself to be such a standard.

3.1 CONSTITUTIONALISM AS STANDARD AND *TERTIUM COMPARATIONIS*

In their introduction to a collection of conference papers on globalization and constitutionalism, Frishman and Muller[1] offer the following with reference to constitutions as the 'pillars of stable societies': '"constitutionalism" can be understood, in general terms, as a legal and political school of thought which holds that any form of governance should be constantly circumscribed by a system of checks and balances derived from a primary legal document or body of principles'. On the next page, however, they add that constitutionalism 'may have different meanings and functions depending on the relevant context and perspective'.[2] Following Louis Henkin, Ramcharan states[3] that to be 'constitutionalist' a constitution 'must secure constitutional legitimacy and constitutional review, authentic democracy and accountable government that will respect and ensure individual human rights and secure basic human needs'.

When dealing with a capricious conception such as religion, one must accept that subjectivity will be part of the equation. Nevertheless, religion is expressly or by implication an important determining factor in the trends of most forms of social regulation and in all environments, being a ubiquitous characteristic of all members of the human race. In many instances religion as such is not mentioned. In most cases it supports ideological goals or ideals such as liberalism, socialism or nationalism. In this view atheists, for example, claiming that they are in awe of the laws of nature, are taking a position closer to religion than anything else. Ideological goals, ideals and ideas about reality are ultimately founded in religion or in preconceptions (even anti-religious ones) so profound that they equate to religion.

When dealing with law, despite its being conceptually less evasive than religion, one must accept that legal norms, concepts, principles and structures established for or by means of law are also not solid or immutable, that is, one cannot scientifically deal with them as enduring, hard data, such as for example the genetic code found in the human

---

[1] Frishman and Muller (2010) 1.
[2] Frishman and Muller (2010) 2.
[3] Ramcharan (2010) 18.

genome.[4] Law is a product of human culture, notoriously varied and variable, subject to the vagaries of unpredictable forces acting upon societies, their leaders and their institutions. These are constantly subject to change, exposed to human passion and historical imperatives.

Part of social reality around the globe and through time is that law and its institutions (the state being at its core) constantly encounter religion. These encounters take many forms, including justifications for the content of legal norms, particular dogmatic approaches to the interpretation or application of the law, motivations for the allocation of authority to legal institutions – and the matter primarily under consideration here – dealing with the omnipresence and diversity of religious convictions.

It is against this background that one must accept that any position that one might take on a preferred approach by the state to the challenges presented by religious pluralism will not meet with universal approval. Any suggested approach will in fact inexorably be met with scrutiny by commentators that will reflect, either expressly or by implication, their normative stances. Such stances may be presented as being political, philosophical, scholarly, historical, objective or neutral, and the precepts upon which they are founded may be unclear, obscure or express, but, and this is the heart of the matter, they will all have their roots in the foundational points of departure of the particular commentator, that is, his or her essentially religious motives. As is argued elsewhere in this book, agnosticism, atheism and secularism all qualify to be classified under religious convictions.

The challenge that is taken up in this chapter is to present constitutionalism as a standard against which the appropriateness of state conduct regarding religion, and especially religious pluralism, may be measured. It must immediately be conceded that general acquiescence on the characterization of constitutionalism is impossible to hope for – the choices that are made will not be indisputable – but it must also be hoped that useful indicators are available in most of the elements of constitutionalism that have gained widespread currency in the constitutional discourse of the early 21st Century around the globe. These notions include, in association with constitutionalism, the constitutional state and the rule of law.

The world is increasingly using similar constitutional vocabulary. However, the denotation of the words in this vocabulary varies in

---

[4] Louis Henkin most certainly could not have had the certainties of the genetic code in mind when he entitled an article 'A New Birth of Constitutionalism: Genetic Influences and Genetic Defects' Henkin (1994).

different contexts and in accordance with local history, current circumstances, dominant ideology and the composition of society. The same terms used by different speakers or in relation to different national orders may therefore not bear the same meaning or have the same connotations. Nevertheless, the shared vocabulary promotes sensible communication (if it is undertaken prudently), enhances the adoption of compatible views, is useful for drawing comparisons and may contribute to an improved sharing of values. This is what allows 'constitutionalism' to be a signifier for a desirable constitutional condition. Unavoidably, however, dogmatic exactitude regarding the details of 21st Century constitutionalism is not at hand. In fact, the notion is being used in an amazing spectrum of contexts. Hans Vorländer,[5] for one, identified the following approaches to or versions of constitutionalism: societal constitutionalism, creeping constitutionalism, compensatory constitutionalism, pluralistic constitutionalism, multilevel constitutionalism (containing the notion of a constitutional compromise or settlement), cosmopolitan constitutionalism and global constitutionalism (with variations in the form of transnational constitutionalism, where mention is made of a constitution of mankind, and global civil constitutions). Among those propounding state (as distinct from international) constitutionalism, Vorländer identified apologists for sovereignty and the national state, theorists on identity and homogeneity, and an approach that considers it possible for the principles of modern democracy to be maintained only in the context of a state-structured order. It is nevertheless considered to be methodologically sound to attribute specific characteristics to the term, particularly for our present purposes. These characteristics are not being sought in the imagination but in a consideration of their manifestation in the world of constitutional law.

The diversity of practical, structural and institutional approaches to constitutional government may be conceived to be such that no single standard, benchmark or yardstick can be devised against which a system can be measured for universally acknowledged integrity. It may also justifiably be argued that a particular constitutional configuration may be good for a specific country or era but inoperable or even debilitating for another. Another valid position to take would be that humanity is so fractured in its understanding of what may be just and good, that there is no sense in assessing all constitutions with one measure. Should one furthermore introduce into the discussion the plurality of religions and world views, not only across the surface of the earth but increasingly

---

[5] Vorländer (2012) 23–24.

within states, it may appear to be hopeless to conceive of a cogent and defensible consolidated framework for an argument in favour of a globally acceptable view on a 'right' way for the state of the 21st Century to deal with the problems of religious pluralism. All these positions are reinforced by the indisputable truth that people, be they believers, scholars or children, look at the world from incalculably divers points of departure. And yet, it does make sense to relate the problems created by religious pluralism to constitutionalism in order to find solutions to otherwise intractable issues. To make this approach viable, it is necessary to construe a cogent position on the nature and content of constitutionalism.

Since the end of World War II constitutionalism has established itself as the vogue around the globe. It is the gift of Europe (including Britain) and the United States to the world of the 21st Century, emanating from the political, economic and constitutional history of what is often referred to as 'the West' (geographically more accurately the slice of the globe Westward approximately of the intersection of 30° Longitude and 30° Latitude up to 60° Latitude). On this point an interesting altercation between Joseph Weiler and Daniel Halberstam was published in 2012.[6] Weiler took the position[7] that constitutionalism is 'a very American' construction, to which Halberstam retorted as follows:[8]

> Constitutionalism was also central to the real-world struggle for liberalism and democracy as it unfolded in Europe. Constitutionalism in one form or another was a key element of the European battles surrounding the legitimate exercise of public power ever since James Whitlocke objected in 1610 to the impositions of James I on the grounds that they were 'against the natural frame and constitutions of the policy [in other words, 'polity'] of his kingdom, which is *ius publicum regni*, and so subverteth the fundamental law of the realm and induceth a new form of State and government.' The struggle in England and, later, on the Continent for liberal self-government quickly came to appreciate the importance of constitutionalism despite the varied forms the latter would take. Whether as the framing of pre-existing political power in England and Germany or the radical founding of political power in the United States and France, constitutionalism and constitutions took centre stage.

From a perspective beyond Europe and the United States, emphasis on the Western roots of constitutionalism may be perceived to be an

---

[6] In De Búrca and Weiler (2012).
[7] Weiler and Halberstam (2012) at 285.
[8] Weiler and Halberstam (2012) at 292–293.

expression of cultural hegemony on the part of the 'dominant West'.[9] Given the less than admirable elements in the colonial legacies of Europe and the often high-handed conduct of American governments over two centuries and particularly of the USA as superpower since World War II, the construction of hegemonic motives is understandable. It must furthermore be accepted that the spread of constitutionalism is indeed to be ascribed to a large extent to colonialism and Americanism. However, that does not mean that constitutionalism currently serves hegemonic purposes: it has in the course of its deployment, whether imposed or willingly received, developed a vitality of its own, rooted in the logic and current modalities of life in a globalized world. To name but one issue that underpins a generalized view of constitutionalism: insistence on individual freedom of choice in the various contingencies of human life as a social phenomenon typical of this era. This desire for individualized freedom of choice is not dependent on Western presence or domination – it is an instinctive human response to be suppressed only by means incompatible with universal notions of morality, and can rightly be considered to be one of the (sometimes unexpressed) drivers of contemporary constitutionalism.

Selecting constitutionalism as the standard is a choice made here on the basis of a preferred comparative methodology. To undertake a useful comparison, one needs to determine what the material that is to be compared is to be compared with. Comparison needs a point of reference: merely finding similarities or differences between compared material can be no more than a preliminary step. Comparing different approaches to the complexities of dealing with religious pluralism requires the identification of a (if necessary, idealized) standard against which all the compared materials can be compared. A notion of constitutionalism, styled for the purpose, can provide us with such a *tertium comparationis*. To realize the utility of this choice, however, requires the making of some choices regarding the nature and content of constitutionalism as preferred *tertium comparationis*.

It must be admitted that the choice of constitutionalism and the allocation of content to the notion as a comparative standard is a paradigmatic choice. Put differently, support for constitutionalism is not a value-free choice, because its characteristics emanate from a philosophical and cultural history. This history is complex and followed many controversial paths, but the notion that has emerged in the course of time contains sufficiently objective and attractive characteristics to provide a

---

[9] Cf. for example, Pollis (1996).

universal vocabulary that allows for valid comparative outcomes that may satisfy a reasonable spectrum of points of departure.[10] A brief consideration of the manner in which constitutionalism is employed in different contexts should be useful for the purpose.

3.2 THE DOMESTIC MEANING OF 'CONSTITUTIONALISM'

In this section 'domestic' is used for lack of a better word. What 'domestic' must here be understood to be is a compact reference to 'intra-statal' or 'constitutional-law-properly-so-called'. Using 'domestic' here at all is actually made necessary only to distinguish what might also clumsily have been called 'constitutional constitutionalism' from the emergent notion of global or international constitutionalism. Indicators such as 'national' or 'classical' would also be misleading because of the wide range of possible national environments and the fact that no specific system can rightfully claim to be the 'classical' or stereotypical constitutionalist example.

As a point of departure for the contemporary scholarly discussion of domestic constitutionalism, the 1938–1939 lectures of C.H. McIlwain,[11] that covered the emergence of the concept from ancient times, continue to be valuable. With reference to the American founding theories of Thomas Paine and Edmund Burke, that a constitution should necessarily be understood to be a written document, McIlwain cited the following statement in 1733 by Lord Bolingbroke on English constitutionalism:[12]

> By constitution we mean, whenever we speak with propriety and exactness, that assemblage of laws, institutions and customs, derived from certain fixed principles of reason, directed to certain fixed objects of public good, that compose the general system, according to which the community hath agreed to be governed. ... We call this a good government, when ... the whole administration of public affairs is wisely pursued, and with a strict conformity to the principles and objects of the constitution.

Even for the moment setting aside the discourse on the 'constitutionalization of international law',[13] one may still, after considering the range

---

[10] For a more detailed exposition of comparative methodology, cf. Venter (2010a) Chapter 2, especially section 2.2.
[11] Published for example, in McIlwain (1947).
[12] McIlwain (1947) 3.
[13] See section 3.3 below.

of meanings currently being given to constitutionalism, tend to despair over the chances of finding a clear and generally acceptable meaning for the word. One should not be surprised by the reality that the more the word is subjected to analysis, the more it is being milked for significance. Nevertheless, as will emerge, the wide-ranging global constitutional intercourse allows for the extraction of the essential elements of constitutionalism.

Let us sample some analyses in different contexts, working from the more or less least likely (Islamic) towards the most refined (European) renderings.

3.2.1 Islam

A discussion of constitutionalism in an Islamic context may be rewarding, though also extraordinarily challenging, since the key components of constitutionalism are historically rooted in soil foreign to Islam. Thus Boozari's book on this theme is, for the purposes of theoretically construing an Islamic form of constitutionalism, launched from a basis wholly non-Islamic.[14] The obvious cause of the difficulty of building an Islamic theory of constitutionalism is the complete dominance of the state, law and culture by the Islamic religion:[15]

> If Islamic civilization, culture, or state ever constituted a regime of any kind, it was one of nomocracy. There has never been a culture in human society so legally oriented as Islam. ... we have come to realize – more than ever – that Islamic law was not merely a legal system that resolved conflicts and negotiated social and economic relationships (the role normally assigned to law in the West), but that it was in addition a theological system, an applied religious ritual, an intellectual enterprise of the first order, a cultural pillar of farreaching dimensions and, in short, a world-view that defined both Muslim identity and even Islam itself.

---

[14] Boozari (2011) 1 ascribes three characteristics to constitutionalism, viz. the limitation of political power, the rule of law and the protection of individual rights, all derived from non-Islamic literature. The foreignness to Western thinking of Islamic doctrine is well demonstrated by Hallaq (2003) at 1706: 'The idea of giving to Caesar what is Caesar's and to God what is God's does not wash in the Muslim world-view, for Caesar is only a man, and men, being equal, cannot command obedience to each other. Obedience therefore must be to a supreme entity, one that is eternal, omnipotent, and omniscient. If modernity has effected profound changes in Islamic culture (and no doubt it has), it has failed in the most important respect, namely, to alter or sever this tie with the divine.'

[15] Hallaq (2003) 1707–1708.

Boozari nevertheless succeeds in drawing examples that evoke a form of constitutionalism from the Shi'ite materials that emerged from the short-lived Iranian revolution of 1905, such as a 'version of popular sovereignty in the service of reconciling constitutionalism with the requirement of compliance to Shari'ah'.[16] According to Khaled Abou El Fadl, writing the introduction to Boozari's book,[17] the Shi'ite arguments offered in favour of constitutionalism apply equally to Sunni Islam.

Another erudite consideration of the possibilities of linking Islam as a form of 'theocratic constitutionalism' to constitutionalism as understood in other contexts is that of Catá Backer. After describing the constitutional dispensations in Iran, Afghanistan, Saudi Arabia, Pakistan, Egypt, Malaysia and Sri Lanka, he acknowledges that theocratic constitutionalism can be very different from the ordering of power hierarchies in Western thinking, but he finds that 'within its own contextual universe, it can provide as sound a basis for ordered and rule of law government as that offered by transnational constitutionalism'.[18] In short, a special kind of constitutionalism needs to be devised in order to apply to Islamic states as a measure comparable to the wider conception. Whether such a construction can be useful as a means to measure appropriate state responses to religious pluralism is doubtful, however.

Ten years before the infamous '9/11' attacks, Reisman correctly predicted,[19] in the context of the 'rise of Islamic fundamentalism' in the Middle East and North Africa, as it was manifested in the Iranian Revolution of 1979 and its consequences, that, although the political ideology of the fundamentalists should not be equated with all of Islam, fundamentalism 'will remain an important political force in countries with considerable Moslem populations'. The course of events in Iran since the publication of the book seems to confirm the following observations of Reisman:[20]

> As a political ideology, Islamic fundamentalism suffers from the same fatal symptoms of communism and other authoritarian régimes. As in communism, it believes in the success of a particular group, irrespective of political boundaries. ... For the Islamic fundamentalists, it is the oppressed Moslems (Moztasaphine). ... In fundamentalism, the actual power of guidance and decision-making is in the hands of a small group of clergy who are responsible to no other authority than God. ... [T]he guaranteed rule of the

---

[16] Boozari (2011) 2.
[17] Boozari (2011) viii.
[18] Backer (2009) 171.
[19] Reisman (1991) 126.
[20] Reisman (1991) 126, including footnote 50.

clergy will eventually, as has already been seen in the Iranian case, lead to personal preference and the exercise of discretion and corruption. ... As some members of the class of clergy move into more political activities and the business of running the government, their principal identity will change. They will begin to lose religious authority, the very basic ingredient of their political legitimacy. They will become vulnerable and susceptible to criticism by the competing clergy for their pursuit and application of power and authority.

3.2.2 China

The notion of constitutionalism is often used as a measure of progress towards a less authoritarian or more democratic dispensation in countries or systems not naturally inclined thereto. Thus, for example, Kellogg[21] and Balme and Dowdle[22] describe some recent developments in China as being indicative of nascent constitutionalism. A consideration of such manifestations of constitutionalism, atypical of the systems concerned, can serve the purpose of highlighting specific elements of an understanding of constitutionalism more often than not by means of contrasting reality with the ideal, but also to demonstrate the persuasive influence of constitutionalist thinking even in circumstances not naturally conducive to it.

Kellogg[23] describes the Chinese constitutional system as one based upon the soviet example of the former USSR. The prevalent Marxist thinking conceives the law as a means of maintaining 'the dictatorship of the proletariat' and is therefore inhospitable to an understanding of the constitution as a mechanism to regulate the relationship between citizens and the state, or of the law as regulating relationships between individuals. Since the 1982 Chinese Constitution places all the power of the state in the hands of 'the people' as represented in the National People's Congress (NPC), the latter is primarily responsible for supervising and enforcing the Constitution. Article 67(1) of the Constitution empowers the NPC Standing Committee to interpret it and to supervise its enforcement. In terms of article 64(1), the Standing Committee (or at least one-fifth of the members of the NPC) may propose amendments to the Constitution, which require the support of at least two-thirds of the members to be adopted. In at least a procedural sense, the Constitution is therefore superior to other laws, which require only an ordinary majority for adoption in terms of article 64(2).

---

[21] Kellogg (2009).
[22] Balme and Dowdle (2009).
[23] Kellogg (2009).

56 *Constitutionalism and religion*

There are indications of a growing importance being ascribed to the Constitution in China. Since the year 2000, laws have been generally required to conform to the provisions of the Constitution, sub-national legal norms may be required to be revised or be nullified if they are found to be unconstitutional, and opportunities for and scholarly argumentation in favour of judicial authority over the Constitution are becoming evident. In fact, it would appear that adherence to Marxist ideology, even on governmental levels, is being diluted. Furthermore, courts have, even as long ago as the 1980s, been exposed to arguments brought before them to adjudicate matters on constitutional grounds. Activists play an important role in this regard. The introduction or growth of constitutionalism in China thus appears to be advanced by society more than by government, and the authorities and the courts have given indications of an inclination to adapt positively, but progress is slow. Stéphanie Balme, for example, concludes[24] that:

> [J]udicial activism is both the cause and the consequence of the central government's emphasis on improving the societal and political role and status of the judiciary. The slogan 'protecting rights is the improvement of justice …' expresses the trajectory of this evolution quite eloquently.

The constitutional deficits in China regarding democracy and the protection of fundamental rights, however, continue to be prominent. Balme and Dowdle[25] see greater possibilities for the development of Chinese constitutionalism in the French example, where they say the mobilization of citizens for the purposes of influencing policy formation is preferred, above the American instincts of challenging governmental behaviour in the courts.

3.2.3 East Asia

The issue of affluence, or economic development as its cause and its relationship to elements of constitutionalism such as democracy, understandably also crops up in the East Asian context. The following telling statement was made by Malaysia's Prime Minister Mahathir at the Europe–East Asia Economic Forum in 1992:[26]

> In the former Soviet Union and the East European countries, democracy was introduced along with the free market. The result is chaos and increased

---

[24] Balme (2009) 197.
[25] Balme and Dowdle (2009) 10.
[26] Cited by Davis (1998) 309.

misery. Not only have the countries broken up, mainly through bloody civil wars, but there is actual recession and more hardship for the people than when the Communists ruled. One may ask whether democracy is the means or the end. Democracy at all costs is not much different from Communist authoritarianism from the barrel of a gun. ... In a number of East Asian countries, while democracy is still eschewed, the free market has been accepted and has brought prosperity. Perhaps it is the authoritarian stability which enabled this to happen. Should we enforce democracy on people who may not be able to handle it and destroy stability?

A systemic constitutional change from authoritarianism to democracy indeed cannot guarantee immediate successes under competitive democracy. Importing the language and constitutional structures normally associated with Western constitutionalism by conscious, cerebral design does not necessarily lead to popular or governmental constitutionalist buy-in. Economic liberalization, often following real or cosmetic constitutional and political change, does seem to induce popular pressure towards democracy. Davis, who considers democratic elections with free and fair multiparty contestation, human rights and freedom of expression, and the rule of law, including adherence to the principles of legality to be the fundamental components of constitutionalism, argues that under the circumstances of a relatively high level of development in the East Asian countries authoritarianism may be 'its own grave digger', because the creation of conditions favourable to economic development depends on the creation of favourable state institutions respectful of human rights.[27]

Consideration of the assumed 'progress' of 'non-Western' states towards constitutionalism confronts one with the reality that culture, be it social, legal, economic or political, is inevitably reflected in the legal and constitutional system of any state. Dealing with the employment of emergency powers in East Asia, Chen,[28] for example, points out that:

> in many countries in Latin America, Africa and Asia, the social, cultural and economic conditions may be such that it is difficult to operate a liberal constitutional democratic system of government. If the conditions are such that an authoritarian system of government is more suitable for a particular nation at a particular stage of its development, then the discourse of emergency may be no more than a substitute or surrogate for the idea that the prevailing circumstances make it impossible or impracticable to practice the liberal constitutional democratic system prescribed in the constitution for 'normal' circumstances.

---

[27] Davis (1998) 305.
[28] Chen (2010) 64.

But must we assume that constitutionalism absolutely requires *liberal* democracy? A factor to be taken into account here is that a large portion of the non-Western world had been under colonial hegemony for long periods during the 17th to the 20th Centuries and, as Beer reminds us, 'the colonialist and pre-colonialist past has cast shadows of different length and shape in each nation'.[29] The colonial era did not eradicate indigenous thinking and legal conceptions and liberal democracy proved not to have been a particularly effective export product. The picture of non-Western understandings of state, constitution and law is therefore a mottled one, incapable of generic detailed description. In his search for an 'omni-directional' and 'transcultural' concept of constitutionalism, Beer settled on 'human rights constitutionalism', human rights now being 'the best test of humane civilization', not being 'vague, abstract or culture-specific'. He bases this approach on the broad acceptance, also by the East Asian states, of the range of 20th Century international instruments proclaiming human rights, 'their worldwide diffusion', their 'transcultural acceptance' and 'their gradually increasing effect in the international law and constitutional law of nations', as well as the notions of nation state sovereignty, the limitation and division of state power, the rule of law, and popular sovereignty.[30] Given their deep roots in Western natural law, individualist and humanist thinking, Beer is more optimistic about the transcultural acceptance of human rights than is warranted by reality. What is true, however, is that human rights have become entrenched in what Beer calls 'a common language of constitutional discourse'.[31]

An important comparative connection that Beer makes[32] is that religion lies at the core of a constitutional culture which provides a coherent set of public values underlying and legitimizing government and law. Religion, he says, represents:

> the most important, most binding ideas at the heart of a culture, those which in the minds and daily lives of the people give ultimate meaning to the state community ... with attendant institutions and customs which embody that community's way of expressing and honoring what it sees as most important.

---

[29] Beer (2009) (the chapter concerned was originally published in 1992) 7.
[30] Beer (2009) 10, 276–277.
[31] Beer (2009) 35 and his discussion of American influence on constitutionalism in Asia.
[32] Beer (2009) 18.

He goes on to identify the religious influences, in addition to Western ideas, on the various Eastern concepts of constitutionalism as Confucian, Islamic, Brahmanic, Buddhist and monarchical quasi-divinity, jointly having in common four tendencies:[33]

> (1) to relate, not separate, religion and the state; (2) to conceptually and institutionally integrate, not divide, the public and the private, the economic, the social and the political; in short, to view community life organically; (3) to see the individual person as achieving fulfilment within a dense network of family and community relationships, rather than as an autonomous individual; and (4) to give the state great formal power, not without restraining responsibilities, but with vagueness about how rulers are to be held accountable.

3.2.4 Eastern Europe

In a paper published in a compilation dealing with the consequences of the entrance into the European Union of eight post-communist countries of Eastern Europe, András Sajó[34] boldly asserts the absence in the new member states of a culture of constitutionalism as it is understood in Western Europe. According to Sajó, East European conceptions of nationalism, independence and sovereignty do not resonate well with the established Western demands for accountability, transparency and predictability. Despite the acceptance of formal legalism in those countries, the political elite have 'a very instrumentalist disregard for the rule of law', and he considers it unlikely that the general public will take to deliberative democracy and tempered majoritarianism while continuing to assume the continuation of the socialistic provision of free public services. Sajó describes the constitutional structure of the countries concerned as a 'cabinet dictatorship' with weak legislative branches, and a 'welfare administrative state.' He describes the attitude of the Eastern European citizens as 'complaint-subjects', meaning 'citizens who behave like subjects of a paternalist state, who refuse to take responsibility for their fate through democratic participation'.

The 'new' European states indeed represent an interesting constitutional environment where the older European notions of constitutionalism are presumed to have been transplanted in the course of their accession to the European Union. In reality, however, the pre-accession communist structures and mentalities did not simply evaporate and were not dissipated by constitutional renewal. This is particularly apparent in the

---

[33] Beer (2009) 19.
[34] Sajó (2006).

appointment procedures and administration of the judiciary and in judicial/executive relationships. Michal Bobek, for example, states:[35]

> If one goes beyond the prophylactic language of various international reports, one discovers that despite the differences in institutional design, the problems of administration of post-communist courts are very similar in nature. Communist judicial cadres cannot become responsible judicial administrators overnight; corruption, incompetence and nepotism are, unfortunately, the defining elements of any system in transition. The same schemes, the same patterns and the same misuses are reproduced in both old and new systems, irrespective of the institutional design.

In March 2013 the dissatisfaction of the Hungarian government with a series of judgments delivered by the Constitutional Court led to some drastic constitutional amendments, leading to pressure being exerted by European institutions on the government to mend its ways. The Council of Europe's Venice Commission, for instance, commented that '[t]he Constitution of a country should provide a sense of constitutionalism in society, a sense that it truly is a fundamental document and not simply an incidental political declaration' and that the 'amendments are not only problematic because constitutional control is blocked in a systematic way, but also in substance because these provisions contradict principles of the Fundamental Law and European standards'.[36]

It appears, therefore, that in Eastern Europe the required 'sense of constitutionalism' has not yet fully taken root.

3.2.5 Africa

In a contribution on constitutionalism from an African perspective produced at the beginning of the last decade of the 20th Century, just when the exponential worldwide surge of constitutionalization following the collapse of the Soviet Union was getting underway, Yash Ghai made the interesting point that the rule of law, understood by him as requiring the authority for executive action to be based on law, historically preceded democracy and that there may be some tension between the 'conservative basis' of the rule of law and the 'dynamic mission of democracy'. This is not necessarily the case, however, and according to

---

[35] Bobek (2010) 268.
[36] European Commission for Democracy Through Law (2013) paras 137 and 141.

Ghai the rule of law is not threatened by democracy at all, and democracy is especially required in Africa in order to sustain the rule of law.[37]

The development of constitutionalism in Europe, Ghai argued, must be ascribed to the emergence of three constituent concepts, viz. secularization, nationalization and the separation and limitation of public powers. Also at its roots lie 'the need of capitalism for predictability, calculability and security of property rights and transactions', which sense of security is nurtured by the concept of the generality of rules to prevent both discrimination and arbitrary government action, simultaneously avoiding both judicial subservience and adventurism.[38] In this account, constitutionalism experienced its apex in the 19th Century when 'the propertied class had achieved political dominance' and the state merely provided the framework for an autonomous and decentralized economy. In the 20th Century the broadening of the franchise, the internationalization of capital and the need for state intervention in aid of economic stability had a dampening effect on the previous century's constitutionalist apogee, but it continues to legitimize 'Western regimes': 'It hides the way in which power is exercised in these societies; it gives the impression of pluralism and competitive political systems, responsive to new interests and change; and it emphasises the primacy of state representative and judicial institutions, thus mitigating the appeal of radical politics.'[39]

Ghai argued that inequality and subordination do not result primarily from the law but from social and economic forces that employ the equality and neutrality of the law for their purposes.[40] When constitutionalism based on this thinking reached post-colonial Africa, he stated, the underlying conditions did not match those that gave birth to the notion. The constitutions of African states generally did not, as in Europe, grow organically from civil society, but started out as a bureaucratic device imposed from above, which was supposed to be capable of dealing with severe socio-economic problems. Those who obtained political power did not also control the market (as in the West), which led to the well-publicized corruption, authoritarianism, instability and political patrimony characterizing post-colonial Africa. However, Ghai did hold out the

---

[37] Ghai (1990–1991) 412.
[38] Ghai (1990–1991) 413.
[39] Ghai (1990–1991) 414.
[40] Ghai (1990–1991) 415.

possibility of change for the better in due course,[41] indications of which have since become visible in some African countries.

Whether Ghai's close linkage of the control over capital with political power should be associated so closely with constitutionalism may be debatable, since it is more often than not the poor masses that take to the streets of African cities when constitutional rights are threatened or trampled upon by authoritarian rulers. Be that as it may, Ghai's explanation of political pathologies in Africa on the basis of wealth distribution does make sense: more than two decades down the line one can still recognize the corrupt client-based politics of many of those in power in Africa, even when they are democratically elected.[42]

A broad empirical study published in 1996 in which the fate of political regimes in 135 countries between 1950 and 1990 was studied found that the following conditions favour the survival of democracy: elections in which the opposition has a chance of success, affluence, growth with moderate inflation, declining inequality, a favourable international climate and parliamentary institutions.[43] Perhaps it is a universal truth: poor politicians obtaining power will be inclined to use their political power to garner wealth, even after they become rich. It would be a sad day for constitutionalism, however, if it could survive only in affluent societies.

Since the end of the Cold War most countries in Africa have produced new constitutions that reflect the intention of becoming part of the world of constitutionalism. Leading examples are Namibia, South Africa and Kenya. Some constitutions are less than effective, and in many African countries constitutional arrangements made in the course of decolonization have influenced post-Cold War constitution-writing. Nigeria's struggle to produce a popularly supported constitution is a case in point, as Femi Falana wrote in 2010:[44]

> There is the urgent need to commence preparations for a people-driven and process-led making of a new constitution. It is only through that process that Nigerians can produce a constitution that will define the limits of the powers of government, the basic duties of citizens, and the social responsibilities of the government to the people under the rule of law.

---

[41] Ghai (1990–1991) 415–423.
[42] This for example, became an unfortunate characteristic of the South African government less than 20 years after the widely admired introduction of constitutionalism. See for example, Lodge (1998) Basson (2012).
[43] Przeworski *et al.* (1996).
[44] Cf. for example, Falana (2010) 141.

Whether it would be possible to divine from the current African constitutions and constitutional practices a distinctly African conception of constitutionalism is doubtful, not only because it is impossible to produce a continentally valid generalization but also due to the wide scope of variation. In this regard Charles Fombad reveals a distinct difference between Anglophone and Francophone African countries when it comes to constitution-writing. Whereas former common-law systems open themselves to be influenced by examples from various jurisdictions, 'many francophone African constitutional draftsmen have continued to rely almost slavishly on what they perceive as the most reliable and unassailable model; the Gaullist Fifth Republic and the timid amendments that have been made to it in the last fifty years'.[45]

3.2.6 Nordic Welfare States

In the Nordic welfare states, judicial review is restrained by a tradition of reticence on the part of the courts to interfere in the responsibility of the state to be actively involved not only in maintaining public order but also in the provision of social services. There the acceptance of all elements of constitutionalism is still in progress, and is significantly affected by the influence of European law in Sweden, Norway and Denmark.[46] It would appear that the theoretical and historical underpinnings of Nordic constitutional thinking are inhibiting the full acceptance of constitutionalism as it is understood in Western Europe. The tension is one of different emphases, either on individual or on social entitlement. Arnáson explains it as follows:[47]

> [I]n the modern Nordic state, basic economic, social and cultural rights can be ranked equally with Locke's classical freedom rights. Without these so-called welfare rights, the possibilities and the freedom of the individual to live an autonomous life in dignity and to seek selfrealisation remain illusory.

The emerging notion of Nordic constitutionalism is considered to require a constitutional document with enhanced legal status that can be enforced by legal means, the rule of law, separation of powers, fundamental rights and 'internationalism', meaning acknowledgement of the domestic applicability of European law and other international conventions.[48]

---

[45] Fombad (2012) 466.
[46] Nergelius (2008).
[47] Arnáson (2008) 159.
[48] Nergelius (2008) 128, citing Martin Scheinin.

3.2.7 United States of America

If it should mean having a written constitution as the 'supreme law of the land', the United States obviously has the longest surviving claim to constitutionalism. How Americans understand constitutionalism is not and cannot be settled, since there are many views on the interpretation of more than two centuries' development and contemporary understanding of the various constitutional elements that may be considered to be characteristic of constitutionalism, be they democracy, the rule of law, constitutional rights, judicial review, procedural limitations or anything else.

Louis Henkin claimed with good reason that the United States was to be credited for establishing and spreading the 'constitutionalist ideology', motivating (and at the same time delineating American constitutionalism) his claim as follows:[49]

> Our Declaration of Independence includes perhaps the most famous articulation of the principles of popular sovereignty, of limited and accountable government, and of individual rights. The United States Constitution ... was the first written constitution – a prescriptive constitution that is supreme law, that governs the governors, that cannot be suspended, and that is not subject to derogations even in national emergency. The United States Constitution is difficult to amend. The United States, which sought an alternative to the Westminster parliamentary system, developed the 'presidential system' as a model of democratic government. The United States adopted the first national, constitutional, lasting Bill of Rights. The United States established constitutional review by the judiciary.

Henkin summarized his understanding of the 'principal demands of constitutionalism' as follows:[50]

> 1. Contemporary constitutionalism is based on popular sovereignty. 'The people' is the locus of 'sovereignty'; the will of the people is the source of authority and the basis of legitimate government. The people alone can ordain and establish the constitution and the system of government. The people remain responsible for the system which they establish. 2. A constitutionalistic constitution is prescriptive; it is law; it is supreme law. Government must conform to the constitutional blueprint and to any limitations the constitution imposes. There can be no legitimate government other than as constitutionally ordained. 3. With popular sovereignty have come related ideas, namely,

---

[49] Henkin (1994) 42.
[50] Henkin (1994) 41–42.

government ruled by law and governed by democratic principles. Constitutionalism therefore requires commitment to political democracy and to representative government. Even in times of national emergency, the people remain sovereign. Constitutionalism excludes government by decree, except as authorized by the constitution and subject to control by democratic political institutions. 4. Out of popular sovereignty and democratic government come dependent commitments to the following: limited government; separation of powers or other checks and balances; civilian control of the military; police governed by law and judicial control; and an independent judiciary. 5. Constitutionalism requires that government respect and ensure individual rights, which generally are those same rights recognized by the Universal Declaration of Human Rights. Rights may be subject to some limitations in the public interest, but such limitations themselves have limits. Some rights may be suspended in times of national emergency, but the derogation from rights in an emergency must be determined by constitutional bodies and subject to democratic review and scrutiny, must be strictly necessary, and must be temporary. 6. Constitutional governance includes institutions to monitor and assure respect for the constitutional blueprint, for limitations on government, and for individual rights. 7. Today, constitutionalism may also imply respect for 'self-determination' – the right of 'peoples' to choose, change, or terminate their political affiliation.

Following this exposition, and despite the claim of the American imprimatur on the 'constitutionalist ideology', Henkin identified certain deficiencies of the United States model measured against the ideological demands of the notion.[51]

Griffen[52] accused his compatriots of 'awed self-congratulation' when anniversaries of the ratification of the US Constitution in 1789 are celebrated. He sets out the theory of constitutionalism and concludes that 'If constitutionalism is understood in terms of the principle that the government must be restrained through written provisions that have the force of law, the American experience with the activist state raises serious questions about the viability of this principle.' According to Griffen, writing from an American perspective and following McIlwain, the essence of the notion of constitutionalism is 'government limited by the rule of law', that is, the opposite of arbitrary rule and despotism. The popularly approved Constitution of the 18th Century was intended to provide such a legal framework, expected literally to be perpetual. The constitutive (as opposed to regulative) provisions are broadly worded, underpinning a wide range of policy choices, and therefore existing in

---

[51] Henkin (1994) 44–48.
[52] Griffen (1990).

'the uncertain boundary territory between law and politics' leading not only to the judicialization of politics but also to the politicization of the law.[53]

Griffen's interpretation of American constitutional history entails strong state and weak federal government at least up to the Civil War in the middle of the 19th Century. The Civil War, bringing about Lincoln's 'quasi-dictatorship', was to him an indication of a failure of the Constitution on the same scale as the Weimar Constitution in 1933. Nineteenth Century 'glorification of the nation', however, saved the text of the Constitution and paved the way for 20th Century adaptations without much fundamental amendment.[54] The New Deal, World War II and the Cold War provided the political branches with the 'authority to maintain a welfare state and generally provide for the nation's economic well-being'; the presidential office became the 'chief legislator' in that the President was expected to propose appropriate measures for dealing with the Depression; and through the Depression, World War II and the Cold War, the President was also placed in control of the military and the intelligence bureaucracy.[55]

American constitutionalism should not, according to Griffen, be ascribed to the longevity of the constitutional text as an exemplary success. Statements to that effect 'are better understood as expressions of national ideology and patriotic sentiment, rather than as a cold evaluation of American political institutions'.[56] To the extent that constitutionalism is intended to mean limited government in terms of the provisions of the Constitution, Griffen concludes, its viability has been neutralized by the constitutional history of the United States.[57]

Griffen's is a crucially important insight: it requires a substantive perspective on constitutionalism, one which requires the existence of a constitutional text but which is not wholly dependent thereupon. It shows convincingly that the actual wording of a supreme Constitution may be of great but decidedly relative importance: its interpretation and application constitute the essence and quality of the constitutionalism for which it provides. This still leaves us, however, with the question of how the constitutionalist essence is to be expressed and how its quality is to be measured.

---

[53] Griffen (1990) 202–204.
[54] Griffen (1990) 207–210.
[55] Griffen (1990) 213–214. This must certainly also apply to the 'war on terrorism' initiated in 2001 by the attacks notorious as '9\11'.
[56] Griffen (1990) 217.
[57] Griffen (1990) 219–220.

The qualifications and criticisms of United States constitutionalism apart, there is no gainsaying the immense debt the world owes the Americans for introducing and spreading the seeds of what has become a globally utilized idea. George Billias traces the influence of American constitutionalism through seven 'echoes' between 1776 and 1989, and concludes (perhaps too enthusiastically):[58]

> American constitutionalism was ... heard round the world for more than two centuries. For Europeans chafing under monarchies and aristocracies, it provided a catalyst for change, a model to follow, and a source of inspiration. For Latin Americans and, later, Asians and Africans throwing off colonial rule, it offered paradigms for new structures of government and a more persuasive definition of the just relationship between governors and the governed. From the American to the European Revolution of 1989, the American model powerfully, if sometimes unevenly, supported constitutional government, greater democracy, and expanded human rights.

However, it is post-War Europe that can claim to be the constitutionalist refinery of our time.

3.2.8 Europe

Going back as far as Aristotle, the foundations of constitutional statehood as we know it today were laid in Europe.[59] There were times, generally well known,[60] when European countries were poor examples of stable and well-balanced government. However, Western European constitutionalism was reborn after World War II to flourish and be established in this era as the key exemplar of the conception.

At the heart of this process was the emergence of German constitutionalism, which continues to serve as the leading illustration of its merits.[61] This is not to say that German constitutional notions dominate the whole of the European constitutional conversation. Historically other systems, particularly those of Britain and France, contributed vital elements to European constitutionalism. They and others (for example, Switzerland

---

[58] Billias (2009) 371.

[59] For example, Vorländer (2012) 33. Friedrich (1964) 3–10 interestingly contested the validity of the idea that the roots of constitutionalism go back as far as that, since the Greek and Roman states were not separated from their religious institutions and were therefore neither church nor state.

[60] National Socialism in Germany between 1933 and 1945 and USSR and Eastern European communism in the course of the largest part of the 20th Century naturally come to mind.

[61] See for example, Brugger and Sarlet (2008).

and the Netherlands) add to the common understanding and practice of constitutionalism in Europe, especially in the interaction of the member states of the European Union. Nevertheless, it is useful as a means of identifying the core of European constitutionalism to refer to the German approach as the constant point of reference.

The essence of contemporary German constitutionalism finds expression in the concept of *Rechtsstaatlichkeit*. Based on the 'chain of ideas' CONSTITUTION–LAW – HUMAN DIGNITY–LIBERTY–JUSTICE–LEGAL CERTAINTY, *Rechtsstaatlichkeit* may, following the authoritative exposition by Klaus Stern,[62] which is itself founded on an extensive survey of the relevant literature, be summarized as follows:[63]

> *Rechtsstaatlichkeit* indicates the exercise of the power of the state on the basis of laws adopted according to the Constitution, with the purpose of guaranteeing freedom, justice and legal certainty. The following are the elements of the *Rechtsstaat* principle:
>
> - the constitutional state (*Verfassungsstaatlichkeit*), meaning the existence of a Constitution as the foundational juridical order and supreme legal norm of the state;
> - human dignity, liberty and equality, indicating the legal regulation of the relationship between citizens and the state by means of fundamental rights, whereby certain personal and political liberties, as well as equality before the law are guaranteed;
> - the separation and control of government authority, meaning the separation and reciprocal limitation of the authority and functions of the state;
> - legality (*Rechtsgebundenheit*), indicating that law provides the foundation and limits for all actions of the state, referring specifically to the law of the Constitution as the foundation for legislative acts and legislation as the foundation for the administrative and judicial branches;
> - judicial protection, meaning the guarantee of extensive and effective legal protection by independent courts following legislatively prescribed procedures against, for example, actions of state authorities (including the legislature);
> - a system of reparation, meaning the legal responsibility of the organs of the state towards citizens, including for damages caused by the state and for violations of rights by the state; and
> - the prohibition of excessive use of government authority, indicating the appropriateness, necessity, and proportionality of state actions.

---

[62] Stern (1984) at 769.
[63] Taken from Venter (2012b) 726–727.

Stern[64] requires the constitution as such, in addition to the classic requirements of the protection of fundamental rights and the separation of powers, to realize certain specific functions and purposes. Thus, the constitution has the function, as does the law in general, of establishing and maintaining order in the state; it should provide stability over an extended period; it should be concerned with essentials rather than be overburdened with transitory detail; it should have an integrational or unifying effect, not merely in the sense of national unity, but should be useful as an instrument for the mobilization of consensus among the citizenry regarding matters of common public concern; it is required to provide effectively for the organization of the organs of government, their competencies, procedures and functioning for the purposes of exercising power and expressing the political will; and lastly it should provide the guiding principles regarding the aims and purposes of the state and must determine the nature of the legal relationship between the citizen and the state.

3.3 INTERNATIONALIZATION OF CONSTITUTIONALISM

For the purposes of reflecting on constitutionalism in the broader context of the European Union, Ton van den Brink identifies the following elements without reference to any particular national jurisdiction:[65]

- the rule of law (as opposed to 'the force of power');
- the distribution of power among various actors, whose mutual relations are regulated;
- the protection of citizens against arbitrary and unlawful treatment by public authorities;
- the protection of human rights as a defensive sphere around the individual that may not be infringed by the authorities;
- the power of individuals to influence the composition of public authorities and their policies;
- a legal relationship of rights and obligations between citizens and their constitutional order;
- a set of legal norms distinct from and prevailing over 'ordinary' legal norms; and

---

[64] Stern (1984) 82–98.
[65] Van den Brink (2010) 126.

- conventions and constitutional principles as part of the traditions of the state concerned.

Although this list of elements does not distinguish between the 'domestic' form of constitutionalism and one that looks beyond the state, involving the EU in the description causes the focus to be adjusted from the state to the supra-national level.

For our present purposes it is necessary to distinguish constitutionalism from the closely associated and bifurcated phenomenon of constitutionalization. This distinction is important because constitutionalism is relevant in the context of the constitutionalization of international law as well as the internationalization of constitutional law, both processes being well underway.[66] Both of these phenomena or processes have the potential to promote internationalized constitutionalism.

Fombad[67] finds the internationalization of constitutional law to have a beneficial effect on the constitutional law of African states in the form of 'a sort of compensatory constitutionalism'. He deals with a manifestation of internationalization, not in the form of the constitutionalization of international law but the internationalization of constitutional law, which he defines[68] as 'the development of the adoption in national constitutional laws of many shared norms whose origins can be traced to international and regional supra-national laws'. In the African context international norms have served as replacements for deficient domestic laws, there has been a 'progressive convergence of constitutional principles and standards' in new African constitutions, and the judiciaries have gained access to broader-based sources supporting progressive judgments.[69]

Conversely, the constitutionalization of international law is advanced for example by Lars Vinx:[70]

> The analogy of constitutional and international law, then, supports the project of international legalization. If legalization is desirable where it is feasible, and if the analogy between constitutional and international law implies that the problems of feasibility that afflict global legalism do not differ in kind from those that afflict domestic constitutionalism, we ought to give support to the project of fully subjecting international politics to the rule of international law. Not to do so would be incompatible with our commitment to domestic

---

[66] See for example, Habermas (2012) and Benvenisti and Downs (2012).
[67] Fombad (2012).
[68] Fombad (2012) 444.
[69] Fombad (2012) 463–464.
[70] Vinx (2013) 122.

constitutionalism, to the goal of subjecting all domestic conflict to the rule of constitutional law. To resist this conclusion, the modern sceptic about international legalization would have to embrace Schmitt's view that constitutional and international law are equally incapable legitimately to resolve any non-trivial political conflict. He would have to deny the legitimacy of domestic constitutionalism along with the legitimacy of the rule of international law.

Turning now to international constitutionalism as such, Dieter Grimm[71] deals with the process unmistakably observable in this era of the decline of statehood characterized by the transfer of public power away from the state to actors not being the state, which is described as a process of 'denationalization', meaning that 'ruling authority is detached from the state and transferred to non-state bearers',[72] and concludes[73] that:

> Just as public power at the international level breaks down into numerous unconnected institutions with sharply limited jurisdictions, so its legal regulation breaks down into numerous unconnected partial orders. A bundling that could make them appear as the expression of unified intention and would also allow a unified interpretation of them is not to be expected even in the long term. Even more, democratic legitimation and responsibility is far off. The aspiration contained in the concept of constitutionalism can therefore not even be approximately realized on the global level. This is no reason to attach little value to the progress connected to the increasing juridification of the world order. To equate it with a constitution, however, is to paper over the fundamental difference and create the impression that the declining significance of national constitutions can be made good at the international level. There is no prospect of that for the time being.

According to Christine Schwöbel,[74] who is even more sceptical than Grimm, 'global constitutionalism' was in 2010 one of the most discussed areas of international law, and there were 'different but overlapping' debates on the subject. She identified three common assumptions, abstractions of reality, about global constitutionalism, viz. that constitutions can exist beyond the domestic legal system and the nation state, that a certain unity or homogeneity of the international sphere exists, and that the idea of global constitutionalism is universal. She categorized the current ideas of global constitutionalism into four dimensions, viz. social

---

[71] Grimm (2008).
[72] Grimm (2008) 82.
[73] Grimm (2008) 91–92.
[74] Schwöbel (2010) 529.

constitutionalism, institutional constitutionalism, normative constitutionalism and analogical constitutionalism. She then finds that the categorization of the contributions to the debate produces 'key themes', all consistent with liberal democratic traditions. These themes are the limitation of the single locus of power through participation (as found in social constitutionalism), the key theme of governance through the institutionalization of power (as found in institutional constitutionalism), the centrality of individual rights (emphasized particularly in normative constitutionalism), an idealistic vision of a social value system (as also found in normative constitutionalism), and the key theme of the systematization or standardization of law (as evidenced in analogical constitutionalism). Her analysis leads her to conclude[75] that 'Global constitutionalism has no content of its own; it has no predetermined values on which it is based and it has no common principles.' In its stead, she proposes[76] the idea of:

> organic global constitutionalism, which rejects stability in favour of flexibility; rejects any pre-political common values in favour of a discursive political determination of constitutionalism; rejects viewing global constitutionalism as a 'positive universal', conceived along the lines of liberal democracy, in favour of viewing it as something that only emerges through contending particulars in the sense of a 'negative universal', and suggests viewing the normative aspect of constitutionalism as a promise for the future, a *constitutionalism to come*.

The powerful qualifications that Schwöbel and Grimm place upon the idea of the constitutionalization of international law are apparently construed on the assumption that global constitutionalism must rely on the existence or creation of a kind of international constitution or binding normative framework endowing a globally legitimized entity with quasi-governmental authority. The difficulty of legitimate constitutionalism is sometimes referred to as the paradox of constitutionalism, indicating the tension between popular constituent authority (perceived by most to be absent beyond the state) and the need to divide, limit and control constitutional institutions entrusted with governmental power.[77] Also evident in the construction of international constitutionalism by commentators such as Schwöbel is the assumption of the universal validity of the precepts of *liberal* democracy, by implication drawing all the paradoxes inherent in liberal theories on law and state into the discussion.

---

[75] Schwöbel (2010) 550.
[76] Schwöbel (2010) 553.
[77] See for example, Fassbender (2007).

Although some universalistic constructions have been made, international constitutionalism is construed in a more qualified manner by others. Otfried Höffe on the one hand insists that globalization 'should not come at the price of political regression' detrimental to democracy by means of global statism or economism, and states:[78]

> Social reality ... extends considerably beyond individual democracies. Economic affairs, science, medicine, technology, culture, migration, environmental pollution, terrorism and organised crime – these concerns create a need for action that extends beyond national borders. Hence, if the demand for action is global, then the idea of an equally global polity cannot be avoided, in other words, a global system of government that would organise itself in a deliberate manner as a global democracy and world republic. In so doing, the accountability of collective actors stretches beyond the borders of states or even groups of states, and the solution to global problems is left neither to market forces (economic neo-liberalism), contingent evolution (systems theory), nor to any possible combination of the two.

Erika de Wet's emphasis is, however, slightly different:[79]

> [T]he intensification of the shift of power and control over decisionmaking away from the nation State towards international actors is increasingly eroding the concept of a total or exclusive constitution. In the increasingly integrated international legal order there is a co-existence of national, regional, and sectoral (functional) constitutional orders that complement one another in order to constitute an embryonic international constitutional order.

In a paper primarily dealing with the evolution of 'comparative constitutional law', Peer Zumbansen explores the 'transnational and pluralist' landscape of the law as such, and posits constitutionalism[80] '[a]s a conceptual framework constituted by an intersection and interplay of both institutional and normative conceptions of political, legal, cultural and economic order.' Zumbansen powerfully argues that the state as the preferred form of political, legal and social organization and its sovereignty can no longer be the primary focus of constitutionalism, which has become a patently transnational notion.[81]

---

[78] Höffe (2007) ix.
[79] De Wet (2006) 75.
[80] Zumbansen (2012) 19.
[81] Zumbansen (2012) 32 *passim*.

When the journal *Global Constitutionalism* was launched in 2012 with the agenda[82] of creating a platform both for the mapping[83] and the shaping[84] of global constitutionalism, the editors followed Anne Peters' definition of constitutionalization, viz. 'the gradual emergence of constitutionalist features in international law which are expected to compensate for globalization-induced constitutionalist deficits on the national level',[85] and proceeded to characterize the notion with 'three "C's"', viz constitution,[86] constitutionalization[87] and constitutionalism, a strategy which involves grappling on a global scale 'with the consequences of globalisation as a process that transgresses and perforates national or state borders, undermining familiar roots of legitimacy and calling for new forms of checks and balance as a result'.[88] From the interdisciplinary literature consulted, the editors identified three schools of thought regarding global constitutionalism, viz. the functionalist, which typically studies 'processes of constitutionalisation which are revealed through bargaining and negotiations in the environment of international organisations such as the WTO, ... and the EU',[89] the normative, which 'sees global constitutionalism as a legal or moral conceptual framework that guides the interpretation, progressive development or political reform of legal and political practices beyond the state to reflect a commitment to constitutional standards',[90] and the pluralist. The scholars in the latter school 'consider mapping and shaping constitutional quality beyond the state as of equal importance', and among them is 'a fair share of universalists'.[91]

---

[82] Wiener *et al.* (2012).
[83] Understood to mean 'describing the shift from globalised to constitutionalised relations and identifying their constitutional substance' Wiener *et al.* (2012) 11.
[84] Understood as 'improving the conditions and substance of this shift according to normative standards' Wiener *et al.* (2012) 11.
[85] Wiener *et al.* (2012) 4.
[86] Described as usual with reference to its establishment to keep politics in check, to serve as a frame of reference for dispute resolution, and an assumed *pouvoir constituant.* Wiener *et al.* (2012) 4–5.
[87] Indicative of 'the shift from globalised towards constitutionalised international relations' Wiener *et al.* (2012) 5.
[88] Wiener *et al* .(2012) 6.
[89] Wiener *et al.* (2012) 7.
[90] Wiener *et al.* (2012) 7.
[91] Wiener *et al.* (2012) 7–8.

In our consideration of the link between constitutionalism and religion, the expanding interest in constitutionalism as a phenomenon with significance in the international sphere is noteworthy as a carrier of broadening acceptance of the possibility of deriving core elements of a 'constitutional good' from diverse points of ideological and ontological departure.

In an insightful overview approximating a summary of views expressed in the literature on the concept, Backer finds constitutionalism to be:[92]

> a system of classification, the principal object of which is to define the characteristics of constitutions, which is used to determine the legitimacy of a constitutional system either as conceived or implemented, based on the fundamental postulate of rule of law and grounded on values derived from a source beyond the control of any individual.

This, he says, amounts to a[93] '*Weltanschauung*, a system of beliefs relating to power in the world, and specifically to that power that is asserted to organize and run a political organization, and its expression through law'.

If, therefore, constitutionalism is rooted in one's perceptions and understanding of the world, a clear connection with religion becomes apparent. Without having for our present purposes to take a dogmatic stance on one or the other approach, school or construction of internationalizing and internationalized constitutionalism, it is clear that significant developments are afoot, legitimately challenging conventional thinking about the nature and operation of the law, its subjects or role players, the sources of its authority, the boundaries between the various disciplines of the law and the role of the state in the global society of the 21st Century. Legal approaches to religion, which is not dependent on the law, the state or supra-statal institutions for its diffusion and defence, must of necessity be influenced by the impact of the internationalization of constitutionalism in its various guises.

Carl Friedrich construed Western constitutionalism as a concept based on religion. The core objective of constitutionalism, he stated,[94] is:

> [S]afeguarding each member of the political community as a political person, possessing a sphere of genuine autonomy ... This preoccupation with the self, rooted in Christian beliefs ... eventually gave rise to the notion of rights which were thought to be natural. ... [W]hat has persisted throughout the

---

[92] Backer (2009) 93.
[93] Backer (2009) 103.
[94] For example, Friedrich (1964) 16–17.

history of Western constitutionalism is the notion that the individual human being is of paramount worth and should be protected against the interference of his ruler, be he a prince, a party, or a popular majority.

Friedrich[95] traced the development of constitutionalism in conjunction with religious doctrine from antiquity, its medieval development (Augustine, Aquinas, Marsilius, Ockham), the Reformation (Luther, Calvin, Hooker, Althusius) and what he calls 'deist' and 'theist' constitutionalism (Locke, Kant) to reach a conclusion that its religious foundations have 'almost vanished' in favour of human rights and their defence, which now lie at the 'humanist core' of the concept. He thus held out the hope of a universalization of constitutionalism regardless of religious conviction:[96]

> The fact that human rights are ever more universally recognized, even by those who seem least inclined to enforce them, is one of the distinguishing characteristics of our time. ... [d]oes it not perhaps justify the legal and political philosopher in hoping that human rights will gradually become more descriptive of the actual behaviour and conduct of government?

3.4 CONSTITUTIONALISM AND THE CONSTITUTIONAL STATE

As was pointed out in the previous section, constitutionalism is a key notion also for the consideration of the role of the state when it is called upon to deal with religious pluralism, not only because constitutionalism has attained the status of political desirability, but also because a system of law aspiring to satisfy the requirements of constitutionalism will approach religious issues in a manner conducive to optimal fairness. Currently the Western notion of constitutionalism is dominant in global constitutional thinking, but the European and American perspectives tend to differ due to their divergent constitutional histories.[97] Consistent with its origins at the end of the 18th Century, the American approach is primarily concerned with individual liberty,[98] whereas the German idea of the *Rechtsstaat* as it matured in the 20th Century has a broader ambit. Nevertheless, it can be stated, at least for the purposes of stabilizing the

---

[95] Friedrich (1964).
[96] Friedrich (1964) 116.
[97] Cf. Venter (2000) 20–36.
[98] Griffen (1990) 202, for example, assigns to constitutionalism 'the idea that just as it is desirable to restrain and empower the individual through the rule of law, so it is desirable to restrain and empower the state'.

terminology that we use, that 'constitutionalism' describes the condition of a domestic system when the state concerned is a constitutional state. This requires the meaning of the expression 'constitutional state' to be clarified.

In plotting the course of the fundamental changes in British constitutional law since 1995, Vernon Bogdanor asserts that Britain is in the process of becoming 'a constitutional state', that is, a state operating in accordance with a codified constitution,[99] one main purpose of which is that:[100]

> government ought to be limited by certain fundamental principles. It is the reference to a pre-existing document laying down basic principles which forms the essence of constitutionalism; and those living under a constitution for any length of time and taking its provisions seriously may be expected to develop a constitutional sense, a sense of what it might be appropriate for governments to do.

Coming from the perspective of British constitutional law, frequently (if not inappropriately) described as 'unwritten', Bogdanor's statement is interesting because it presupposes a 'codified constitution' but also suggests a more substantive characterization of a constitutional state. The term 'constitutionalism' does seem to imply the existence of a constitution. If so, the idea of the United Kingdom as a constitutional state would counter a demand that the constitution should be a single, codified legislative object. This would suggest that it would be acceptable to speak of constitutionalism where structural arrangements such as the establishment, empowerment and limitations of the organs of the state are clear, where public opinion has an important effect on executive and legislative governance, where the judiciary is independent from the government and the legislature and is generally considered to deliver fair judgments, and citizens perceive themselves to be free and equal and that their rights are appropriately protected. Where constitutionalism of this nature resides, one would be justified to speak of a constitutional state.

Possibly the best extant example of attaching a relatively solid meaning to the expression 'constitutional state' is to be found in its explicit employment in South African constitutional jurisprudence. There the notions of the rule of law and the *Rechtsstaat* have systematically been

---

[99] Bogdanor (2009) xiii: 'We are now in transition from a system based on parliamentary sovereignty to one based on the sovereignty of a constitution, albeit a constitution that is inchoate, indistinct and still in large part uncodified.'
[100] Bogdanor (2009) 21.

merged into a single concept: reference to the South African 'constitutional state' gives expression to a set of characteristics of the country's constitutional law.[101]

The South African approach can naturally not be said to have exclusive claim to the definition of a constitutional state. Its relatively rare conceptual combination of attributes both of the rule of law rooted in the Common Law and the Germanic conception of the *Rechtsstaat* cannot be considered to be a prerequisite to allow the use of the term 'constitutional state' to indicate compliance with the requirements of constitutionalism. One must also accept that the characteristics of constitutionalism vary in different jurisdictions, for example in the nature and manner of the protection of the range of acknowledged fundamental rights, and the distribution and counter-balancing of governmental authority.

Allowing for variations in emphasis and institutional structure and for possible additions, and accepting that political reality and constitutional theory rarely coincide fully, the following characteristics of the constitutional state identified by the South African Constitutional Court, it is submitted,[102] may be seen as indicators of the presence of constitutionalism in a system: the constitution serves as a guide for the interpretation of the law and for all actions of the state; fundamental rights are acknowledged and protected through the independent authority of the judiciary; the state as a whole has a duty to protect fundamental rights; the separation of powers is maintained; all government action is required to be legally justified; legal certainty is promoted; democracy is maintained; clear constitutional principles apply; and an objective system of values is established to guide the executive, the legislature and the judiciary.

It is becoming more difficult to maintain constitutional equilibrium in contemporary societies characterized by the globalization-enhanced plurality of religious adherence. To achieve such a balance, a large measure of universal inter-religious tolerance or comity would have been helpful – if such a state of generosity were imaginable in the context of humanity's history of severe religious conflict. The question is whether or not the law can enforce the semblance of such comity. The notion of the constitutional state provides a legal environment which is best capable of maintaining religious peace in a multi-religious society, although the law alone can never be sufficient for this purpose. A minimum consensus regarding the ethical values that guide the making,

---

[101] See Venter (2012b).
[102] This was demonstrated in Venter (2012b) and summarized at 736.

administration and adjudication of the law is crucial. The constitutional state as the end product of domestic constitutionalism may provide a platform for such consensus.

3.5 CONSTITUTIONALISM AS COMPARATIVE TOUCHSTONE

In 1987 a project on comparative constitutionalism inspired partly by the upcoming bicentennial of the US Constitution but with widespread international participation was initiated by the American Council of Learned Societies. The results were published in 1993. The editors reported that two 'thrusts' in defining constitutionalism emerged in the course of a series of conferences held around the world, the one formalistic, mostly concerned with the structural features of constitutional documents, the other dynamic, projecting constitutionalism as a process founded upon the social realities of the state concerned.[103] As is shown in the descriptions cited above, 20 years later this dichotomy is still in evidence. These two lines of thinking are, however, not the only ones encountered when searching for the essential meaning of constitutionalism: a surprising variety of emphases are to be found in different environments, despite the frequent overlap of vocabulary.

The fact that constitutionalism is the flavour of the century obviously does not mean that all and sundry, including dictatorships and pseudo-democracies, are conforming to the good standards of constitutionalism. In fact, the real constitutional states are still in the minority among the member states of the United Nations, although they are significantly among the more successful and powerful states, and are endowed with political influence and economic power far exceeding their numbers.

There are very few states in the world of the 21st Century that do not have written and often procedurally entrenched and consolidated constitutions. In a great many of these cases one cannot say with justification that constitutionalism prevails in a normative sense. Examples would be constitutions that do not ensure a balanced separation of powers, the independence of the judiciary, freedom of expression or legitimate democracy. This means that the presence or absence of a written constitution may not be the key to the realization of constitutionalism.

The systems where constitutionalism is established serve, despite the fact that there cannot be any perfect instance, as role models for those

---

[103] Greenberg *et al.* (1993) xvii.

who have learnt merely to talk the talk of good governance, despite their failings in walking the walk. Put bluntly, the iconic desirability of constitutionalism causes the acknowledgement by the political leaders of a state, before their peers, that constitutionalism does not prevail in their state, to be a cause for embarrassment.

Constitutionalism therefore does provide us with a general benchmark for balanced state conduct in the exercise of executive, legislative and judicial authority, *inter alia* when confronted with the realities of religious pluralism.

A condensed description of a system of law and governance conforming to a generalized conception of constitutionalism is one that centres upon effective and preferential constitutional norms designed to provide for a balanced exercise of authority and the effective protection of fundamental rights. Reducing it to a slogan (which is the form in which it is probably employed most frequently), the expression 'constitutionalism' may be used in the sense of a universally recognized measure of constitutional good. Beyond sloganism (which is seldom useful in scholarship or legal practice) it should be possible to catalogue the elements of constitutionalism.

Although it has been argued not to be an absolute requirement, a prominent element indicative of spreading constitutionalism is the fact that the largest proportion of current constitutions are 'supreme', that is, they represent the highest form of law in the system concerned.[104] Introducing effective constitutional supremacy in a system previously characterized by parliamentary sovereignty[105] or ideological dominance,[106] especially where a set of entrenched fundamental rights is included,[107] often results in the reorientation or even reconstruction of the whole of the legal system concerned. This does not absolutely require the adoption of a supreme constitutional document, although the trend in this

---

[104] Hirschl and Eisgruber (2006) 203 reported 'constitutional supremacy' to prevail in more than 100 countries.

[105] Canada and South Africa are good examples, and the United Kingdom appears to be following a similar route: see for example, Bogdanor (2009) *passim*.

[106] See for example, Sadurski, Czarnota and Krygier (eds) (2006).

[107] Canada for example, retained a degree of parliamentary sovereignty, but the Chief Justice of the Supreme Court of Canada was reported in 1992 (Hirschl and Eisgruber (2006) 204, citing Jeff Sallot in the *The Globe and Mail* of Toronto on 17 April 1992) to have stated that 'the introduction of the Charter has been nothing less than a revolution on the scale of the introduction of the metric system, the great medical discoveries of Louis Pasteur, and the invention of penicillin and the laser'.

direction might be considered to be an indication that the desirability of constitutionalism is in the ascendant.

The next obvious characteristic of constitutionalism is the special place allocated to constitutionally protected rights. This is an area of greater contestation than one might suspect because of the many differences in emphasis that are found in bills or charters of rights.[108] Despite the divergence on this account, it is interesting to note that catalogues of constitutional rights consistently boast the protection of religious and related freedoms.[109] This naturally does not mean convergence regarding the efficacy or content of the freedom of religion.

Should one survey the spectrum of characteristics that have been attributed cogently to constitutionalism in different systems and contexts as described above, at least three categories of elements would emerge: structural, substantive and doctrinal. The structural (or formal) elements concern primarily the manner in which a constitutional order is organized and the procedures prescribed for the different elements. It is necessary to make a subdivision here: on the one hand there would be rules, mechanisms and procedures with which a constitutional order must comply to qualify for constitutionalism, and on the other, rules, mechanisms and procedures that create a framework within which such a system operates. Substantive (normative or material) elements of constitutionalism are those that posit demands for 'good' or 'moral' or 'desirable' qualities of the state. The doctrinal category is made up of complex notions or ideas expressing dogmatic constitutional desirability, often in a manner incorporating or overlapping with structural and substantive constitutional elements.

In tabulated form, the key elements of constitutionalism (primarily reflected in its domestic form) can be represented as shown in Table 3.1.

This catalogue of elements must be understood to have fuzzy boundaries and variable descriptions because different proponents of constitutionalism see things differently. It is therefore useful to focus on the essence of one core doctrinal element, namely the rule of law/ *Rechtsstaat*/constitutional state and what it entails.

---

[108] For example, Hirschl and Eisgruber (2006) 209, referring to 'dissimilarities in constitutional legacies and structures, historical inheritances and formative experiences, as well as the nontrivial differences in value systems between Canadians and Americans'.

[109] Martínez-Torrón and Durham (2012) 8 claim that 'most constitutions' have provisions which prohibit discrimination on the grounds of religion.

Table 3.1   Elements of constitutionalism

Structural (formal)		Substantive (normative) qualities	Doctrinal components
Strict requirements	Mechanisms and procedures		
Legally (usually constitutionally) regulated division of the authority of the state among institutions and persons	Free and fair elections with multiparty contestation	Legitimate, non-arbitrary government and recognition of human dignity	Rule of law / *Rechtsstaat*/ constitutional state
Independence of the judiciary	Judicial review jurisdiction	Legality and legal certainty	Democracy
Binding legal regulation of mutual relations between organs of state and of relations between individuals and the state	Civilian control of the armed and security forces	Respect for the separation of powers	Popular sovereignty
Fixed procedures for legislation, administration and adjudication	Legal protection against arbitrary and unlawful state conduct	Popular respect for (the legitimacy of) the constitution	
Ability of the state to maintain public order	Representative and accountable government		
Specific protection of fundamental rights			

Attempting to focus on this element may in one sense be understood to be like jumping from the frying pan into the fire, which would indeed be the case if the vagueness surrounding the notion were not addressed. The rule of law presents itself in a number of forms, justifications and theories, but is better capable of reductionist definition than constitutionalism. The instinctive desire to trace the historical and conceptual route of the development of this concept with its overwhelming current presence in constitutions, international instruments and constitutional jurisprudence has to be resisted in order to facilitate the simple presentation of a conclusion regarding this element of constitutionalism's essential, reduced meaning formulated elsewhere,[110] and more specifically in the sense of *the constitutional state* referred to above in section 3.4.

At the heart of the constitutional state lie value-determined considerations which may also vary according to one's point of departure. However, broad agreement on the following two elements as being characteristic of the constitutional state can be expected:

- the recognition of human dignity, that is, the acceptance that the individual person has inherent dignity; and
- the denunciation of arbitrariness, that is, the acceptance that the fairness of actions performed in the exercise of public authority must be capable of and subject to open, rational explanation.[111]

The reason for these elements having true potential to be generally accepted is to be found in the ethical norm of reciprocity, that is, dealing with others as you want them to deal with you. Although this is not identically motivated by all, the soundness of the principle of reciprocity, which is often described as 'the golden rule', means that it enjoys truly universal acceptance.[112] The sources of support for reciprocity are found in the major philosophies (beginning with Confucianism) and major religions (including Judaism, Christianity and Hinduism). The golden rule manifests itself intuitively as a universal truth[113] on a par with the universal acceptance that murder, theft and dishonesty constitute reprehensible conduct.

Both of the above mentioned essential characteristics of the constitutional state, the inherent dignity of a person and the need for fair, non-arbitrary government, naturally and self-evidently flow from reciprocity. This can serve us well as the inevitably reduced essence of constitutionalism as *tertium comparationis*, as we contemplate the role the constitutional state should perform when dealing with religious pluralism.

---

[110] Venter (2014).

[111] Cohen (2010) for example, represents the thesis that a substantial (as opposed to a procedural) definition of the rule of law should require the giving of reasons by legal decision-makers as a central component of the notion.

[112] See also section 1.5 above.

[113] See for example, Wattles (1996) and Flores (2013) Chapter 6. This is the case despite its rejection by philosophers such as John Locke, and no doubt by cynical postmodernists as well.

PART II

Religion in law

Against the background provided in Part I of the considerations regarding the relationship between law and religion, the impact of globalization on the state, the citizen and on the world's religious demography, constitutional comparison and the nature of constitutionalism, this part addresses the interface between law and religion where constitutional and international legal reality, as well as the jurisprudence of the courts, meet religion.

To do so first requires an exposition and broad categorization in Chapter 4 of the modalities of the regulation of religious interests in representative groups of constitutions. This is followed in Chapter 5 by a consideration of the role of religion in and its impact on international law. Chapter 6 contains a comparative excursion into the world of the adjudication of religion-related cases.

4. Religion in constitutions

4.1 UBIQUITY OF RELIGION IN CONSTITUTIONS

It is remarkable that protective mention of religion is made in one or another form in the overwhelming majority of contemporary constitutions – be they constitutions of constitutional states or of states with dubious credentials in terms of their standards of constitutionalism.[1] At the end of an authoritative review of eight models of the relations of states to religion, the models being the atheist state, assertive secularism, separation as state neutrality towards religion, weak religious establishment, formal separation with the *de facto* pre-eminence of one denomination, separation alongside multicultural accommodation, religious jurisdictional enclaves and strong establishment, Ran Hirschl concludes as follows:[2]

> Unlike the conventional image of a 'clash of civilizations' or the 'west' and the 'rest', there is actually a strong echo of religion in each and all of these models. In fact, all constitutions, every single one of them – from France to Iran and anywhere in between – address the issue of religion head on. Some constitutions despise it, others embrace or even defer to it, and yet others are agnostic but are willing to accommodate certain aspects of it. But not a single constitution abstains, overlooks or remains otherwise silent with respect to religion. With the exception of the concrete organizing principles and prerogatives of the polity's governing institutions, the only substantive domain addressed by all modern constitutions is religion. What could be a more telling illustration of religion's omnipresence in today's world, or a stronger testament to constitutionalism's existential fear of religion?

Hirschl's notion that the fear of religion is a built-in theme of constitutionalism can probably best be understood as one inspired by a separationist view. A more universal perspective on constitutionalism, such as that proposed above in Chapter 3, is that constitutionalism is generally

---

[1] Cf. Martínez-Torrón and Durham (2010) 6–7 note 36, and the abbreviated version, Martínez-Torrón and Durham (2012) 8, stating that 'most constitutions' have provisions which prohibit discrimination on the grounds of religion.
[2] Hirschl (2011) 438.

more accommodating and does not constitute a threat to religion nor is religion a threat to a constitutionalist polity, even amidst religious pluralism.

If it were possible to produce a neat classification of every constitution in one of the categories 'secular or non-establishment', 'dubious protection of religion' and 'constitutional promotion of a preferred religion', or in any other set of categories, that might be tidy and orderly. But such a water-tight classification is not possible, since exceptions tend to crop up immediately following the placement of a constitution in a category. Obvious examples of this are the 'laic' France and Belgium where many clerics receive their salaries from the state and church-run institutions and church buildings are maintained to a significant degree with funding from the public fiscus.

Despite the exceptions, the three categories mentioned above will serve here as a mechanism for ordering – in broad terms – the description of different approaches to religion found in constitutions. It would naturally be impossible to cover all existing constitutions, and therefore the instances that are discussed are intended to serve as exemplars (often with exceptions) of the category in which they are placed.

In view of the indications set out in Part I that law (and specifically constitutional law) cannot be isolated from religion, the ubiquitous allusion to religion in constitutions is to be expected. Furthermore, in view of the challenges to the state that globalized religious pluralism presents, and leaving aside the phenomenon of states ostensibly existing for and as a consequence of a particular religion (such as some of the Islamic states), it should not come as a surprise that some states seek refuge in 'non-establishment' and ostensible neutrality; others put up a false image of themselves as being fair and open-minded;[3] and yet others maintain an historical, but mostly tenuous, allegiance to specific religions or religious institutions.

---

[3] Perhaps one of the most cynical examples is to be found in article 68 of the *Socialist Constitution of the Democratic People's Republic of Korea* of 2009:

(1) Citizens have freedom of religious belief. This right is granted through the approval of the construction of religious buildings and the holding of religious ceremonies.
(2) Religion must not be used as a pretext for drawing in foreign forces or for harming the State or social order.

4.2 NON-ESTABLISHMENT CONSTITUTIONS

Constitutional secularity is expressly manifested in the constitutions of France and Turkey as characteristic of the national identity of the citizenry.

4.2.1 Turkey

The fifth paragraph of the preamble to the Turkish Constitution,[4] which in terms of article 2 reflects the 'fundamental tenets' upon which the state is built, states *inter alia*:

> In line with ... [t]he recognition that no protection shall be afforded to thoughts or opinions contrary to Turkish national interests, the principle of the indivisibility of the existence of Turkey with its State and territory, Turkish historical and moral values or the nationalism, principles, reforms and modernism of Ataturk and that, as required by the principle of secularism, there shall be no interference whatsoever of the sacred religious feelings in State affairs and politics ...

The first sentence of article 2 provides that '[t]he Republic of Turkey is a democratic, secular and social state governed by the rule of law'.

The founder of modern Turkey, Mustafa Kemal Pasa, better known as Kemal Atatürk, dogmatized secularism for the Turkish state in the 1920s and 1930s as a means of modernizing the country in the face of majority Islamism.[5] Recent internal political developments have, however, brought about indications that Turkish secularism is under increasing pressure from Sunni Muslims, the majority in the country.[6]

4.2.2 France

The first article of the French Constitution[7] lays down the nature of the state in the following clear words: 'France is an indivisible, secular,

---

[4] Constitution of the Republic of Turkey, 1982, English translation found on the website of the Turkish Ministry of Foreign Affairs at http://www.constitution.org/cons/turkey/turk_cons.htm (accessed 19 March 2014).

[5] Adams (2009) 23–24.

[6] See for example, Dabestani, Sevinclidir and Erol (2012).

[7] Constitution of the Fifth Republic adopted in 1958 and amended in 2008, English translation at http://www.servat.unibe.ch/icl/fr00000_.html (accessed 19 March 2014).

democratic and social Republic' (La France est une République indivisible, laïque, démocratique et sociale). The term 'laïque' is generally understood to give expression to the fullest form of secularity. Its historical roots are to be found (at least) in the French Enlightenment and the French Revolution, when the influence of the Catholic Church was targeted in particular. This led to the French notion of freedom *from* religion – *laïcité*.[8] Nevertheless, the French state is deeply involved in the financial support of religious institutions, such as paying the salaries of clerics, in supporting religious schools and hospitals, and in maintaining cathedrals.[9]

4.2.3 Belgium

Although secularity is not mentioned expressly in the Belgian Constitution,[10] various provisions are indicative of a secular approach – and support for religion similar to that in France. Article 20 prohibits forced participation in the acts and ceremonies of a religious service or in the observance of its days of rest. Article 21 provides that the state does not have the right to intervene either in the appointment or in the installation of ministers of any religion whatsoever or to forbid those ministers from corresponding with their superiors or from making the acts of those superiors public, subject to normal accountability regarding the press and publication. Article 21 furthermore requires that, subject to statutory exceptions, a civil wedding precedes the religious blessing of a marriage.

Article 24§1 guarantees respect for the religious beliefs of parents and pupils and a choice in public schools between the teaching of one of the recognized religions and the teaching of non-denominational ethics. Remarkably, article 181 provides that the state awards remuneration and pensions to ministers of religion and to representatives of organizations recognized by the law as providing moral assistance according to a non-religious life view.

Thousands of priests, pastors, chaplains, rabbis and 'moral consultants' benefit in this manner from public funds. Since 2007 a significant number of imams have been included, and Buddhism has been subsidized since 2008. The historically sourced intention of these arrangements is that the state deals with the spectrum of religious and world views

---

[8] See for example, Nirenberg (2013) 156.
[9] Adams (2009) 8 and see the discussion of some cases below in Chapter 6, sections 6.2.3, 6.3.2 and 6.3.3.
[10] Dutch text found at http://www.senate.be/doc/const_nl.html (accessed 19 June 2014) – translation by the author.

present in society in a neutral manner in order to facilitate the free exercise of religion for the purposes of avoiding conflict.[11] Although the French and Belgian examples are considered to be manifestations of a strict separation between church and state, it is remarkable that these secular states are deeply involved in religious matters, although in a studiously 'neutral' manner.

4.2.4 The United States of America

The notion of non-establishment comes from the wording of the First Amendment of the Constitution of the United States. The American example of non-establishment has been followed in a large number of constitutions around the world.[12] Essentially, it is understood to indicate a strict separation between 'church' and state – a prohibition imposed on the state to favour any religious institution. The understanding of non-establishment in the USA makes it unthinkable that the salaries of clerics might be paid or religious schools be subsidized from public funds.

The second part of the First Amendment, the other side of the coin, as it were, guarantees the 'free exercise' of religion, which in turn makes it unthinkable in the USA for example to prohibit Muslim women from wearing a headscarf or a burqa in schools and universities.

James Whitman contrasts American non-establishment and tolerance of religion with secularism in European countries, emphasizing the profound role that religion continues to play in political and forensic life in the USA, whereas religion is said to be anathema in continental European law and politics.[13] These contrasts are explained by Whitman as the result of the different religious histories and traditions in Europe and the USA. He contests the explanation that they are related to contrasting Catholic and Protestant views, and credibly ascribes the causes for the divergence in the historical sociology on the opposite sides of the Atlantic to the following factors:[14]

> [O]n the one hand, we have northern continental countries (like France, Germany and the Scandinavian countries) in which *the state, over many centuries, has gradually assumed many of the historic functions performed by the medieval Church.* This has happened differently in different parts of the

---

[11] Adams (2009) 8–9.
[12] Cf. the discussion above in Chapter 1, section 1.4.
[13] Whitman (2008) 86–90.
[14] Whitman (2008) 91–92.

northern continent. But in one way or another it has happened in all of the countries that lie north of the Alps, east of the Pyrenees, and west of the Elbe ... . In the Anglo-American tradition, medieval Church functions have, by and large, never been assumed by the state. Quite the contrary: in America, *historic church functions have generally either been left to the churches, or else they have died out entirely.*

Whitman also shows that the roots of French *laïcité* are deeper than is often assumed, reaching back as far as the Edict of Nantes of 1598.[15] He furthermore points out[16] that, whereas the confrontation of Europeans with Islam tends to evoke a degree of intolerance, the American 'promiscuous mixing of religion and politics' can create the impression (in international relations) that the USA functions as 'a paladin in the Christian cause'.

Given the historical and practical inconsistencies in non-establishment and laic legal orders, one might conclude that one should not wonder at the confusion that accompanies attempts to proclaim neutrality in the constitutional law of states professing secularity.

4.3 DUBIOUS CONSTITUTIONAL PROTECTION OF RELIGION

4.3.1 China

As has been mentioned above, it would appear that contemporary constitutions almost consistently provide for the protection of freedom of religion. It is not unusual, however, for such provisions to be qualified in the text or to be flouted in practice. Thus, for example, article 36 of the Constitution of the People's Republic of China of 1982 (as amended)[17] opens, under the heading 'the fundamental rights and duties of citizens', with the statement that Chinese citizens 'enjoy freedom of religious belief', followed, however, by a prohibition of 'activities that disrupt public order, impair the health of citizens or interfere with the educational system of the state', and by the statement that 'religious bodies and religious affairs are not subject to any foreign domination'. Under the heading 'general principles' article 24 provides as follows:

---

[15] Whitman (2008) 93–95.
[16] Whitman (2008) 99–101.
[17] English text found on the government website at http://english.gov.cn/2005-08/05/content_20813.htm (accessed 24 March 2013).

The state strengthens the building of socialist spiritual civilization by promoting education in high ideals, ethics, general knowledge, discipline and legality, and by promoting the formulation and observance of rules of conduct and common pledges by various sections of the people in urban and rural areas.

The state advocates the civic virtues of love for the motherland, for the people, for labor, for science and for socialism. It conducts education among the people in patriotism and collectivism, in internationalism and communism and in dialectical and historical materialism, to combat capitalist, feudalist and other decadent ideas.

In their categorization of religious control regimes, Martínez-Torrón and Durham point out[18] that in China there are very high governmental restrictions on religion, but that the level of social restrictions (hostile acts by individuals) is not much higher than that in the USA, Japan or Italy. Furthermore, in keeping with the communist style, freedom *from* religion is emphasized for ideological reasons and to prevent religious communities from becoming a competing source of legitimacy in society.

4.3.2 Pakistan

Article 20 of the Constitution of the Islamic Republic of Pakistan, 1973 (as amended)[19] provides:

Subject to law, public order and morality, –

(a) every citizen shall have the right to profess, practise and propagate his religion; and
(b) every religious denomination and every sect thereof shall have the right to establish, maintain and manage its religious institutions.

Articles 21 and 22 go on to provide safeguards against taxation for the purposes of any particular religion and regarding educational institutions in respect of religion. However, article 2 unambiguously states that 'Islam shall be the State religion of Pakistan'. Article 19 allows 'reasonable restrictions' on the freedom of the press 'in the interest of the glory of Islam', and article 31 requires the state to promote 'the Islamic way of life', *inter alia* by providing appropriate facilities to this end. To qualify for election as president or prime minister one must be a Muslim (articles

---

[18] Martínez-Torrón and Durham (2012) 3 and 7.
[19] Text found on the Pakistani government website http://punjablaws.punjab.gov.pk/public/dr/CONSTITUTION%20OF%20PAKISTAN.doc.pdf (accessed 25 March 2014).

41(2) 91(3)), and for election to Parliament a candidate must not be 'commonly known as one who violates Islamic injunctions' and must have 'adequate knowledge of Islamic teachings and practice[s] obligatory duties prescribed by Islam' and be one who 'abstains from major sins' (article 62(d) and (e)), but ten seats are reserved for non-Muslims (article 51(4)). The Constitution furthermore establishes the Federal Shariat Court (article 203C) with the jurisdiction to 'examine and decide the question whether or not any law or provision of law is repugnant to the injunctions of Islam'.

Against the background of the overwhelming constitutional promotion of Islam in Pakistan, the protection of non-Muslim religious freedom appears to be hollow.[20] This is confirmed by the practice in the country, which is not only discriminatory against religions other than Islam but is openly suppressive of minority Muslims, that is, those who do not belong to the Sunni sect: in constitutional terms, this is effected by the definition of 'Muslim' and 'non-Muslim' in article 260(3).[21] Criminal prosecution for blasphemy is said to be a 'widespread phenomenon' which is frequently abused.[22] According to Michael Bohlander:[23]

> The oft repeated protestations that Muslims do respect other faiths and would not harm adherents of other religions purely because of that fact appear to be given the lie in everyday Pakistani life where reactionary and aggressive Islamism has the upper hand. If Islam is a religion of peace, then Pakistan would not seem to be a land of Islam, no matter what its constitution says.

4.3.3 Greece

Article 13 of the Constitution of Greece (as revised in 2008)[24] provides that 'freedom of religious conscience is inviolable' and that the enjoyment of other rights is not influenced by individual religious beliefs. It goes on (paragraph 2) to protect 'all known religions' and 'their rites of worship', but significantly subject to the following: 'The practice of rites

---

[20] Hassan (2002) nevertheless argues that Pakistan is essentially a secular state.
[21] Cf. also Levey and Modood (2009) 95.
[22] Bohlander (2012) 42–43.
[23] Bohlander (2012) 65–66.
[24] To be found on the website of the Hellenic Parliament at http://www.hellenicparliament.gr/UserFiles/f3c70a23-7696-49db-9148-f24dce6a27c8/001-156%20aggliko.pdf (accessed 25 March 2014).

of worship is not allowed to offend public order or the good usages. Proselytism is prohibited.'[25] Further qualifications then follow:

3. The ministers of all known religions shall be subject to the same supervision by the State and to the same obligations towards it as those of the prevailing religion.
4. No person shall be exempt from discharging his obligations to the State or may refuse to comply with the laws by reason of his religious convictions.

Article 3 contains the following extensive exposition under the heading 'Relations of Church and State':

1. The prevailing religion in Greece is that of the Eastern Orthodox Church of Christ. The Orthodox Church of Greece, acknowledging our Lord Jesus Christ as its head, is inseparably united in doctrine with the Great Church of Christ in Constantinople and with every other Church of Christ of the same doctrine, observing unwaveringly, as they do, the holy apostolic and synodal canons and sacred traditions. It is autocephalous and is administered by the Holy Synod of serving Bishops and the Permanent Holy Synod originating thereof and assembled as specified by the Statutory Charter of the Church in compliance with the provisions of the Patriarchal Tome of June 29, 1850 and the Synodal Act of September 4, 1928.
2. The ecclesiastical regime existing in certain districts of the State shall not be deemed contrary to the provisions of the preceding paragraph.
3. The text of the Holy Scripture shall be maintained unaltered. Official translation of the text into any other form of language, without prior sanction by the Autocephalous Church of Greece and the Great Church of Christ in Constantinople, is prohibited.

Encountering constitutional provisions containing religious doctrine and the institution of church structures inevitably raises questions concerning the sincerity and status of the protection of religious freedom in terms of other provisions. According to Martínez-Torrón and Durham these constitutional arrangements do not render the Greek Orthodox Church the official state religion but merely the 'prevailing' religion in the state, which, however, causes other religions to 'clearly lack many of the privileges of the Orthodox faith'.[26]

The Greek Constitution clearly displays a tension between the 'prevailing' and the other 'known' religions. Despite official protestations that

---

[25] Prosylatism is in fact a punishable crime in Greece: cf. for example, *Kokkinakis v Greece*.
[26] Martínez-Torrón and Durham (2010) 9.

the religion practised by the Orthodox Church is not the state religion, the reality seems to be that 'existing case law and the prevailing opinion in Greek legal theory generally support the interpretation of Art 3 as establishing a state religion, either in its traditional or majoritarian version'.[27]

4.4 HISTORICAL CHURCH/STATE ALLIANCES

Various examples of constitutional arrangements exist that reflect a history of close relations between the state and one or more religious denominations. The consequences of arrangements of this nature for the degree of even-handedness in state conduct regarding religion vary, but in most of the legal orders in this category notions of secularism tend to counter outright favouritism, or to support an intention to phase out favouritism.

4.4.1 The Church of England

One of the better-known examples is the United Kingdom, where the Queen is the 'Supreme Governor of the Church of England'. The Queen appoints archbishops, bishops and deans of cathedrals on the advice of the prime minister. The two archbishops and 24 senior bishops have seats in the House of Lords, where the senior bishop ('Lord Spiritual') reads a Christian prayer at the beginning of sittings of the House. On the official website of the UK Parliament[28] the following information is offered:

> Sittings in both Houses begin with prayers. These follow the Christian faith and there is currently no multi-faith element. Attendance is voluntary.
>
> The practice of prayers is believed to have started in about 1558, and was common practice by 1567. The present form of prayers probably dates from the reign of Charles II. Members of the public are not allowed into the public galleries during prayers.

The Church of England's exposition of its history[29] takes the reader back to the 3rd Century, when a Christian missionary church was established in

---

[27] Kyriazopoulos (2001) 530.
[28] http://www.parliament.uk/about/how/business/prayers/ (accessed 31 March 2014). See also Woodhead (2013) 148–149.
[29] To be found on its official website at http://www.churchofengland.org/about-us/history/detailed-history.aspx (accessed 31 March 2014).

Britain while it was still part of the Roman Empire. Between the 7th and 16th Centuries the *Ecclesia Anglicana* acknowledged the authority of the Catholic pope. The Reformation of the 16th Century, however, brought about a break with Rome:

> The catalyst for this decision was the refusal of the Pope to annul the marriage of Henry VIII and Catherine of Aragon, but underlying this was a Tudor nationalist belief that authority over the English Church properly belonged to the English monarchy.[30]

At the end of the turbulent times of civil war and the Cromwellian *interregnum*, when the church was abolished, the restoration of the monarchy brought about the restoration of the official status of the church, and eventually, in 1689, the 'settlement', which continues to be:

> the basis of the constitutional position of the Church of England ever since, a constitutional position in which the Church of England has remained the established Church with a range of particular legal privileges and responsibilities, but with ever increasing religious and civil rights being granted to other Christians, those of other faiths and those professing no faith at all.[31]

Charlotte Smith[32] argues that establishment demands a place for religion in the public sphere but that a human rights framework tends to remove religion into the private sphere. This suggests a particular, strictly liberal approach to human rights, disregarding the possibility that a constitutional arrangement is possible in which the significance of religion beyond mere personal belief is recognized. Smith's contribution nevertheless provides some useful insights into the implications of English establishment, particularly with reference to the 2001 and 2003 judgments of the Court of Appeal and the House of Lords in *Aston Cantlow v Wallbank*.[33] According to Smith[34] the judgments expose:

> [T]he significance of the gap between modern and historical assumptions about the role of religion in the public sphere; the difficulties created by the nature of development and reform in the English constitution; and the relevance of different reactions within the church to social and political change.

---

[30] *Ibid.*
[31] *Ibid.*
[32] Smith (2009) 167 *et seq*.
[33] In 2001 and 2003. Smith (2009) sets out the facts and salient points of the judgments at 167–169.
[34] Smith (2009) 170.

The 17th Century assumption was that to be English meant to be a member of the Church of England, which 'was tied into the very fabric of state and nation by a system of organisation which made provision for every geographical area of the state'.[35] Following the Reformation, the legislative granting of religious freedom to persons of other religious persuasions occurred in the 18th Century. Eventually religious conformity was detached from civic participation, but some remnants of a relationship between parochial residents and the parish church continue to exist. According to Smith:[36] 'The continued assumption that all individuals have rights in respect of their parish church demonstrates continuity with old ideas of Establishment as making public provision for religious services.'

The judgment of the Court of Appeal deemed a church council endowed with the statutory authority to levy contributions for the maintenance of the church on all parish residents, regardless of their religious affiliation, to be a public function, subject to the provisions of the Human Rights Act, whereas the House of Lords considered it to be a matter of private law, and therefore unaffected by UK or European human rights law. The Lords saw the church to be a private religious institution, exercising certain public functions, but not as a representative of the state.[37] There is some irony in this: were the established church considered to be associated closely enough with the state to be competent to exercise public functions, non-members would have been able to avoid contributing to the maintenance of church property; on the other hand, considering the church to be detached from the state as a private entity allowed it to impose obligations on non-members.

Here one must conclude that the constitutional position in which the Church of England finds itself is, to say the least, contradictory. The established church no doubt enjoys significant privileges in England but its traditional position can hardly be maintained in the long run, given the simultaneous pressures of the constitutional transformation of English law within the European context and the pluralization of religion of British society. Nevertheless, Javier Oliva concluded in 2010:[38]

> [T]he religious establishment today protected by law in England and Scotland would seem to be perceived by many leaders of the mainstream religious traditions as unproblematic, by the European Union as a legitimate exercise in

---

[35] Smith (2009) 171.
[36] Smith (2009) 175.
[37] Smith (2009) 168.
[38] Oliva (2010) 504.

4.4.2 Ireland

In its preamble the Irish Constitution[39] unambiguously sets out the Christian convictions under which Éire is established. It opens with the following words:

> In the Name of the Most Holy Trinity, from Whom is all authority and to Whom, as our final end, all actions both of men and States must be referred,
>
> We, the people of Éire,
>
> Humbly acknowledging all our obligations to our Divine Lord, Jesus Christ, Who sustained our fathers through centuries of trial ...

Article 44.1 provides that '[t]he State acknowledges that the homage of public worship is due to Almighty God. It shall hold His Name in reverence, and shall respect and honour religion.' Before 1972 two further subsections added (in 44.2) that the state 'recognises the special position of the Holy Catholic Apostolic and Roman Church as the guardian of the Faith professed by the great majority of the citizens' and (in 44.3) that the state 'also recognises' various named churches, Jewish congregations and other religious denominations existing in Ireland. Articles 44.2 and 44.3 were repealed by the Fifth Amendment of the Constitution of Ireland in 1972, thereby terminating the distinction between the 'special position' of the Catholic Church and the position of other faiths. Since this recognition did not mean that the Catholic Church was established as the official church of Ireland, the amendment did not change the position significantly.

The recognition of Catholicism as 'the Faith professed by the great majority of the citizens' explains some other constitutional provisions reflecting Catholic morals. Among these is article 41, concerning the family. In article 41.1.1 'The State recognises the Family as the natural primary and fundamental unit group of Society, and as a moral institution possessing inalienable and imprescriptible rights, antecedent and superior to all positive law.' Article 41.3 purports to provide for special protection of the institution of marriage. Until 1996 the granting of divorce was prohibited, but the *Fifteenth Amendment of the Constitution Act* of 1995

---

[39] *Bunreacht na Héireann*, 1937.

repealed the prohibition and now permits divorce under certain prescribed conditions.

Articles 44.2–44.6 meticulously guarantee the freedom of conscience and the free profession and practice of religion, but 'subject to public order and morality'; the state is prohibited 'to endow any religion'; the imposition by the state of 'disabilities' or discrimination on religious grounds is precluded; state aid may be granted to schools under the management of different religious denominations without discriminating among them; and the property rights and independence of all denominations are protected. The moral if not religious foundation upon which these provisions are built is to be found in article 44.1: 'The State acknowledges that the homage of public worship is due to Almighty God. It shall hold His Name in reverence, and shall respect and honour religion.'

4.4.3 Germany

It could not justifiably be said that a specific church or denomination stands in close alliance with the German state, but in Germany a unique and comprehensive body of law dealing with church and state (*Staatskirchenrecht*) has emerged from history. Some of the principles of *Staatskirchenrecht* are state neutrality in matters of religion and world view, a prohibition of the founding of a state church or the favouring of any religious creed,[40] religious freedom and the equality of religions.[41] However, denominational religious education is allowed in schools, as well as religious activity in state institutions.[42] Religious communities are allowed to raise 'church tax' through the mechanisms of the state,[43] church property is specially protected by law,[44] and Sundays are recognized as days of rest and spiritual worship.[45] Interestingly, and in conflict with this notion, the Federal Constitutional Court has made it clear that the recognition of Sundays as a day of rest is not founded upon limited religious grounds, but 'in the secularised society and constitutional

---

[40] See for example, Kokott (1996) and the judgment of the German Constitutional Court in *BverfGE* 19, 206 (216).
[41] See Ehlers (1996).
[42] Art. 141 of the *Weimarer Reichsverfassung* (WRV) as incorporated by art.140 *Grundgesetz* (GG).
[43] Art. 137 WRV.
[44] Art. 138 Abs(2) WRV.
[45] Art. 139 WRV.

system', and that it includes the pursuit of 'profane' goals such as 'personal rest, contemplation, relaxation and diversion'.[46]

4.4.4 Switzerland

A rather curious recent instance of social resistance to state neutrality in religious matters occurred in 2009 in Switzerland. The preamble to the Swiss Constitution of 1999 opens with the words 'In the name of God Almighty!' and article 15 guarantees the freedom of faith and conscience and the usual concomitant rights such as the right to profess one's religion alone or in community with others. Article 72 is headed 'Church and State'. Sub-article (1) makes the regulation of this relationship a cantonal matter and sub-article (2) allows both the Federation and the Cantons to 'take measures to maintain public peace between members of the various religious communities'. Sub-article (3) simply states: 'The building of minarets is prohibited.' This provision was inserted in 2009 'by popular vote', that is, after a federal referendum was held following a campaign by the Swiss People's Party in which it was argued that minarets have nothing to do with the Muslim religion but served as symbols of power.[47]

When Swiss Muslims complained to the European Court of Justice that the constitutional amendment prohibiting the building of minarets impaired their freedom of religion and the right not to be discriminated against on religious grounds, as protected by the European Convention on Human Rights (articles 9 and 14), the Court found the complaints to be inadmissible on the grounds that the complainants did not under the circumstances qualify to be deemed victims of a violation of the Convention.

The constitutional prohibition of the building of minarets has brought about considerable scholarly reaction regarding the justification or otherwise of citizen-initiated referenda as a possible means by which a majority may dominate unpopular minorities.[48] Be that as it may, this instance demonstrates how difficult it is to resolve preferences related to religion under circumstances of the migration and pluralization of religions.

---

[46] BVerfG, 1 BvR 2857/07 delivered on 1 December 2009.
[47] Randall and McGregor (2010) 428. See section 4.5 below for more details on the referendum.
[48] Cf. Randall and McGregor (2010) 428–429 and Spadijer (2012) and the publications cited in footnote 2 of the article.

Some further examples of states that award a special status to 'national' churches are Norway[49] and Argentina.[50]

4.5 RELIGION IN THE STATE AMIDST GLOBALIZATION

Religion is an attribute of humanity which is at least as foundational as but is probably even more foundational than the need for government. No wonder then that the guarantee of freedom of religion may be considered to be the oldest claim of the individual against the state. Nor should one wonder why the history of constitutional law has over many centuries and across the globe been characterized by a contest between religious and political claimants of power over society and the individual.

The vastly increased mobility of contemporary humanity is transforming populations within state boundaries in many countries into plural societies in terms of socio-economic, racial and cultural diversity.

As has been shown above, the state continues to be the primary role-player in law, internally as the legislator, administrator and adjudicator, and internationally as the representative and protector of the inhabitants of its territory. The contemporary state continues to function within the superannuated theoretical framework of its assumed origin as the embodiment of a nation. Whereas 'nations' (as more or less cohesive conglomerates of culturally compatible tribal or feudal sub-groups) living in defined geographical spaces in the 19th and partly in the 20th Centuries were assumed to form the core of intra- and extra-statal authority and identity, the 'nation state' has since begun to lose its credibility as a consolidated entity which displays internal cultural solidarity, and this trend is proceeding apace.[51] The terminology of the era of nation-forming

---

[49] Thus for example, the still operational Constitution of the Kingdom of Norway of 1814, the official English version available at http://www.constitution.org/cons/norway/dok-bn.html (accessed 9 April 2014) provides in Article 2: 'All inhabitants of the Realm shall have the right to free exercise of their religion. The Evangelical-Lutheran religion shall remain the official religion of the State. The inhabitants professing it are bound to bring up their children in the same.'

[50] Section 2 of the Constitution of the Argentine Nation of 1853 (English text at http://www.servat.unibe.ch/icl/ar00000_.html (accessed 9 April 2014)) provides: 'The Federal Government supports the Roman Catholic Apostolic religion.'

[51] Glenn (2013) 98 concludes that 'states today are not coincident with nations'.

nevertheless remains with us, as for example in the expression 'inter-*nation*al', and politicians are still fond of employing expressions such as 'nation-building' and 'national honour'.

Statehood or 'nationhood', however, hardly ever coincided with religious solidarity. Religious considerations were prominent at the time of the inception of statehood in Europe. The Peace of Westphalia of 1648 concluded a period of bloody religious warfare and initiated the recognition of a right to religious freedom.[52] It was also during the negotiation of the peace treaty that the word 'secularization' was introduced (by a French ambassador) to indicate the abolition of religious principalities and the state expropriation of church property.[53]

Although it is not a new phenomenon, the extent of religious pluralism, by which is meant the practising of a spectrum of religious creeds by the inhabitants of a single constitutional jurisdiction, whether all, none or only some of the religious practices and institutions are recognized by the state as such or not, is growing along with global migration.

A broad taxonomy of types of religion is possible, but the diversity thereof, even within the various streams, is immense.[54] Thus most sources identify Christianity as the largest religion, although widely diverse groupings that are at odds with one another on fundamental points of faith such as Eastern Orthodox churches, Quakers and Jehovah's Witnesses are included in such statistics. The second largest grouping is normally considered to be Islam, which is also fundamentally divided politically and religiously between (mostly) Shi'ites and Sunnis. Hinduism, lacking single or consolidated scriptures and teachings, with its largest adherence in populous India and Nepal, can probably be considered to be the third largest religion, followed by Buddhism, Sikhism, Judaism, Mormonism, Jehovah's Witnesses, Baha'ism, Jainism,

---

[52] Croxton and Tischer (2002) 69, under the entry 'CUIUS REGIO; EIUS RELIGIO':

> The Peace of Westphalia sharply limited the doctrine by setting 1624 as the 'normal year' for religious affairs: whatever religion was practised at that time was allowed to continue, and although the ruler could change the state church, he could not interfere with the public worship of his other subjects. The Peace of Westphalia also diverged from the *cuius regio* principle because it guaranteed freedom of worship in private homes and the right of religious dissidents to emigrate.

[53] Hunter (2009) 40.

[54] Some internet resources regarding world religions are http://www.bbc.co.uk/religion/religions (accessed 28 February 2013) and http://www.adherents.com/Religions_By_Adherents.html (accessed 28 February 2013).

Rastafarianism, Zoroastrianism, Unitarianism and religious splinter groups such as Santerianism.

It is not always agreed that some not insignificant groupings such as Spiritualism, Shintoism, Unitarianism and Taoism may accurately be classified as religions, and in many African and South American societies (but also in parts of Australasia and the Arctic North) there are naturalistic, syncretistic and traditional groupings and rituals that may under some circumstances also have to be accounted for in the context of religious pluralism. Finally, an amorphous though significant segment of the human population that may contest the validity of their inclusion in religious demographics, but whose views are extraordinarily influential, are the agnostics, atheists and secular humanists. Within and across all these categories, uncounted variations exist. None of them is confined to a single geographic area on the globe and due to the ever-growing mobility of people their adherents are increasingly establishing a presence in many countries, sometimes causing social tensions due to the strangeness to the local population of their beliefs and modes of worship.[55]

In the case of states where religious practices were banned (for instance in communist systems) but were reinstated as being concordant with a process of democratization and economic development, old religious practices have revived (in Russia, for example) or there has been an explosive growth of religions from abroad through missionary activity (for example in China). In many African countries centuries of Christian or Islamic penetration have had the effect of the elaborate growth of syncretism, but also of religious division, such as between the Muslim North and Christian South of Nigeria.

In most cases the escalation of religious pluralism is a function of increased mobility and migration. Put differently, the driver behind religious pluralism is not so much religious as economic or political. Social disturbances, generally of a political nature, cause the swelling of the number of refugees, many of whom become migrants. More significant, however, are the attractions of wealth in economically stronger countries which draw migrants from weaker economies. The religious

---

[55] Highly interesting demographic statistics on the spread of the adherents of the various religious groupings are available. In this regard the intensive reporting by *The Religion and State Project* of the Bar-Ilan University in Tel Aviv, which is affiliated to the Association of Religion Data Archives (ARDA), to be found on the internet at http://www.thearda.com/ras/ (accessed 5 April 2013) provides valuable information regarding statistics relating to religion in all countries of the world.

affiliation of refugees and economic migrants, regardless of the fact that their creed is in the minority or even alien to the majority of the population of the receiving destination, is more often than not of incidental significance to the migrant seeking better living conditions. Only after arrival and settlement in the host society do considerations arise such as the acquisition of citizenship, cultural and religious accommodation, and dealing with possible social tensions.[56]

Constitutional regulation by different states of religious and cultural matters varies vastly and is for obvious reasons largely determined by local circumstances. Two contrasting examples, Saudi Arabia and the USA, demonstrate the divergence of possible approaches. Article 1 of the Saudi *Basic Law of Government* of 1992, which serves as an instrument to provide structure to the government of that autocratically ruled country, provides as follows: 'The Kingdom of Saudi Arabia is a sovereign Arab Islamic state with Islam as its religion; God's Book and the Sunnah of His Prophet, God's prayers and peace be upon him, are its constitution, Arabic is its language and Riyadh is its capital.' The open practice of any religion other than Islam is prohibited in Saudi Arabia and the death penalty may be imposed upon a person who attempts to convert a person to any other religion.

The well-known opening words of the US Constitution's First Amendment, 'Congress shall make no law respecting an establishment of religion', represent a diametrically opposed approach. Over more than two centuries this 'non-establishment clause' has been interpreted and applied in various often contradictory manners, but it is generally thought to require state neutrality (however understood)[57] in religious matters.

The manner in which states respond to the challenges of religious pluralism varies according to constitutional, statutory and common-law norms and their jurisdictional interpretation, but consistent and clearly predictable responses by courts, legislatures and administrations are not in evidence anywhere in the world.

Despite the huge spectrum of contemporary constitutional approaches to the legal regulation of religious matters, the rising challenge that religious diversity of the population poses is common to almost all states.[58] In reputable constitutional states a large volume of jurisprudence

---

[56] Cf. Bosniak (2006) 1, Smith (2009) 912 and Glenn (2013) 200.

[57] Cf. for example, Laycock (2010) 225 *et seq*, who distinguishes between formal neutrality, substantive neutrality and disaggregated neutrality.

[58] Even of Saudi Arabia it is said that approximately one-tenth of the total population, mostly foreign labourers from countries with Christian populations, is composed of non-Muslims. Cf. for example, Israel (2008).

on religious freedom and its implications for government and law has accumulated and seems to grow steadily. A survey of the cases[59] does not reveal a clear, recognizable set of common guidelines for dealing with this thorny issue – on the contrary, divided benches in such cases seem to be the norm rather than the exception. The issue will not go away, however, and it seems likely that its intensity will continue to escalate due to the large-scale migration of people and the concomitant spread of religions. In states (mostly Islamic) where religious freedom is suppressed vigorously, finding solutions may be postponed, but it is unlikely that the issue will be avoided in the long run.

Under these circumstances it may be asked how the adherents of diverse religions can peacefully share a common constitutional space. Where justice and equal treatment are striven for, legal dilemmas constantly occur regarding the need to allow or to prohibit religious conduct which offends or disturbs citizens professing different religions. Situations that notoriously crop up in this regard include controversies arising from religious dress, rituals considered to be unusual, cruel or unhygienic practice by non-adherents, dietary prescriptions strange or offensive to those not bound thereby, and the reservation of varying times, days and periods for prayer, rituals, commemorations or observations. It is noteworthy that such controversies often arise in the context of education. Offending the religious, moral or legal principles held by some components of a society or community is one thing; causing tension regarding local notions of visual or auditory aesthetics and hygiene, however, brings about another set of challenges to legal peacekeeping.

It is self-evident that where a population was characterized by a single prevalent religion large-scale immigration causing the society to become religiously plural will require the state to respond to the likelihood of increased social tensions occurring within the population. In some instances, especially where Islam prevails, stringent measures to protect the status quo are adopted. In other cases, such as those of most Western European countries, a *laissez faire* approach allowed previously foreign religious groupings to gain a foothold, causing a slow but discernable popular backlash. Thus, for instance, in Switzerland a referendum was held in November 2009 at the initiative of conservative parties on the question of whether the building of minarets was to be prohibited. At the time there was a Muslim population of approximately 400 000 (out of approximately 7 million) living in the country, hailing mostly from the

---

[59] See Chapter 6 below.

former Yugoslavia and Turkey. To the surprise of many, after an unusually high rate of participation in the election (54 per cent), a majority of 57.5 per cent of voters supported the prohibition.[60]

The question that now arises is what good may be harvested from the emergence of constitutionalism around the globe. In a world that has put the 20th Century behind it, a century characterized by brutal mass wars, a 'cold' war waged in response to fears of a nuclear catastrophe, the results of the previous century's self-serving colonialism and the quadrupling of the world's population, one might wish to be able to think in terms of the 21st Century as being the human race's age of maturity. Unfortunately such a utopian vision is easily dulled, even by a brief glimpse at the state of the world seen through the eyes of the law. One cannot look beyond the reality that the most serene norms of international law are constantly being subjected to military and economic power, the fact that constitutionalism is frequently made to serve the aspirations of corrupt or self-centred rulers, that cold commercial interests will not allow moral limitations upon the global expansion of concentrated wealth, and that the law is increasingly being over-extended while it attempts to bear the responsibility for maintaining social stability.

Such a glum outlook may be qualified, however, by dwelling on the merits of the constitutional values and principles to be found in many jurisdictions, despite the divergent life and world views that prevail in the states to which they apply. There is at least some hope that the tired and fictitious constitutional artefacts inherited from centuries gone by which do not contribute to the merits of constitutional law may eventually be replaced.

Where, however, might one find such universal principles and values? Here lies another irony: while globalization is in some respects a blight on the ambitions of the hypothetically sovereign individual, preventing him from attaining freedom from poverty, economic suppression and ecological devastation, it simultaneously serves as the primary vehicle for the dissemination and reception of constitutionalism. This dissemination, although far from complete, solid or final, holds the promise of the laying of sound and just foundations for good governance in many places on the globe. This often takes the form of collectively attractive notions such as the rule of law.

Establishing what the rule of law, its principles and underlying values mean globally requires stringent comparative study, thus inescapably

---

[60] See for example, *Zeit Online* 29 November 2009 at http://www.zeit.de/politik/ausland/2009-11/schweiz-minarett-wahl (accessed 4 June 2015).

requiring constitution-makers to become avid comparatists. The South African Constitutional Court, one may be pleased to observe, has produced some exemplary constitution-making jurisprudence on this theme by propounding a doctrine of constitutionalism under the banner of the rule of law in which continental principles were elegantly grafted on to the common-law vine. According to this Court the South African constitutional state may be defined as a state in which the Constitution prevails over all law and all actions of the state, where fundamental rights are acknowledged and protected through the independent authority of the judiciary to enforce the Bill of Rights and the Constitution, a separation of powers is maintained, all government action is required to be legally justified, the state has a duty to protect fundamental rights, legal certainty is promoted, democracy and the rule of law are maintained, a specific set of legal principles applies, and an objective normative system of values guides the executive, the legislature and the judiciary.[61] These are obviously not novel ideas at all, but their systematic integration as a compound description of what is globally accepted to be elements of constitutional 'good', even in differing social, political and dogmatic contexts, promises their utility in the promotion of good governance.

Even if the globally confessed dictates of good governance, constitutionalism and the rule of law do not provide us with absolute guarantees against the abuse of power, corruption and hardship, they afford us, at the very least, strong and widely supported arguments against these endemic character weaknesses of humanity, and may therefore, under relatively favourable conditions, serve as a shield behind which constitution-makers and courts may combat decay – especially where governors feel themselves obliged, under the pressure of their actions being observed by a global audience, to employ the language of constitutionalism for the purposes of justifying their conduct even when their actions actually fall lamentably short of moral justification.

4.6 RELIGION AND CONSTITUTIONALISM

In their comprehensive overview of the extent of religious freedom in a wide range of constitutions, Martínez-Torrón and Durham offer a significant distinction between *secularity* and *secularism*.[62] According to them, in secularism 'secularization is sought as an end itself', which is an ideology or system of belief which leads in its extreme form to the repression and

---

[61] Cf. Venter (2012b) 721–747.
[62] Martínez-Torrón and Durham (2010) 3.

persecution of religion, or in its more typical, milder form, prefers neutrality to freedom of conscience and relegates religion to the private sphere, completely removing the expression of religion from public life.

Martínez-Torrón and Durham see secularity as being less rigid and placing 'greater emphasis on protecting freedom of conscience':[63]

> Secularity favors substantive over formal conceptions of equality and neutrality, taking claims of conscience seriously as grounds for accommodating religiously-motivated difference. Separation in this model is clearly recognized as an institutional means for facilitating protection of freedom of religion or belief, rather than as an ideal endstate in itself. The secular state is understood as a framework for accommodating pluralism, including individuals and groups with profoundly differing belief systems who are nonetheless willing to live together in a shared social order.

This distinction between secularism and secularity is useful for the characterization of a state as one that allows for a degree of religious freedom on a continuum from theocracy via neutrality to abolitionism. Martínez-Torrón and Durham accordingly devised an informative graphic 'loop' for the purposes of showing the range of possibilities regarding the approach of states to religion. Secularity appears around the turn of the loop representing optimal religious freedom, either as a positive freedom or a negative freedom, depending on the nature of the concept of neutrality prevalent in the state concerned (Figure 4.1).

For the purposes of considering the appropriate approach of a constitutional state to religion, the representation shown in Figure 4.1 is significant because of what it reveals about the relative impact that secularism has on the degree and nature of the recognition of the freedom of religion of the inhabitants of a particular state. Although the recognition of the right to religious freedom lies close to the core of the constitutional and political attitude of the society and the state towards religion, it does not reflect the whole of the picture. Equally important is the prevailing understanding of constitutionalism in the legal order concerned: it is necessary to assess the impact that constitutionalism, properly understood, should have on the manner in which the state deals with religious pluralism.

There is irony in the phenomenon that some of the constitutions most often cited as pillars of constitutionalism, such as those of Canada and France, drive (or allow) secularist agendas most ardently. This cannot mean that constitutionalism by definition favours hostility to religion,

---

[63] Martínez-Torrón and Durham (2010) 3.

110   *Constitutionalism and religion*

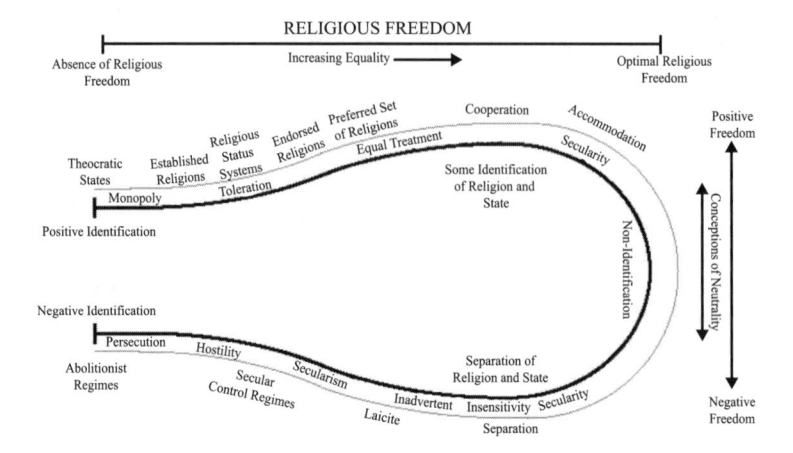

Source: Martínez-Torrón and Durham (2012) 9. Reproduced here with kind permission of the author and Springer Science+Business Media.

Figure 4.1   States' approach to religion

except if there is only one form of constitutionalism, viz. liberalist constitutionalism.

On the contrary, it is remarkable that a high degree of accommodation of religious pluralism can often be observed in constitutional orders such as England and Germany where there are established churches or long-standing special relationships between state and church without the quality of constitutionalism or the existence of exemplary constitutionalism being impugned thereby.

Despite the merits of their distinction between secularity and secularism, Martínez-Torrón and Durham's approach amounts to subscribing to the notion of the secular state. If the only alternative to the secular state were theocracy, supporting the notion might have been acceptable. However, there is a conceptual problem not only with secularism but also with secularity: despite the 'mildness' of the latter as presented in the graphic loop of Figure 4.1, it still implies state neutrality, an attitude that will be argued below is impossible to achieve and undesirable when it comes to matters of religion. The contention here is that not secularism but constitutionalism provides the 21st Century state with a viable and defensible foundation for doing objective justice to all under the prevailing trend of increasing religious pluralism.

5. Religion in international law

As we have seen in Chapter 1, it is not always clear what the concept 'religion' entails, since there are divergent views on the matter. The application of the notion in international law is no different and, due to the inevitably global (as opposed to national) spectrum of variation, perhaps even more complex.

It is possible and desirable to approach the theme of this chapter from two perspectives. First, religion has had, and perhaps surprisingly still has, a profound influence on the history and present state of international law. In the first section a brief exposition is given of the influence of religion on the development of international law. Secondly, international law impacts significantly on religion around the world and in international intercourse. In section 5.2 an overview of the manner in which international law deals with religion and religion-related matters is presented. In the third section the manner in which religion figures in diplomacy and international discourse is discussed and in the fourth section the role of religious institutions in international law is described.

5.1 RELIGION IN THE DEVELOPMENT OF INTERNATIONAL LAW

In 1990 Mark Janis compiled a collection of astute essays on the influence of religion on the development of international law[1] which has retained its value over more than two decades. Janis' preface opens with the following striking remarks:

> The connection between religion and international law is close but nowadays surprisingly little studied or analyzed. This lack of attention has, I think, two causes. First is the effort made in the 19th and 20th centuries to turn international law into a 'science.' Those who do this often feel that doing law 'scientifically' means keeping religion entirely out of the discipline. Second is the addition in recent decades of more than a hundred new mostly non-Western states to the international political community. Conscious that

---

[1] Janis (1991).

Western values are not necessarily shared with other cultures, many international lawyers are unwilling to discuss religion, ethics and morals for fear of excluding those whose beliefs may be very different from their own.

These remarks reveal the dilemma, also in constitutional law, of the dominant liberal scholarly and judicial approach to law (primarily in the dominant West) which tends to attempt to drain morality from legal normativity in the name of neutrality, instead of addressing the real need for a conscionable public legal response to religious pluralism.

The essays collected by Janis provide a uniquely useful historical overview, warranting a brief summary of the essential findings in three of the contributions.

David Bederman found that religion played an important, but not exclusive, role in international legal obligation in the pre-Christian Near East, the Greek city states, the Indian states until 150 BC and the Mediterranean until 168 BC. In addition to fearing divine retribution, a 'dread of chaos' and pragmatism underpinned ancient international law, the first principle of which was that breaking faith with another nation embracing a national religion 'brought punishment, whether godly or human, immediate or delayed, terrible or trivial'.[2]

In his analysis of the role of religion in the writings of six authors of standard international law texts – Hugo de Groot (Grotius) in the 17th Century, Emmerich de Vattel in the 18th Century, John Austin and Henry Wheaton in the 19th Century, Lassa Oppenheim in the early 20th Century and Ian Brownlie in the late 20th Century – Janis finds that to Grotius religion was proof, 'problem to Vattel, and sanction to Wheaton' and to Oppenheim, mostly history:[3]

> Unlike Grotius who relied so heavily on philosophical and religious sources or Wheaton who saw religion as a moral sanction or even Oppenheim who at least took some account of the philosophical and religious antecedents of international law, Brownlie gives neither philosophy nor religion much attention in what is a formal court-oriented text. Brownlie seems to care for religion as little as Vattel without even Vattel's concern for religion as a problem.[4]

This course of religion through the development of international law is stated even more concisely by David Kennedy: 'Religion begins as a social force, is transformed into a "philosophy" and survives only as a set

---

[2] Bederman (1991) 24.
[3] Janis (1991) 75.
[4] Janis (1991) 79.

of "principles," guiding the practice of institutions.'[5] This statement is not only apposite when it comes to international law, but actually describes in broad terms the main line along which Western scholarly and scientific thinking has evolved since the golden age of the 17th Century natural philosophers to the contemporary era of astounding scientific achievement that inspires the intellectually arrogant assumption that man is the sovereign master of his own fate.[6]

Janis nevertheless concludes that, despite the different approaches to religion that are to be found, it is to be expected that any author dealing with international law doctrine will give religion 'a more or less distinctive role'.[7]

5.2 RELIGION IN INTERNATIONAL LAW

James Nafziger suggested in 1991 that '[r]eligion and international law often appear to be congruent':[8]

> They share elements of ritual, tradition, authority and universality that 'connect the legal order of any given society with that society's beliefs in an ultimate transcendent reality.'[9] There is, too, a certain sanctity to any body of law, just as there is an authoritative and often constitutive structure in religion.

But, as is to be expected, he also finds it necessary to address the problem of the definition of 'religion'. For the purposes of his contribution, he describes religion[10] as 'A practice of ultimate concern about our nature and obligations as human beings, inspired by experience and typically expressed by members of a group or community sharing myths and doctrines whose authority transcends both individual conscience and the state.'

---

[5] Kennedy (1991) 138.
[6] Cf. for example, the relentless assault on religiosity by Michael Shermer in his monthly column 'Skeptic' in *Scientific American*. For example, he closed his column in Shermer (2014) under the title 'The Awe Delusion' with an explanation of the attitude of 'those of us who find our spirituality in the awe of the natural world without a need for supernatural agenticity' as follows: 'Instead of fear and trembling, we feel wonder and gratitude in discovering that the author's hand is nature's laws and nothing more, but also nothing less.'
[7] Janis (1991) 81.
[8] Nafziger (1991) 151.
[9] The quotation is from Berman (1974).
[10] Nafziger (1991) 150.

In 2003, against the background that, despite the prevalence of various important guarantees of fundamental rights concerning religion, neither international law nor national constitutions provide a definition, Jeremy Gunn also addressed the complexity of the challenge to define religion for the purposes of international law. He maintained[11] that the widespread misunderstandings of the concept and definition of religion lead to 'the failure to take sufficient cognizance of the nature of religious discrimination and persecution and can preclude meritorious claimants from receiving deserved relief'. Citing an unpublished study prepared for the UN High Commissioner for Refugees by Karen Musalo, Gunn lists the following typical misunderstandings by judges of the nature of religion and religious persecution in refugee cases in the United States, Canada, Australia and New Zealand:[12]

- assessing claimants' credibility on the basis of their knowledge of and the consistency of their personal behaviour with the doctrines of their religions;
- failing to understand that religions sometimes persecute members of their own religious communities in order to ensure conformity with doctrines and practices;
- failing to understand the sometimes complex interrelationship of religious persecution and gender or ethnicity;
- failing to understand that what might initially appear to be only a minor inconvenience might reasonably constitute persecution to a claimant;
- failing to understand that persecutors' attitudes towards religion may be more relevant for adjudicating a religious persecution claim than scholarly definitions of 'religion'; and
- incorrectly assuming that 'neutral laws' or 'laws of general applicability' cannot cause religious persecution.

This list strongly suggests that the adjudication of religious cases is prone to injustice and subjectivity where neutrality is assumed to be the solution to the resolution of the difficulties presented by religious pluralism.

Gunn aptly characterizes the deficiencies in legal definitions of religion, which are usually called for in the 'complicating contexts' of the

---

[11] Gunn (2003) 215.
[12] Gunn (2003) 192.

protection of the freedom of religion, or the prohibition of religious discrimination or persecution, in the following passage:[13]

> Legal definitions do not simply describe the phenomenon of religion, they establish rules for regulating social and legal relations among people who themselves may have sharply different attitudes about what religion is and which manifestations of it are entitled to protection. Legal definitions, as a result, may contain serious deficiencies when they (perhaps unintentionally) incorporate particular social and cultural attitudes towards (preferred) religions, or when they fail to account for social and cultural attitudes against (disfavored) religions.

The two 'complicating contexts' that Gunn identified (freedom of religion and non-discrimination) certainly are real, but it is remarkable that they tend to overshadow most legal discussions of religion, thereby limiting the perspective considerably. It is suggested that this limitation can be diminished by not approaching religion as a phenomenon relevant in law only from the perspective of the individual requiring protection against incursion of guaranteed rights. Religion is relevant in law (and society for that matter) in the broader context of the function of the state to balance not only the religious rights among and between persons and institutions within its jurisdiction, or its constitutional obligation not to discriminate between persons, institutions, denominations and beliefs in the exercise of its authority, but also in the stances that the state and its various organs take regarding their own conduct; for example, in the making of policies for education, migration and labour, financial and tax governance, and ceremonial and legislative procedures. Official stances on matters of this nature of course do often impact on religious rights, but not always. Perhaps understandably, however, international instruments tend to deal with religion almost exclusively from a human rights perspective.

In a world where mono-religious countries are becoming rare or where the traditional prevalence of a single religion or of compatible religions is dissipating, the maintenance of social peace is becoming a growing priority for modern governments and the international community. It is therefore to be expected that the protection of religious rights has developed into an important theme in international law. Various well-known international and regional or supra-national instruments have been developed in terms of which the various facets of religious freedom are purported to be protected.

---

[13] Gunn (2003) 195.

Among the most prominent of these provisions are article 18 of the *Universal Declaration on Human Rights* of 1948 (UDHR), article 18 of the *International Convention on Civil and Political Rights* of 1966 (ICCPR) and the *Declaration on the Elimination of all Forms of Intolerance and of Discrimination Based on Religion or Belief* of 1981 (DRI). Article 18 of the UDHR is considered to be the standard-setting norm in this regard[14] and provides that:

> Everyone has the right to freedom of thought, conscience and religion; this right includes freedom to change his religion or belief, and freedom, either alone or in community with others and in public or private, to manifest his religion or belief in teaching, practice, worship and observance.

Three rights are identified by this provision: the right to believe, the right to change one's religion or belief and the right to manifest one's belief.[15] In terms of article 29.2 of the UDHR these rights may be limited, but:

> In the exercise of his rights and freedoms, everyone shall be subject only to such limitations as are determined by law solely for the purpose of securing due recognition and respect for the rights and freedoms of others and of meeting the just requirements of morality, public order and the general welfare in a democratic society.

Being intended to apply globally, the phrase 'meeting the just requirements of morality, public order and the general welfare in a democratic society' must be expected, perhaps especially where religion comes into play, to engender diverse responses as to the nature of justice, morality, public order, general welfare and democracy.

Flowing from the UDHR, the ICCPR provides for more detail regarding the right to freedom of religion against the broader context of freedom of thought and of conscience. Article 18 of the ICCPR reads as follows:

1. Everyone shall have the right to freedom of thought, conscience and religion. This right shall include freedom to have or to adopt a religion or belief of his choice, and freedom, either individually or in community with others and in public or private, to manifest his religion or belief in worship, observance, practice and teaching.
2. No one shall be subject to coercion which would impair his freedom to have or to adopt a religion or belief of his choice.

---

[14] Cf. for example, Van der Vyver (2005) 499–500.
[15] Also Van der Vyver (2005) 500–502.

3. Freedom to manifest one's religion or beliefs may be subject only to such limitations as are prescribed by law and are necessary to protect public safety, order, health, or morals or the fundamental rights and freedoms of others.
4. The States Parties to the present Covenant undertake to have respect for the liberty of parents and, when applicable, legal guardians to ensure the religious and moral education of their children in conformity with their own convictions.

The limitation of these (and other) rights provided for in the ICCPR is regulated, in addition to article 18.3, by article 5.1:

> Nothing in the present Covenant may be interpreted as implying for any State, group or person any right to engage in any activity or perform any act aimed at the destruction of any of the rights and freedoms recognized herein or at their limitation to a greater extent than is provided for in the present Covenant.

The limitation of the rights again involves considerations that one should expect not to be understood uniformly around the world: legitimacy of the limitation by law, what is needed to protect public safety, health and morals, and what these are understood to entail in a particular legal order.

Article 1.2 of the DRI states: 'No one shall be subject to coercion which would impair his freedom to have a religion or belief of his choice.' And article 4 provides as follows:

1. All States shall take effective measures to prevent and eliminate discrimination on the grounds of religion or belief in the recognition, exercise and enjoyment of human rights and fundamental freedoms in all fields of civil, economic, political, social and cultural life.
2. All States shall make all efforts to enact or rescind legislation where necessary to prohibit any such discrimination, and to take all appropriate measures to combat intolerance on the grounds of religion or other beliefs in this matter.

Various international instruments also relate the protection of religious freedom to educational rights. International law is intended to warrant, among others, the following rights concerning education, at least potentially related to religion:

- a right to establish educational institutions;
- rights relating to one's choice of educational language and culture;
- rights concerning equality and non-discrimination in education; and

- parents' right to choose the religious and moral nature of the education of their children.

Article 26(2) and (3) of the UDHR provides:

2. Education shall be directed to the full development of the human personality and to the strengthening of respect for human rights and fundamental freedoms. It shall promote understanding, tolerance and friendship among all nations, racial or religious groups, and shall further the activities of the United Nations for the maintenance of peace.
3. Parents have a prior right to choose the kind of education that shall be given to their children.

An elaboration on this right is found in article 18(4) of the ICCPR, where states are constrained to maintain the freedom of parents 'to ensure the religious and moral education of their children in conformity with their own convictions'. Somewhat curiously these provisions of the ICCPR and the UDHR focus on the rights of *parents* to choose the kind of education that their children receive and the freedom of the *parents* to ensure that the religious and moral education of their children conforms to 'their own convictions', but are not concerned with the rights of their children. Whether these rights should be primarily or exclusively rights of the parents, or when the rights of the children concerned, such as the right to have their best interests considered, will be in conflict with those of their parents is a complex question. In this regard the United Nations *Convention on the Rights of the Child* of 1989 provides in article 14:

1. States Parties shall respect the right of the child to freedom of thought, conscience and religion.
2. States Parties shall respect the rights and duties of the parents and, when applicable, legal guardians, to provide direction to the child in the exercise of his or her right in a manner consistent with the evolving capacities of the child.
3. Freedom to manifest one's religion or beliefs may be subject only to such limitations as are prescribed by law and are necessary to protect public safety, order, health or morals, or the fundamental rights and freedoms of others.

Determining when, under which circumstances and according to which criteria parental control is exercised 'in a manner consistent with the evolving capacities of the child' can be agonisingly difficult. Courts have indeed had to decide questions of the life and death of children and about their education under or outside denominational guidance, not infrequently against parents' religious views.[16] The combination of the facts in such cases, the international obligations of the state concerned, the local legal position and the nature of the religious convictions of those concerned and affected by the outcome confronts the judges squarely with religious considerations and the inescapable obligation to deal with the difficulties emanating from the interface between law and faith. It is inconceivable that a judge, when placed in such a position, would humanly be capable of severing his or her own religious convictions, regardless of what they might be, from the consideration of the matter. A secular attitude is most certainly one possible subjective attitude that a judge may have. It would therefore be as questionable to adjudicate in matters of a religious nature from an expressly secular basis as it would be to do so from the basis of a particular faith. Justice demands that a better solution be found.

Returning again to the field of education, the UN Committee on Economic, Social and Cultural Rights published in 1999 its General Comment No. 13 on the right to education. This has become an influential standard for educational governance. The Committee created a conceptual framework which has become known as 'the four As'. According to this framework all forms of education shall exhibit the features of availability, accessibility, acceptability and adaptability, and each was elaborated upon:

- Availability includes 'functioning institutions and programmes'.
- Accessibility entails *inter alia* the non-discriminatory provision of free primary education and the progressive introduction of free secondary and higher education.
- Acceptability demands that 'the form and substance of education, including curricula and teaching methods, have to be acceptable (for example, relevant, culturally appropriate and of good quality) to students and, in appropriate cases, parents'. Here the teaching approach to subjects such as history and religion is obviously relevant. Acceptability also applies to 'the form and substance of education, including curricula and teaching methods' mentioned in Comment No. 13. Education is more than imparting knowledge, notoriously making it a sensitive matter concerning philosophy and often also religion. Teachers, parents and learners on all levels are confronted with dogmatic, methodological and organizational

---

[16] Cf. the judicious description, analysis and commentary on such cases in the United Kingdom, South Africa and Germany by Robinson (2003) and Robinson (2004).

choices. Some of these are constantly being debated. For example should creation or evolution be used as point of departure? Should religion or information about religions be taught? Which approaches to history should be followed? Is outcomes-based education, problem-solving, Montessorian constructivism or rote learning the appropriate teaching method? What should the balance in the curriculum be between the humanities and natural sciences? – and so on.

- Adaptability promotes education that is flexible, 'so it can adapt to the needs of changing societies and communities and respond to the needs of students within their diverse social and cultural settings'. The need for educational authorities to deal fairly with the increasing challenges of religious pluralism is clearly relevant in this regard.

Globalization can be seen as a process that is propagated top-down by powerful liberal democratic states, international organizations and agencies, and transnational corporations, often to the detriment of deprived societies and individuals. Globalization also has another aspect, however, viz. a bottom-up involvement of local communities, non-governmental organizations and minority societies in the promotion of their rights and the exposure of injustices to a global audience. The latter form of globalization is logically reinforced by the sweeping expansion of access to social media, information and mobility, and may be considered to promise increased democratization and pressure on states to fulfil their international obligations.

When it comes to education, we have to take into consideration that the size of the human race is approaching 7 billion souls, every one of them dependent on taught and learnt knowledge. The acquisition in the 21st Century of effective education and skills is essential for the survival and prosperity of individuals, societies and states. Failure by a state to honour its educational responsibilities as defined in international law therefore amounts to a failure to bear the responsibilities of good governance.

In the end, it should not be forgotten that the products of our educational system must be capacitated to live, work and thrive in a globalized world in which knowledge and skills have become very important, if not the most important capital that a person and a country can acquire.

A prominent difficulty regarding the development of norms of international law on the relation and conduct of a state in matters concerning religion is that whereas 'High Contracting States have to comply with international human rights which are codified within established international forums, these forums have no clear competence on the question of how to organize the state internally'.[17] Nevertheless the UN Human Rights Committee does not refrain from investigating internal state practices concerning religion,[18] a fact which is indicative of the subtle emergence of global norms, albeit in a 'soft' form. Temperman concludes[19] that:

> Though they may not be in a position to dictate in detail how states ought to organize their political system internally, their official interpretations and applications of internationally adopted fundamental norms could very well, in themselves, have a bearing on the legitimacy and, ultimately, the tenability of certain forms of political organization.

In addition to the possibility of intervention by the Human Rights Commission (now Council), Johan van der Vyver also points out the other international means of enforcement of the freedom of religion, including UN Security Council intervention, proceedings provided for in international covenants and conventions, and prosecution before the International Criminal Court.[20] Limiting his comprehensive exposition to international instruments that apply globally, Van der Vyver usefully classifies and discusses 'international concerns pertinent to religion or belief' in three categories:[21] freedom to entertain and to manifest a particular religion or belief; the religious rights of a child; and the right to self-determination of peoples (especially of religious communities).

In the first category are the rights – and their limitations – to entertain a particular religious or other belief, the right to change one's religion or belief, and the right to manifest one's religion or belief through teaching or practising the same, or in worship and observance.[22] In the second category we find the freedom of the child to manifest its religion or belief, family values, parental interests and the best interests of the child – and the applicable limitations.[23] In the third category Van der Vyver discusses self-determination and the right to secession and 'unbecoming' religious practices.[24]

---

[17] Temperman (2010a) 2.
[18] Temperman (2010a) 4.
[19] Temperman (2010a) 339.
[20] Van der Vyver (2005) 530–535.
[21] Van der Vyver (2005).
[22] Van der Vyver (2005) 499–513.
[23] Van der Vyver (2005) 513–519.
[24] Van der Vyver (2005) 519–530.

Following the example of international instruments with global application, the protection of the freedom of religion is usually also dealt with in regional instruments. Suffice it here to cite two prominent examples. First article 9 of the *European Convention on Human Rights* (Rome, 1950) provides:

1. Everyone has the right to freedom of thought, conscience and religion; this right includes freedom to change his religion or belief, and freedom, either alone or in community with others and in public or private, to manifest his religion or belief, in worship, teaching, practice and observance.
2. Freedom to manifest one's religion or beliefs shall be subject only to such limitations as are prescribed by law and are necessary in a democratic society in the interests of public safety, for the protection of public order, health or morals, or the protection of the rights and freedoms of others.

Similarly article 8 of the *African Charter on Human and Peoples' Rights* of 1981 (the Banjul Charter) provides: 'Freedom of conscience, the profession and free practice of religion shall be guaranteed. No one may, subject to law and order, be submitted to measures restricting the exercise of these freedoms.' It speaks for itself that regional international instruments create their own enforcement or persuasive mechanisms and procedures.

In conclusion regarding religion in international law, it should be observed that the importance of the influence of religion, at this level comprehensively, that is, involving religion in all its manifestations around the globe, cannot be denied, nor can the indications that it is growing be ignored. This should provide good cause for further consideration of the merits of expanding the use of the precepts of constitutionalism in some form in international law.[25]

5.3 RELIGION IN INTERNATIONAL DIPLOMACY AND POLITICAL BATTLES

In the world of international diplomacy and politics, opposing religious groupings tend to promote their causes by means of contesting the interpretation of religion-related provisions of international instruments.

---

[25] Since the focus here is on constitutional law viewed comparatively, pursuing the issues of constitutionalism in the international context will not now receive further attention.

Thus, for example, the provision 'no one shall be subject to coercion which would impair his freedom to have a religion or belief of his choice' in article 18(2) of the ICCPR and in paragraph 2 of the UN *Declaration on the Elimination of all Forms of Intolerance and of Discrimination Based on Religion or Belief* (2008)[26] is interpreted by some to guarantee the freedom of religious choice, and by others as a prohibition on proselytism.[27]

In his thorough discussion of the difficulties attending the resolution of the tensions inherent in the protection of religious rights Peter Danchin[28] gives the following examples of divergent approaches to proselytism:

- The Catholic Church distinguishes between 'proper acts of Christian witness' and improper acts of proselytism, the latter apparently being understood as attempted religious coercion.
- The Evangelical Lutheran Church in America regards 'evangelical outreach' to be a religious obligation.
- The Jehovah's Witnesses and Mormons notoriously have active global programmes for the recruitment of converts and the distribution of soliciting literature.
- Some Islamic traditions prohibit the proselytism of Muslims while it is regarded as a religious duty of Muslims to proselytize non-Muslims.

Danchin argues that conventional liberal thinking does not offer the means for the resolution of the divergent religious approaches to matters such as proselytism in international law, and prefers an (albeit adapted liberal) approach of 'toleration rather than neutrality and the need to balance competing claims of similar validity rather than to prescribe a universal regime'.[29]

Another similarly selective utilization of international law for the purposes of the protection or promotion of specific religious interests plays out in attempts to bind the international community by means of the adoption of specific resolutions or protocols favourable to such

---

[26] General Assembly Resolution 63/181 adopted 18 December 2008. In para 2 the General Assembly – *Stresses* that the right to freedom of thought, conscience and religion applies equally to all people, regardless of their religions or beliefs, and without any discrimination as to their equal protection by the law.

[27] Cf Taylor (2005) 24 *et seq.*

[28] Danchin (2008) 256–257.

[29] Danchin (2008) 320.

interests. A prominent example has been the campaign of the Organization of Islamic Conference (OIC) in the United Nations since 1999 to have resolutions passed to combat 'defamation of religion' in order to counter measures limiting Muslim activities in countries where Islam is a minority religion. These proposals, if adopted, would limit free speech.[30] Support for these attempts to brand as defamation certain measures that states had taken with reference to Muslims steadily waned, but eventually the efforts of the OIC did result in 2012 in the adoption by the UN General Assembly of a resolution on *Combating intolerance, negative stereotyping, stigmatization, discrimination, incitement to violence and violence against persons, based on religion or belief*.[31] The Resolution reiterated[32] a call made by the Secretary General of the OIC on all states to take actions to promote *inter alia*: '[u]nderstanding the need to combat denigration and the negative religious stereotyping of persons, as well as incitement to religious hatred, by strategizing and harmonizing actions at the local, national, regional and international levels through, *inter alia*, education and awareness-raising'. Significantly the Resolution also calls upon all states[33] '[t]o make a strong effort to counter religious profiling, which is understood to be the invidious use of religion as a criterion in conducting questioning, searches and other law enforcement investigative procedures'.

However, this did not put an end to the attempts to bring the 'defamation of religion' back onto the international agenda.[34] The OIC's *Ten-Year Programme of Action (To Meet the Challenges Facing the Muslim Ummah in the 21st Century)* has a section under the heading 'Combating Islamophobia' in which 'the responsibility of the international community, including all governments, to ensure respect for all religions and combat their defamation' is emphasized.[35]

---

[30] Cf. for example, Seiple (2012) 175.
[31] A/RES/66/167 adopted on 19 December 2011.
[32] Para. 5(g) of the Resolution.
[33] Para. 6(d) of the Resolution.
[34] See for example, http://blog.unwatch.org/index.php/category/defamation-of-religion/ (accessed 7 May 2014).
[35] Para. VII 1, accessible at http://www.oic-oci.org/english/conf/is/ex-3/TYOAP_Makkah_2005.pdf (accessed 7 May 2014).

5.4 RELIGIOUS NON-STATE INTERNATIONAL ACTORS

Nafziger identifies five functions of religion that 'define the more or less positive side of the relationship between religion and international law': creative, aspirational, didactic, custodial and mediative. He finds that his survey reveals not only the role that religious institutions play in international law but also that of other leading non-governmental institutions and ideas. This demonstrates, he maintains, that international law is 'invented, applied and appraised both within and beyond the corridors of sovereign power'.[36]

The creative role of religion, according to Nafziger,[37] takes both institutional and doctrinal forms. In addition to the active involvement of various religious organizations and denominations, he mentions the generally accepted scholarly opinion (following Oppenheim) that 'much of modern international law grew out of Christian civilization', but also cites various other religious sources that underpinned the development of the notions of extradition (religious formulae practised by the ancient Chaldeans, Egyptians and Chinese), asylum (ancient Greece), self-determination and the peaceful resolution of conflict (Ghandi's Hinduism) and the non-litigatory resolution of international commercial disputes (Confucian ideology). He also discusses the influences of the fragmentation of medieval Christendom on the development of international law, especially relating to the controversy of the notion of 'just war' and the emergence of the universal reception of human rights.

Nafziger argues that the aspirational content of international law which qualifies Austinian positivism and legal realism in order not to reduce it to mere power politics but to represent it as an expression of morality is also due to religious influences.[38] Furthermore, he argues, religion didactically opens up an understanding of the involvement of international law in matters such as hunger and family planning, in which religious institutions are inevitably involved.[39] A custodial function is performed in international law by frequent communication by religious institutions and their leaders to political leaders of their views on matters concerning international law,[40] and finally he cites a number of instances

---

[36] Nafziger (1991) 163.
[37] Nafziger (1991) 153–159.
[38] Nafziger (1991) 159–160.
[39] Nafziger (1991) 160–162.
[40] Nafziger (1991) 162.

of religious institutions performing a mediative function in keeping the peace and maintaining global order.[41]

Citing S.H. Rudolph and referring to Sufi orders, Catholic missionaries and Buddhist monks that 'carried word and praxis across vast spaces before those places became nation-states or even states', John Madeley and Jeffrey Haynes[42] open their discussion of 'transnational religious actors' with the statement that '[r]eligious communities are among the oldest of the transnationals'. This they offer as 'a long perspective' as opposed to a 'shorter perspective more appropriate to the modern world' in terms of which '[t]ransnational religious actors have typically had to operate in environments dominated by territorial state authorities which have jealously contested the legitimacy of any outside interference in their affairs, whether by religious or other international instances'. They then proceed to point out that the influence of religious bodies in recent centuries has been exerted as a 'soft power', 'by means of preachment or argumentative persuasion' and that globalization has brought about improved opportunities to do so. This, they say, contrasts with forceful proselytizing by Christianity and Islam until it was outlawed in the 17th Century by the emergence of secular states in Europe. Currently Madeley and Haynes consider the secularity of the state to be under threat due to 'the resurgence of the religious factor in politics in international as well as certain national contexts, not least through the impact which transnational religious actors have once again managed to exert across ever more permeable territorial borders'.

Although religious and state institutions have for centuries generally been separated in non-Muslim countries, religious intervention in matters of state still occurs from time to time. For example, the Catholic Church is well placed to arbitrate between states where Catholicism is prominent. A remarkable example of this was the successful resolution of a border dispute between Argentina and Chile in 1978: the populations of both these states largely associate themselves with the religious authority of the church and its head, the Pope, which made it possible for papal arbitration to prevent a very likely war in Latin America. According to Mirow:[43]

> Consistent with the Church's mission of making peace, the Vatican brought several unusual attributes to the process of mediation. These included the religious authority of the Church, the ability to control information regarding

---

[41] Nafziger (1991) 162–163.
[42] Madeley and Haynes (2011) 63–64.
[43] See Mirow (2004) 28.

the mediation, neutrality stemming from its lack of military and earthly ambitions, and highly trained and patient bureaucratic machinery accustomed to dealing with power and evil.

Other recent examples of religious involvement in matters of state (albeit not directly international in nature) include the overthrow of the Pahlavi dynasty (the Shah of Iran) in the Iranian Islamic revolution of 1979 and the role of the Catholic Church in the Polish Solidarity Movement leading to the transition from communism to democracy in the 1980s. Madeley and Haynes furthermore discuss the role of the World Council of Churches, which has been known to support liberalization, decolonization and democratization in various parts of the world, and the OIC's efforts to promote dialogue between Western and Muslim countries.[44]

However, the examples of religion-driven efforts to promote peace and to facilitate progress do not detract from the reality that various religions and denominations have over time figured prominently, and still do, in inter-religious disputes, civil disturbances and even war and revolution. Islam is currently particularly prominent in this role, considering for example the revolutionary overthrow of authoritarian regimes in North Africa, known as the Arab Spring,[45] and Al-Qaeda's violent activities in its attempts to restore and promote its fundamentalist national and international ambitions for Islam.[46]

5.5 CONCLUSION

In an insightful analysis of the role that religion is allowed to play in international law, Tawia Ansah argues that the separation between law and religion is porous. She states that 'God has been banished from the realm of public international legal discourse' and that 'God has been relegated to the realm of the private conscience'.[47] This is consistent with liberalism, which has no doubt been highly influential in post-1945 developments of international law. Seen from the perspective of the accepted terminology and vernacular of international law, Ansah's is a legitimate position to take.

However, we have also seen that, historically, religion has had a profound impact on the development of international law and that,

---

[44] Madeley and Haynes (2011) 65–69.
[45] Cf. Mancini and Rosenfeld (2014) xv–xvi.
[46] Madeley and Haynes (2011) 69–73.
[47] Ansah (2005) 14.

although incidental or peripheral, religious institutions have been known, even recently, to have influenced matters of international concern in significant ways.

International norms can notoriously not rely for their validity and enforceability on the kind of authority that is provided by states for their internal legal orders. Reliance on other forms of authority such as prevailing notions of morality is therefore called for. In this context there are indications that religion in its diverse manifestations does provide moral and ethical guidance in international law. Johan van der Vyver for example holds that:[48]

> International standards for the promotion and protection of basic human rights and freedoms, though perhaps lacking in effective enforcement mechanisms, contribute in no small measure to the development of an international moral code. That code over time becomes the criterion of national introspection and reform. Governments do not like being seen as violators of international standards of human rights protection.

---

[48] Van der Vyver (2005) 537.

6. Travails of the judges in religious cases

6.1 INTRODUCTION

In the all too frequent emergence arising in societies of controversies involving religion and law – an occurrence seemingly on the increase in many jurisdictions around the world – it is mostly judiciaries that are called upon to resolve the disputes. The judicial forum is therefore the site where expression is most often given to the approach of the particular state's version of constitutionalism insofar as it impacts on religious matters. This chapter focuses on the manner in which religious disputes are dealt with by courts.

For this purpose a categorization of kinds of dispute is made, and selected cases from various jurisdictions are then discussed as examples of how courts compose their interpretative arguments in the process of resolving religious issues. The intention is not to construct best judicial practice or to extract some kind of *communis opinio iudicis*, but to collect a range of responses by courts when confronted with the vexed questions of disputes concerning religion. At the end of the chapter an attempt is made to determine what judges have in common when dealing with cases involving religious considerations, despite having to function in legal orders that respond in fragmented ways to the issues concerned.

For the purposes of this discussion the choice of jurisdictions from which judgments are selected is important, since the range of legal orders arranged according to standards of constitutionalism is wide. Moreover, although we are not primarily focusing here on the quality of the constitutional protection of the right to religious freedom that is afforded to the citizens of different states, the degree of religious freedom in different places does provide us with a useful measure of categorization.

In this regard the credible findings of the *Pew–Templeton Global Religious Futures Project* concerning the restrictions that countries impose on religion[1] make for interesting reading: despite the finding that

---

[1] Pew Research Center (2012).

the constitutions of 144 of the 197 countries surveyed provided for freedom of religion,[2] in terms of three levels of restrictions (low, moderate and high/very high) 37 per cent of the countries were in the (steadily rising) 'high' category by mid 2010, but those countries' population represented 75 per cent of the global population.[3]

In accordance with the centrality of the protection of fundamental rights in the notion of constitutionalism, judgments for consideration in this chapter are chosen from jurisdictions where the level of restrictions on religious freedom is low or moderate. The aim here is not to provide a comprehensive review of jurisprudence of this nature – that would indeed require a titanic, encyclopaedic volume. The purpose is rather to present examples of important or noteworthy judgments in the process of drawing a broad picture of tendencies in judgments on religion.

The spectrum of situations in which the state may be called upon to deal with religious issues is potentially as broad as the scope of social activity, because of the implicit or explicit role of religion in many societal interactions. A certain recurrence of categories within this spectrum, by no means packed in water-tight compartments, can be observed, however.

Dieter Grimm[4] made the following interesting classification of liberty and equality claims that may be encountered in the context of religion:

I. Freedom claims
   1. More freedom in favour of religion
      (a) Permission to do what is generally prohibited
      (b) Permission not to do what is generally required
   2. Less freedom in favour of religion
      (a) Permission to prohibit what is generally allowed
      (b) Permission to require what is generally optional

II. Equality claims
   1. Equal treatment of religious groups
      (a) Equal treatment of all religions
      (b) Privileges for some religious groups
   2. Equality within religious groups
      (a) Permission to differentiate where equal treatment is generally required
      (b) Permission to treat equally where differentiation is generally required

---

[2] Pew Research Center (2012), GRI.Q.1 on page 66 of the Pew Forum Report.
[3] Pew Research Center (2012) 'Summary of Findings' on page 9.
[4] Grimm (2009) 2377–2378.

For the purposes of the broader approach that is followed here regarding the forms of state engagement with religion, that is, including but not limited to the protection of religious freedom and the prohibition of religious discrimination, the jurisprudence will be approached from the perspectives of three categories of state functions, activities and actions. The first deals with the performance of general functions of the state with incidental religious implications, the second contains actions having direct religious implications in which the state has the initiative, and the third contains activities that are initiated from a religious perspective. The following scheme is used for this classification:

General functions of the state having an incidental impact on religion:

- Education
- Migration and citizenship
- Animal protection
- Prevention of public disturbance
- Governance of state institutions
- Conscientious objection
- Balancing rights

State-initiated activity concerning religion:

- Preventing or countenancing discrimination on religious grounds
- Religion-related funding, subvention and taxation
- Labour relations, hours of business and public holidays

Inspired by religion:

- Recognition of religious institutions
- Religious dress and symbols
- Intra- and inter-religious disputes

With reference to the relevant constitutional arrangements in the jurisdictions concerned, examples from the jurisprudence of the selected courts will be described in the following sections according to this categorization.

6.2 GENERAL FUNCTIONS OF THE STATE WITH INCIDENTAL RELIGIOUS IMPLICATIONS

A consideration of religion in education presents a useful point of entry to this theme because it is remarkable – but also to be expected – that a great many controversies about the exercise of fundamental rights relate to the role of the state in public education. The religious garb of students and teachers, religious symbols in the form of personal jewellery and appearance, including hair styles, the teaching of religion and religious perspectives on teaching content, school discipline, working hours and public holidays, gender issues, maintaining peaceful inter-religion relationships, freedom of opinion and of expression, and so on are all issues that tend to crop up in the educational context around the world, although not all can be discussed in this chapter.

6.2.1 Education

The acceptance by the state after the Middle Ages of primary responsibility for education did not occur very long ago.[5] Not much historical imagination is needed to assume that the education of the young started out as the passing on of knowledge and skills from parents to children, later became formalized as a community activity and, in at least the Western and Islamic worlds, eventually became an important task in which religious educators took the lead.[6] Education has, however, never been reserved for the state or parents or the church. Training, culture, belief, upbringing and imparting knowledge are all elements of education which can hardly be separated into silos. Elements of even the most remote historical phases in the history of education are woven into our present understanding of education, and the main role-players (parents, religious institutions, society, the state) are still concerned with the nature, content and quality of education. None of these, not even the state, has or should have a monopoly. Thus, for example, Elizabeth Lawrence wrote with reference to the history of education about[7] 'the Greeks, with their ideal of the whole man, and of education as concerned not with the intellect only, but with the good life, with wisdom. To the Greek and the Christian, education was a spiritual, not a commercial matter.'

When considering the state-led governance of schooling in our day, one should not forget that the state as we know it today, as a consolidated entity which effectively exercises authority over most dimensions of human existence by means of a nationally and regionally coordinated administrative and legislative infrastructure, really emerged only in the

---

[5] The following exposition is taken from Venter (2012a) 436–438.

[6] Elizabeth Lawrence described the history of education interestingly in Lawrence (1970).

[7] Lawrence (1970) 21.

course of the 19th Century and ripened throughout the 20th Century.[8] It may be that the Sumerians, some of the Greek city states and empires founded in antiquity in the Middle East, Egypt, Rome, China and India were exceptions in this regard. Despite the influence of these classic cases on modern thinking about the relationships between religion, culture, state and authority, the times immediately preceding the emergence of modern statehood saw a discontinuity in the development of the modern state and of its responsibility for education.

According to Stephen Ward and Christine Eden, state education systems, which began to develop in Europe in the 19th century, became a feature of the nation state and the means of establishing nationalism and a commitment by the whole of society to the state.[9] They also point out[10] that globalization has since the second half of the 20th Century brought about a steady decline in the power of nation states to dictate educational policy in favour of 'the marketisation of schooling and the development of education as consumerism to feed the requirements of the global marketplace'. In reaction to this trend, states tend in the 21st Century to insist on controlling education through legislation and policies, because their control over global commerce is declining steadily.

It is understandable that in the process of the emergence of state responsibility for education, the teaching of religion to children in school did not suddenly disappear, especially in Western countries where the citizenries maintain a strong though diversified Christian ethos. Equally understandably a similar pattern was established in the far-flung European colonies where annexation more often than not was closely accompanied by forceful missionary activity, particularly involving the establishment of educational institutions.[11]

Various leading post-war constitutions explicitly impose educational responsibilities on the state, often specifying arrangements regarding religious education. Examples of contentious judgments on religion in education can be found in a number of such jurisdictions. Some show attempts to assimilate constitutional or social notions of neutral secularity, often with differing results and based on different lines of argument. In many constitutional states, teaching religion in state schools has recently undergone significant changes, due both to secularization and increasing multiculturalism. A concise review of a selection of these must suffice here.

---

[8] Cf. Chapter 2 above and Venter (2010a) 11–29.
[9] Ward and Eden (2009) 2.
[10] Ward and Eden (2009) 3.
[11] Cf. for example, Le Roux (2011) 57–86.

6.2.1.1 Canada

Probably the clearest recent example of the process of secularization is the developments in Canada over the last three decades. Although the constitutional arrangements in Canada do not exclude state support of religion (as in the United States), the courts, responding to legislative, executive and administrative actions, took the lead in the establishment of the idea that 'sponsorship of one religious tradition amounts to discrimination against others'.[12] A relatively extensive exposition is required to put this into perspective.

Although it did not deal with education, the often cited Canadian Supreme Court judgment of 1985 in *Big M Drug Mart* concerning Sunday trading heralded a turning point away from the toleration of religious tradition towards secularism: secularism was thereby endorsed in Canadian law and religion was branded as 'sectarian'. A significant *dictum* in that judgment reads as follows:[13]

> To the extent that it binds all to a sectarian Christian ideal, the *Lord's Day Act* works a form of coercion inimical to the spirit of the *Charter* and the dignity of all non-Christians. In proclaiming the standards of the Christian faith, the Act creates a climate hostile to, and gives the appearance of discrimination against, non-Christian Canadians. It takes religious values rooted in Christian morality and, using the force of the state, translates them into a positive law binding on believers and non-believers alike. The theological content of the legislation remains as a subtle and constant reminder to religious minorities within the country of their differences with, and alienation from, the dominant religious culture.

In 1988 the Ontario Court of Appeal emphasized the need for the state to maintain neutrality in religious matters when it struck down a regulation made under the *Education Act* of 1980 which made the saying of Christian prayers compulsory (except where an exemption was granted) in public schools. The Court stated[14] that,

> [o]n its face, [the regulation] infringes the freedom of conscience and religion guaranteed by s.2(*a*) of the [Canadian] Charter [of Rights and Freedoms]. The recitation of the Lord's Prayer, which is a Christian prayer, and the reading of Scriptures from the Christian Bible impose Christian observances upon non-Christian pupils and religious observances on non-believers.

---

[12] *Commission scolaire* (2012), para. [17].
[13] *R v Big M Drug Mart Ltd*, [1985] 1 S.C.R. 295, para. 97.
[14] *Zylberberg v Sudbury Board of Education (Director)* (1988), 65 O.R. (2d) 641, 654.

In 1990 the same court found that provincial legislation that regulated religious education in public schools amounted to state-authorized religious indoctrination, causing the imposition of majoritarian religious beliefs on minorities, thereby offending against the Canadian Charter. The court then went on to state that a programme that taught *about* religion and moral values without indoctrination in a particular faith would not cause such a breach.[15]

Section 76 of the British Columbia *School Act* of 1996 provides:

(1) All schools and Provincial schools must be conducted on strictly secular and non-sectarian principles.
(2) The highest morality must be inculcated, but no religious dogma or creed is to be taught in a school or Provincial school.

What 'secular' was intended to mean was interpreted by the Supreme Court of Canada in 2002 while reviewing a school board's decision to exclude books about same-sex families from a kindergarten curriculum. The majority of six judges of the Court held as follows:[16]

> The Act's insistence on strict secularism does not mean that religious concerns have no place in the deliberations and decisions of the Board. Board members are entitled, and indeed required, to bring the views of the parents and communities they represent to the deliberation process. Because religion plays an important role in the life of many communities, these views will often be motivated by religious concerns. Religion is an integral aspect of people's lives, and cannot be left at the boardroom door. What secularism does rule out, however, is any attempt to use the religious views of one part of the community to exclude from consideration the values of other members of the community. A requirement of secularism implies that, although the Board is indeed free to address the religious concerns of parents, it must be sure to do so in a manner that gives equal recognition and respect to other members of the community. Religious views that deny equal recognition and respect to the members of a minority group cannot be used to exclude the concerns of the minority group. This is fair to both groups, as it ensures that each group is given as much recognition as it can consistently demand while giving the same recognition to others.

In this *dictum* 'secular' does not seem to have been defined as 'detached from religion' but rather as 'equal consideration of everyone's values'. The obvious difficulty here, although it seems that the Court did not

---

[15] *Canadian Civil Liberties Assn. v Ontario (Minister of Education)* (1990), 71 O.R. (2d) 341.
[16] *Chamberlain v Surrey School District No. 36* [2002] 4 S.C.R. 710, 728–729.

realize or accept the implications, is that secular morality and values based on secularism (or for that matter on secularity) would clash in many ways with religious convictions. In later cases the Court did not maintain this approach which, despite its implications for religious morality, seemed to be sympathetic towards 'the religious concerns of parents'.

The telling *Commission scolaire* judgment of the Canadian Supreme Court concerning religion in school education was delivered in 2012.[17] The background of the case was that in 2008 Catholic parents requested the local school board to exempt their children from attending the prescribed course at their public school on Ethics and Religious Culture (ERC) developed by the Quebec Ministry of Education. The grounds for their request was that their children would, in the language of a provision of the *Education Act* of Quebec, suffer 'serious harm' by attending the course. The harm that the parents feared took the form, *inter alia*, of the children '[b]eing exposed, through this mandatory course, to the philosophical trend advocated by the state, namely relativism'.[18]

The ERC programme is divided into instruction in ethics and instruction in religious culture. Its purpose is officially described as follows:[19]

> For the purposes of this program, instruction in ethics is aimed at developing an understanding of ethical questions that allows students to make judicious choices based on knowledge of the values and references present in society. The objective is not to propose or impose moral rules, nor to study philosophical doctrines and systems in an exhaustive manner.
>
> Instruction in religious culture, for its part, is aimed at fostering an understanding of several religious traditions whose influence has been felt and is still felt in our society today. In this regard, emphasis will be placed on Québec's religious heritage. The historical and cultural importance of Catholicism and Protestantism will be given particular prominence. The goal is neither to accompany students in a spiritual quest, nor to present the history of doctrines and religions, nor to promote some new common religious doctrine aimed at replacing specific beliefs.

The parents' request for exemption from the course was refused on two administrative levels, whereupon the parents took the matter to the Superior Court of Quebec, seeking a declaration that the ERC programme infringed their and their children's right to freedom of conscience and religion, and judicial review of the decision denying their

---

[17] See full citations in the Table of Cases under Canada.
[18] *Commission scolaire* (2012) para. [28].
[19] *Commission scolaire* para. (2012) [34].

requests for exemption from the course. In 2009 the Superior Court, and subsequently in 2010 also the Court of Appeal, denied the application. On appeal the Supreme Court of Canada had to decide whether the trial judge erred in holding that the school board's refusal to exempt the appellants' children did not infringe the parents' freedom of conscience and religion. This question turned on whether or not the trial judge was correct in finding that the appellants had not proven that the ERC programme itself infringed their freedom of religion.

All nine judges of the Court agreed that the appeal had to be dismissed primarily on the ground that the parents had not objectively proven that the ERC programme interfered with their ability to pass their faith on to their children. However, seven of the judges followed one line of argument and two of the judges motivated the dismissal differently. This is consistent with the phenomenon that multi-member benches in various jurisdictions that are called upon to adjudicate matters relating to religion very seldom deliver unanimous judgments. The majority judgment opened with the following statement:[20]

> The societal changes that Canada has undergone since the middle of the last century have brought with them a new social philosophy that favours the recognition of minority rights. The developments in the area of education that have taken place in Quebec and that are at issue in this appeal must be situated within this larger context. Given the religious diversity of present-day Quebec, the state can no longer promote a vision of society in public schools that is based on historically dominant religions.

Citing various scholarly sources, Deschamps J for the majority pointed out[21] that:

> [t]he place of religion in civil society has been a source of public debate since the dawn of civilization. The gradual separation of church and state in Canada has been part of a broad movement to secularize public institutions in the Western World. ... Religious neutrality is now seen by many Western states as a legitimate means of creating a free space in which citizens of various beliefs can exercise their individual rights.

The two minority judges also subscribed strongly to state neutrality and secularism. Also citing previous judgments and scholarly literature, they put it as follows:[22]

---

[20] *Commission scolaire* (2012) para. [1].
[21] *Commission scolaire* (2012) para. [10].
[22] *Commission scolaire* (2012) para. [54].

Under the constitutional principles governing state action, the state has neither an obligation to promote religious faith nor a right to discourage religious faith in its public education system. Only such true neutrality is in keeping with the secularism of the state.

Justice Deschamps for the majority cited census findings indicating that there were some 95 separate religious institutions in the country, and that 23 per cent of Canadians supported non-Christian religions or had no religious identity at all. This diversity was attributed to 'globalization of trade and increased individual mobility' and imposed the need for 'the adoption of a policy of neutrality' in Canada as a whole.[23]

To prove infringement of the right to freedom of religion, the Court required not only a sincere belief that a practice must be observed, but more specifically proof on a balance of probabilities that actual infringement occurred, in this case by requiring children to attend the ERC course. The court *a quo* was not convinced by the parents that the course was not neutral.[24] They therefore failed in their appeal because the Supreme Court agreed that there was no evidence, presented on the basis of *objective analysis*, that the ERC programme 'interfered with their ability to pass their faith on to their children'.[25] Reacting to the opinion of the parents that exposing children to various religious facts would confuse them, the Court referred to its 2002 judgment in *Chamberlain*, where it was stated that 'cognitive dissonance' encountered by children was 'simply part of living in a diverse society' and 'part of growing up'.[26] The majority therefore concluded:[27]

> The suggestion that exposing children to a variety of religious facts in itself infringes their religious freedom or that of their parents amounts to a rejection of the multicultural reality of Canadian society and ignores the Quebec government's obligations with regard to public education.

In their minority judgment, the two judges expressed their opinion that the approach established in the *Amselem* case of 2004 had not been adhered to by the trial court. This would have required the court first to establish that the parents' religious belief was sincere and that the ERC

---

[23] *Commission scolaire* (2012) para. [11].
[24] *Commission scolaire* (2012) para. [36].
[25] *Commission scolaire* (2012) paras [2], [23], [24] and [27].
[26] *Commission scolaire* (2012) para. [39].
[27] *Commission scolaire* (2012) para. [40].

programme infringed that aspect of their freedom of religion.[28] According to them, the error of the trial court was that it 'turned this matter into a debate about the incorrect nature of the parents' belief, ... did not consider the program's content or its impact on the alleged belief' and then held that their belief was wrong, based on the evidence of a theologian.[29] What was needed according to the minority judges was to find answers to the following questions:[30]

> [I]s it a program that will provide all students with better knowledge of society's diversity and teach them to be open to differences? Or is it an educational tool designed to get religion out of children's heads by taking an essentially agnostic or atheistic approach that denies any theoretical validity to the religious experience and religious values? Is the program consistent with the notion of secularism that has gradually been developed in constitutional cases, particularly in the field of education?

Because of 'the state of the record' of the original trial, the minority declared themselves[31] 'unable to conclude that the program and its implementation could not, in the future, possibly infringe the rights granted to the appellants and persons in the same situation'. With reference to the textbook for the course that was filed in the record, the minority judges were potentially concerned. They wondered if, for example,[32] 'the content of the Christmas-related exercises for six-year-old students encourage the transformation of an experience and tradition into a form of folklore consisting merely of stories about mice or surprising neighbours?'

Less than a year after the delivery of this judgment, the Quebec Court of Appeal decided[33] that a private Catholic high school was also lawfully required to teach the prescribed ERC course instead of a similar course offered by the school from a Catholic point of view. On appeal the Supreme Court of Canada however decided in March 2015 that prohibiting the school to teach the ethical elements of the programme from a Catholic perspective would constitute a disproportionate limitation on the freedom of religion.[34]

---

[28] *Commission scolaire* (2012) paras [48], [49] and [50].
[29] *Commission scolaire* (2012) para. [51].
[30] *Commission scolaire* (2012) para. [53].
[31] *Commission scolaire* (2012) para. [58].
[32] *Commission scolaire* (2012) para. [58].
[33] *Québec (Procureur général) c. Loyola High School* 2012 QCCA 2139.
[34] *Loyola High School v Quebec (Attorney General)* 2015 SCC 12.

From both the judgments in the *Commission scolaire* case it would appear at first blush that all members of the Supreme Court bench are in agreement about secular neutrality as a principle of Canadian constitutional law. However, considering the need felt by two judges to hand down a separate judgement, it would appear on closer investigation that there are some significant differences in emphasis.

The difficulties surrounding religious neutrality were acknowledged in the majority judgment with reference to the literature. Citing Richard Moon, Deschamps J recognized that 'trying to achieve religious neutrality in the public sphere is a major challenge for the state'.[35] The following passages from Moon's book were cited:[36]

> If secularism or agnosticism constitutes a position, worldview, or cultural identity equivalent to religious adherence, then its proponents may feel excluded or marginalized when the state supports even the most ecumenical religious practices. But by the same token, the complete removal of religion from the public sphere may be experienced by religious adherents as the exclusion of their worldview and the affirmation of a non-religious or secular perspective ... .
>
> Ironically, then, as the exclusion of religion from public life, in the name of religious freedom and equality, has become more complete, the secular has begun to appear less neutral and more partisan. With the growth of agnosticism and atheism, religious neutrality in the public sphere may have become impossible. What for some is the neutral ground on which freedom of religion and conscience depends is for others a partisan anti-spiritual perspective.

Commenting on this, the Court then explicitly stated[37] that '[w]e must also accept that, from a philosophical standpoint, absolute neutrality does not exist', but found consolation in the fact that 'absolutes hardly have any place in the law', thus concluding that:[38]

> following a realistic and non-absolutist approach, state neutrality is assured when the state neither favours nor hinders any particular religious belief, that is, when it shows respect for all postures towards religion, including that of having no religious beliefs whatsoever, while taking into account the competing constitutional rights of the individuals affected.

By implication 'state neutrality' would therefore be a principled position to take. It would entail equal respect for all religions and ostensible

---

[35] *Commission scolaire* (2012) para. [30].
[36] Moon (2008) 231.
[37] *Commission scolaire* (2012) para. [31].
[38] *Commission scolaire* (2012) para. [32].

non-religions, and recognition of the individual right of everyone to believe what he or she prefers to believe and to express and practise such belief, limited only by the competing rights of others. Inevitably, however, religious or anti-religious beliefs are foundational for ethics and morals. Put differently, the expression 'neutral ethics and morality' is oxymoronic.

Considered rationally, ethics and morals based on secularity will be different from and likely even offensive to a range of religions. The state's efforts to impose secular ethics and morals on those who subscribe to other religious precepts is therefore as prejudicial to others as it would be if the state prefers or supports a specific religion.

The Court's argument is not logical: it assumes that absolute state neutrality is not possible, but should nevertheless be pursued by imposing on all state conduct based on secular beliefs. By finding acceptable the ambitions of the ERC programme to develop an understanding of ethical questions and knowledge of values, the Court does not detach the state (or itself) from moral guidance for its conduct from whatever source. Apparently the Court finds secular guidance to be good but religious guidance to be bad in law. This leaves the question open as to how it might be possible that considerations of *Weltanschauung* (which inevitably reflects atheism, agnosticism or some religion) be pushed aside successfully by judges in their adjudication, or by other organs of the state in their legislative, administrative or executive conduct. It follows that a state's choice of secularity is a choice hostile to religion.

On the face of it the difference between the majority and minority in the *Commission scolaire* judgment is procedural: the majority was not concerned with the fact that the trial court weighed the correctness of the parents' belief that their rights were being infringed, whereas the minority would have required proof that the ERC programme as such did or did not contain elements offensive to religion. Under the circumstances it did not make a difference to the outcome of the case, but the minority suggested that, in a similar case properly presented to a court, the court would have to determine if the programme was actually neutral.

The Canadian Supreme Court seems to have been caught in a conceptual trap. It does not use the term 'neutral' when it deals with proof of the infringement of a fundamental right on a balance of probabilities:[39]

> The subjective part of the analysis is limited to establishing that there is a sincere belief that has a nexus with religion, including the belief in an

---

[39] *Commission scolaire* (2012) para. [24].

obligation to conform to a religious practice. As with any other right or freedom protected by the *Canadian Charter* and the *Quebec Charter*, proving the infringement requires an objective analysis of the rules, events or acts that interfere with the exercise of the freedom. To decide otherwise would allow persons to conclude themselves that their rights had been infringed and thus to supplant the courts in this role.

Here *objective* analysis is contrasted with *subjective* belief. The question emerges whether objective analysis is neutral, or is it something different? The Court did not explain, but it did imply that it is possible to approach a matter objectively (as distinct from subjective belief), while it acknowledged the impossibility of being fully neutral. This is a distinction that will be considered further in Chapter 9.

At the end of a thorough analysis of the Canadian courts' use of neutrality in cases concerning religion, Richard Moon made the following cogent observations:[40]

> Behind the courts' uneven application of the religious-neutrality requirement lies a complex conception of religious commitment in which religion is viewed as both an aspect of the individual's identity that should (sometimes) be excluded and insulated from politics and as a set of judgments made by the individual about truth and right that must (sometimes) be subject to the give and take of politics. The challenge for the courts is to fit this complex conception of religion into a system of constitutional rights that distinguishes between choices or commitments that are protected as a matter of human liberty but are subject to laws that advance the public interest and immutable or deeply rooted traits that must be respected by the state as part of a commitment to human equality. Because religious beliefs are deeply held, and because they have sometimes given rise to social and political conflict, the courts have said that the state should remain neutral in spiritual matters. The state should take no position on the truth of religious beliefs, because (or even though) they address matters of the utmost importance to the individual. Yet, at the same time, the courts seem to recognize that religious beliefs sometimes touch on civic concerns and so cannot simply be removed from politics. ... The problem, of course, is that the distinction between the spiritual and civic elements of religion cannot be drawn clearly and cleanly. Indeed, not all belief systems accept that such a line can be drawn. More generally, any line the courts may draw between spiritual (private) and civic (public) will reflect a particular (non-neutral) view about the proper scope of state action and the ordinary forms of religious worship.

---

[40] Moon (2012) 548–549.

6.2.1.2 The United States

The Canadian instance of the conceptual confusion regarding secular education is but one of many from around the world. Disputes over religion in education in the United States since the end of World War II required the attention of the courts in many cases, from which a diverse range of judgments emanated. Some of these judgments are dealt with elsewhere in this book.

Frank Ravitch[41] highlights the running battle in the United States between the supporters of secular education and those promoting 'intelligent design' as an alternative, purportedly scientific approach to education intended to satisfy the constitutional restraints of the First Amendment. He describes it as a daily raging battle 'over where humanity came from, or more specifically how humans came to be human' and identifies Eastern Europe as a specific target of the 'growing movement' of intelligent design.[42] He argues that the constitutional provisions in the United States, Canada and Japan can counter the movement effectively to 'protect science' without demeaning religion or interfering 'with its free exercise in areas, unlike science, where religion has its place'. He praises England and Australia as examples where the educational authorities have achieved this institutionally 'on the basis of sound educational judgement'.

As is demonstrated by the ongoing debate between religious and anti-religious natural scientists on naturalism and theism in science,[43] an assessment of a state's approach to religion in education is all but neutral: it is a matter of religious conviction regardless of how ardently it is averred to be 'neutral'.

6.2.1.3 Germany

It is interesting to note that, in contrast to some other legal orders, whereas the German legal discourse concerning religion in education also employs the usual liberal concepts of secularism and neutrality, terms that incidentally are not found in the *Grundgesetz*, public prayer in schools has been found by the Federal Constitutional Court (*Bundseverfassungsgericht*) to be allowable under particular circumstances,[44] denominational religious education is expressly permitted, and tolerance of difference is considered to be a matter of the optimal balancing of rights and interests. Article 7 of the German *Grundgesetz* of 1949 places

---

[41] Ravitch (2012) 200.
[42] Ravitch (2012) 191–192.
[43] See for example, Lennox (2011), as opposed to Dawkins (2006).
[44] *BVerfGE* 52, 223 of 16 October 1979 – 1 BvR 647/70 and 7/74.

the entire school system under the supervision of the state, and then provides for the right of parents and guardians to decide whether or not children should take part in religious instruction.[45] The next provision renders religious instruction in public schools (with the exception of schools designated to be non-confessional (*bekenntnisfrei*)) to be part of the regular curriculum. Reserving a right for the state to supervise the instruction and prohibiting teachers to be obliged to give religious instruction against their will, the provision requires religious instruction to be given in accordance with the tenets of the religious community concerned.[46]

In Germany children of school-going age are compelled by law (set out extensively in the regional (*Länder*) constitutions) to attend school. When parents refused in 2001 to send their children to school on the grounds that they wished to home-school them in accordance with their religious beliefs that differed from the approach to sex education, evolution theory and value pluralism taken by the school, their conduct was found to be punishable under law. Eventually the mother in this case submitted a constitutional complaint (*Verfassungsbeschwerde*) to the Federal Constitutional Court, where the complaint was refused.

In a decision by the panel of three judges in which the status of the law regarding education and religion was reflected concisely,[47] it was pointed out that the parents' rights were restricted by the constitutional duty of the state to provide education. In the performance of its educational functions the state is required to respect everyone's serious religious convictions, only refraining from punishing contravention of the law in cases of a concrete conflict between the legal duty concerned and a religious injunction which will put a person in spiritual distress (*seelische Bedrängnis*) and impinge upon his human dignity if the law were to be obeyed. Considering the facts, the panel found that this was not such a case. The panel considered the educational responsibility of the state not to be merely the mediation of knowledge and the development of independent personalities, but also the development of responsible citizens capable of participating responsibly in the democratic processes in a

---

[45] Article 7(2): 'Die Erziehungsberechtigten haben das Recht, über die Teilnahme des Kindes am Religionsunterricht zu bestimmen'.

[46] Article 7(3): 'Der Religionsunterricht ist in den öffentlichen Schulen mit Ausnahme der bekenntnisfreien Schulen ordentliches Lehrfach. Unbeschadet des staatlichen Aufsichtsrechtes wird der Religionsunterricht in Übereinstimmung mit den Grundsätzen der Religionsgemeinschaften erteilt. Kein Lehrer darf gegen seinen Willen verpflichtet werden, Religionsunterricht zu erteilen'.

[47] *BverfG* 2 BvR 1693/04 of 31.5.2006.

pluralistic society. The state was prohibited from exerting any focused influence in support of a particular political, ideological or philosophical (*weltanschauliche*) approach, and also may not identify itself with a particular religion or a specific *Weltanschauung*, thereby endangering religious peace in society. The public schools in a free democratic polity should be open to a broad spectrum of opinions and outlooks and the complainant had not presented evidence of contravention of the injunction of state neutrality and tolerance in education. The complainant had no right to insist that her children be completely isolated from confessions and opinions with which she did not agree. The state had an interest in preventing the development of parallel societies and minorities: social integration and dialogue between people thinking and believing differently was to be promoted in education in the open pluralistic society. The complainant was to accept that her children will be confronted with the views and values of a predominantly secular plural society despite its conflict with her own views.

A particularly interesting interpretative mechanism used by the German courts to find solutions to difficult issues concerning conflictual constitutional claims and responsibilities, including state conduct in matters of religion, is known as *praktische Konkordanz* (practical concordance). With reference to a previous judgment in 1995 concerning a Bavarian law requiring crucifixes to be hung in all classrooms,[48] it was pointed out in the above mentioned panel decision of the *Bundesverfassungsgericht* of 2006 that in cases where a conflict arose between the right of parents to educate their children and the educational responsibilities of the state, *praktische Konkordanz* would have to be employed.

In the crucifix case of 1995 the bench was (not unexpectedly) split in its opinion. The freedom of religion protected in Article 4 of the *Grundgesetz* was found to include both positive and negative freedom, which in the concrete situation had to be balanced in a manner that does not prefer any one of the conflicting legal positions or allow the full realization of either, but brings about *the most accommodating equilibrium*.[49] A question that arises here is whether this really is neutrality, or does it require the court to approach religious differences objectively,

---

[48] *BVerfGE* 1 BvR 1087/91 16.05.1995.

[49] *BVerfGE* 1 BvR 1087/91 16.05.1995, 51: 'Dieser Konflikt zwischen verschiedenen Trägern eines vorbehaltlos gewährleisteten Grundrechts sowie zwischen diesem Grundrecht und anderen verfassungsrechtlich geschützten Gütern ist nach dem Grundsatz praktischer Konkordanz zu lösen, der fordert, daß nicht eine der widerstreitenden Rechtspositionen bevorzugt und maximal behauptet wird, sondern alle einen möglichst schonenden Ausgleich erfahren.'

taking into account the applicable positive constitutional and statutory provisions?

6.2.1.4 Europe

Considering the matter of state neutrality in public school education from a European and international law perspective, Jeroen Temperman emphasizes the state's 'positive obligation to ensure that sufficient public schools with appropriate curricula are available at all times'. In the milieu of religion and education he identified the following as 'main failures and objectionable policies' in states' public school systems:[50]

- religious education is made compulsory for children;
- the state has 'contracted out' the issue of education to religious institutions, thus not actively making available sufficient adequate – in terms of international obligations – education;
- the state fails to frame a supposedly neutral subject on religion in a truly non-confessional manner;
- the state practises defective opt-out policies;
- the state tolerates traditional forms of religious symbolism, affecting the compulsory non-confessional character of state schools; or
- the state bars access to public school education, *de facto*, by virtue of other policies, for instance, regulations on dress codes.

Although he argues strongly for the inclusion of 'neutral subjects about religions and beliefs' in public school curricula, he concedes that 'strict educational secularism' may not be feasible. Citing Carolyn Evans,[51] a secular curriculum would make it impossible to explain the causes of various European wars, to discuss art and music, or to participate in contemporary debates:[52]

> In other words, as religion and beliefs will inevitably be touched upon in the curriculum, public school officials should reflect upon these issues. In doing so officials should develop an informed approach to deal with issues of religion so that the school justly observes the rights of children and their parents. Conversely, if the topic of religion is obstinately avoided, pupils may learn to avoid religion at all costs.

---

[50] Temperman (2010b) 868.
[51] Evans (2008) 451.
[52] Temperman (2010b) 895–896.

Following the trend to prefer secularism and neutrality in public education, the Chamber judgment of November 2009 of the European Court of Human Rights in the case of *Lautsi v Italy* concerning the presence of crucifixes in classrooms, construed European Convention law relating to the right to education and religious freedom to have established 'an obligation on the State to refrain from imposing beliefs, even indirectly, in places where persons were dependent on it or in places where they were particularly vulnerable, emphasising that the schooling of children was a particularly sensitive area in that respect'. However, in 2011 the Grand Chamber of the European Court of Human Rights overturned the Chamber judgment of 2009, finding on a vote of 15 to 2 that the applicable law had not been violated, since the state enjoyed a wide enough margin of appreciation to respect the right of parents to have their children educated 'in conformity with their own religious and philosophical convictions'.[53]

This judgment, like various others in different jurisdictions,[54] once again highlighted the fact that religious pluralism represents a severe test for all involved at the interface between culture, history, education, law and religion.

6.2.2 Migration and Citizenship

The sociologist Bryan Turner made the point in a 2012 article that 'religion is often inseparable from ethnic identity, so that debates about secularization and liberalism cannot be separated from the question of citizenship in multicultural societies'.[55] According to Turner the liberal paradox lies in the fact that in the post-secular society both secular and

---

[53] *Lautsi v Italy* (Grand Chamber, 2011), para. 76 of the judgment, inspiring the publication of Temperman (2012).

[54] Some interesting examples are: the decision of the Bavarian Constitutional Court on the wearing of headscarves by teachers (*VerfGH* 60,1 (Bayern), 15.1.2007); the decision of the South African Constitutional Court in 2007 on the wearing of a Hindu-related nose stud by a school-going girl published as *MEC for Education, KwaZulu-Natal v Pillay* 2008 (1) SA 474 (CC); the 1983 decision of the House of Lords in *Mandla v Dowell Lee* [1983] 2 AC 548 concerning a Sikh schoolboy who refused to refrain from wearing a Sikh headdress and have his hair cut; and *Grzelak v Poland* App. No. 7710/02, Eur. Ct. H.R. (22 Nov. 2010) dealing with discrimination against the child of agnostic parents in Poland who was not given access to instruction in ethics as an alternative to the religion course, and was therefore given a blank for the course on his school reports.

[55] Turner (2012) 1059.

religious citizens are called upon to provide reasoned arguments for their world views:[56]

> [T]his debate takes place in a context where the state is increasingly called upon to intervene in the management of religions in the interests of civil harmony. Liberalism champions freedom of religion, but liberal states are compelled to exercise some oversight or management of religion in the interests of liberal values, 'negative freedoms' (such as freedom of conscience) and in the quest for civil stability.

The following example from Canada demonstrates the point.

The Ontario Superior Court of Justice was called upon to decide on the constitutionality of the statutory requirement that affirming allegiance must be sworn to the British Queen as head of state when taking up Canadian citizenship.[57] The applicants had different motivations, being an Irish-born republican immigrant, an immigrant from Israel who opposed royal privilege and a Jamaican Rastafarian immigrant who considered the Queen to be 'the head of Babylon'. The application was based on arguments of freedom of expression, equality and freedom of religion, but failed on the finding that the oath was a reasonable limit on the freedom of expression, and no violation of equality or religious freedom.

The Court found that the oath does not have a religious purpose, and although the *Act of Settlement* of 1701 still prohibits Roman Catholics from ascending the throne, 'the purpose of the oath in Canada is the strictly secular one of articulating a commitment to the identity and values of the country'.[58] Citing Supreme Court authority,[59] the Court found that the claim that the oath offended a sincerely held religious belief 'runs counter to the very object of holding up constitutional values for new citizens' and:[60]

> To the extent that the oath to the Queen reflects a commitment not to inequality but to equality, and not to arbitrary authority but to the rule of law, it is not only a unifying statement but a rights-enhancing one. In taking the position that the mere recitation of the oath is an infringement of her subjectively held religious belief, [the applicant] runs up against the settled

---

[56] Turner (2012) 1060.
[57] McAteer (2013).
[58] McAteer (2013) para. [85].
[59] *Alberta v Hutterian Brethren of Wilson Colony*, [2009] 2 S.C.R. 567 and *Bruker v Markovitz*, [2007] 3 S.C.R. 607.
[60] McAteer (2013) paras [89] and [90].

notion that the rights of some cannot be a platform from which to strike down the rights of others.

With reference to the Supreme Court's 2012 judgment in *Commission scolaire*, allowing the applicant to obtain citizenship without making the oath 'would be analogous to a public school board accommodating a religious group by de-secularizing its curriculum'. The Court resisted the idea of relativizing the distinguishing nature of citizenship as a status defining the state concerned: 'one simply cannot have citizens without non-citizens, or members of the state without non-members; and since the non-citizens define the citizens, their very status cannot be discriminatory'.[61]

The *McAteer* judgment has the interesting implication that, among various other factors, the precepts of one's religious convictions can preclude one from obtaining Canadian citizenship. Although the Court wished to avoid deciding the matter on the basis of religious freedom, it essentially found (in the case of one of the litigants) that if the religious convictions of an applicant for naturalization did not resonate with the Canadian 'identity and values', that was the end of the matter: despite an applicant's 'subjective religious beliefs' being affected, such 'religious particularity' could not be accommodated 'in the face of the secular universality of the Act and the oath'. Such accommodation, the Court considered to run counter to the values enshrined in section 2(a) of the *Charter*, which protects the freedom of conscience and religion as being fundamental.[62] It seems that what the Court said was that swearing the oath of allegiance to the Crown should be understood to ensure that new citizens subscribed to secularism as the civil religion of Canada. It may be asked, however, if this is a sustainable stance in this post-secular era.

Religion is not infrequently a factor, albeit indirectly, in applications brought before the courts by immigrants and refugees, especially if the application is founded on religious persecution. Such was the situation in a recent case before the European Court of Human Rights, where a young Iraqi man's deportation by Sweden was found not to clash with the protection afforded to life and inhuman and degrading treatment in terms of articles 2 and 3 of the *European Convention on Human Rights* despite strong evidence that his family had been subjected to severe religious persecution at home. This case demonstrates the high degree of

---

[61] *McAteer* (2013) para. [106].
[62] *McAteer* (2013) para. [92].

defensive protection that the law still provides for when it comes to immigration control. The Court explained it in the following terms:[63]

> The Court reiterates that Contracting States have the right, as a matter of well-established international law and subject to their treaty obligations, including the Convention, to control the entry, residence and expulsion of aliens.... However, the expulsion of an alien by a Contracting State may give rise to an issue under Article 3, and hence engage the responsibility of that State under the Convention, where substantial grounds have been shown for believing that the person in question, if deported, would face a real risk of being subjected to treatment contrary to Article 3 in the receiving country. ...
> However, it must be shown that the risk is real and that the authorities of the receiving State are not able to obviate the risk by providing appropriate protection.

In the end the Court found it acceptable that the applicant be deported to another part of Iraq, where animosity against the applicant's faith was less acute.

6.2.3 Animal Protection and Hygiene

The ritual slaughter of animals, especially bulls, has a long history and continues to be practised in various religious contexts.[64] The Zulu of South Africa maintain an annual ritual known as *Umkhosi ukweshwama* involving, *inter alia*, the killing of a bull by a group of 14-year-old boys using only their hands to strangulate the animal and to break its neck. In 2009 the KwaZulu-Natal Provincial Division heard an application of an animal rights trust to interdict the slaughtering of a bull at that year's *Ukweshwama* festival. The Court did not grant the interdict, but the judgment[65] contained various interesting dimensions.

The Court acknowledged the 'great public importance' of the matter concerning 'the Constitutional rights of the Zulu nation to practise their religion and culture and to observe their customs'. The Court did acknowledge that applications of this nature were:

> symptomatic of an intolerance of religious and cultural diversity. They are often an attempt to force the particular secular views and opinion held by one

---

[63] *N.A.N.S. v Sweden* EUCtHR (Application no. 68411/10) decided on 27 June 2013, paras 23 and 24.
[64] See for example, Rautenbach (2011); Peté and Crocker (2012) *Obiter*; and Mnyongani (2012).
[65] *Smit NO v King Goodwill Zwelithini Kabhekuzulu* 2009 JDR 1361 (KZP) (Juta's unreported judgments, case no. 10237/2009).

faction on others. The traditional African form of culture, religion and religious practices may not be embraced by many who subscribe to the mainstream cultures and religions in Western societies, and were historically often discriminated against and in some instances its followers were persecuted and punished.

This was not, however, the basis for the dismissal of the application. Considering the fact that the application was made shortly before the ceremony was to take place, and recognizing the impossibility of postponing the ritual because it would cause the specific traditional community to have to forego the right to engage in the practice of their religion and culture, the Court employed the mechanism of a 'balance of convenience' (apparently developed in the English equity tradition and adopted in many Anglo-American jurisdictions). The balance of convenience test is understood to mean that the inconvenience suffered by the respective parties caused by the outcome of a decision is weighed in order to give rise to the least inconvenience. In this context the balance was in favour of the Zulu traditional community. It is interesting to note that the 'balance of convenience' analysis resonates well with the German instrument of *praktische Konkordanz* referred to in section 6.2.1.3 above.

Ritual slaughter according to Jewish and Muslim custom offends against the requirement, usually provided for in European countries, that the suffering of the animal must be minimized by stunning it before it is killed and slaughtered. Founded in Talmudic laws *inter alia* preventing the consumption of blood, ritual slaughtering in accordance with orthodox Jewish demands of *kosher* certification involves the killing of an animal with a single stroke with a sharp knife through the trachea, the oesophagus, the carotid arteries and the jugular veins, thus ensuring that as much blood as possible will be drained from the carcass. In France such ritual procedures may be performed in slaughterhouses by persons officially authorized to do so, being 'in the general interest to avoid unregulated slaughter, carried out in conditions of doubtful hygiene, and that it is therefore preferable, if there is to be ritual slaughter, for it to be performed in slaughterhouses supervised by the public authorities'.[66]

When an ultra-orthodox association was refused such authorization by the French authorities after it was granted in 1982 to an association representing the majority of orthodox Jews in France, the matter eventually came before the European Court of Human Rights in the *Cha'are*

---

[66] *Cha'are Shalom Ve Tsedek v France* [GC] Application no. 27417/95, EUCtHR 27 June 2000 para. 77.

Shalom case. In a split decision the Court found that this arrangement did not violate the ultra-orthodox applicant organization's rights to freedom of religion (article 9 of the European Convention) and that it was not being discriminated against (article 14), since its members could obtain meat that satisfied the prescribed ritual requirements, except only for their additional demand that the lungs of the slaughtered oxen and sheep were to be inspected thoroughly in accordance with their specific rules. The Court did not expressly find that the additional inspection required by the applicant association was not really a religious requirement, but the outcome of the case may be considered to imply such a finding. The minority judgment, however, considered the arrangements to be without an objective or reasonable justification and disproportionate, leading to the discriminatory infringement of religious freedom.

6.2.4 Prevention of Public Disturbance

Courts have to consider applications to prohibit or limit sound emanating from religious buildings that is conceived by others to constitute a public nuisance or disturbance from time to time. Two examples are discussed here.

In 1999 a South African High Court considered an application for an interdict preventing the amplification of the call to prayer from a mosque ('madressah') through loudspeakers.[67] The applicant was a township developer who sold land reserved for use for religious purposes to the Islamic Society concerned under the express condition that the call to prayer would not be made from the mosque, but would be replaced by a light at the top of the minaret to be switched on during the hour of prayer, as long as such light was 'used in such a way not to be a nuisance or disturbance to other owners of erven in the township'. The Islamic Society stated before the Court that it never intended to abide by the contractual condition, since the call to prayer was one of the basic tenets of Islam, and argued that the condition offended against the constitutionally guaranteed right to freedom of religion.

In response to the respondent's argument that the electronic amplification of the call to prayer was not so loud as to be a disturbance, the Court found that, if that was the case, an unamplified call (to which the applicant would not further object) 'might as well be made by the unassisted human voice'. The Court therefore upheld the 'sanctity' of

---

[67] *Garden Cities Incorporated Association not for Gain v Northpine Islamic Society* 1999 (2) SA 268 (C).

the contractual agreement, even if it were to be assumed that the constitutional protection of the right came into play. Due to the concession by the applicant that the original agreement that a light should replace the call to prayer was not to be enforced, the Court was able to provide a pragmatic solution to the dispute without really delving into the constitutional issue: in effect it was found that the contractual protection of the interests of other members of the community allowed for an understanding of the freedom of religion that did not impose an unwanted burden on non-adherents of the particular religion.

In 2012 the European Court of Human Rights dealt with an application of a Catholic parish priest in Tilburg, Netherlands, on whose parish limitations on the loudness of the ringing of the church bell before 7:30 am were placed by the local authorities: the bell was rung to call parishioners to services early in the morning, but the neighbouring residents complained that the noise nuisance was intolerable and disturbed their night's rest.[68]

The priest's complaint was that the imposed sound limitation infringed on his right to manifest his religion in contravention of article 9 of the *European Convention on Human Rights*. Although appropriate legislation was not originally in place to allow the imposition of the limitation (the dispute arose in 2007), this was rectified later on. The Court accepted in its judgment that the limitations interfered with the right to manifest one's religion, but found that it was properly sanctioned by law having the purpose of the protection of the rights of others. The limitation on the ringing of the bell, as opposed to a full prohibition thereof, the Court found to be justified as necessary in a democratic society, being a fair balance between competing interests.

The outcome of these two cases is interesting in that they represent examples of solutions to disputes where the religious parties showed a degree of inflexibility but were required by law to take the interests of others into consideration without having to compromise their practices.

6.2.5 Governance of State Institutions

Contemporary states maintain and govern a wide range of institutions including civil services, prisons, the police and the military. As in the case of education, although not necessarily so directly, issues concerning religion inevitably crop up in the governance of state institutions, ranging

---

[68] *Schilder v the Netherlands* EUCtHR 2158/12 Decision 16.10.2012 [Section III].

from the accommodation of the religious convictions of officials and citizens to the granting or withholding of access to persons and official actions. Two examples, one from Croatia and the other from South Africa, demonstrate the nature of the issues sufficiently.

In 2011 a dispute between the Croatian government and a union of Protestant churches concerning the relations between the churches and the state came before the European Court of Human Rights.[69] What was at stake was the churches' ability 'to provide religious education in public schools and nurseries, to provide pastoral care to their members in medical and social-welfare institutions, as well to those in prisons and penitentiaries, or to perform religious marriages with the effects of a civil marriage'.[70]

The state's refusal to register the churches concerned was based on their failure to comply with the required standards, such as the number of their members (a membership of at least 6000 was required) and their history (their presence in Croatia since 1941), despite the fact that 42 other churches, some with even smaller numbers of members, were indeed registered.

The Court confirmed the government's position that article 9 of the European Convention (freedom of religion) did not oblige the state to recognize religious marriages as equal to civil marriages or to allow churches to provide religious education in public schools, but considered the fact that other religious communities had been granted these rights to justify the complaint of discrimination in terms of article 14 of the Convention.[71]

The Court reiterated its view that the meaning of 'discrimination' was 'treating differently, without an objective and reasonable justification, persons in relevantly similar situations'[72] and that the imposition of criteria for the granting of the status of a religious community 'raised delicate questions, as the State had a duty to remain neutral and impartial in exercising its regulatory power in the sphere of religious freedom and in its relations with different religions, denominations and beliefs'.[73]

---

[69] *Savez Crkava* (2011).
[70] *Savez Crkava* (2011) para. 7.
[71] *Savez Crkava* (2011) paras 58, 92 and 93. However, the provision of the applicant churches of pastoral care to their members in medical and social welfare institutions, prisons and penitentiaries was found not to be hindered by the government.
[72] *Savez Crkava* (2011) para. 85.
[73] *Savez Crkava* (2011) para. 88.

In South Africa a 'neutral' dress code policy for officers of the Correctional Services Department concerning the length and neatness of their hair styles was found to be discriminatory after the dismissal of male officers who refused to remove their dreadlocks. The dress code explicitly forbade 'any punk style, including a Rastaman hairstyle'. Some of the dismissed officers were indeed Rastafarian adherents, and others pleaded that their long hair style was related to a cultural process of becoming traditional healers.

Before the Supreme Court of Appeal the Department conceded that it discriminated against male officers preferring to wear dreadlocks, but that 'the discrimination was justifiable because it sought to eliminate the risk and anomaly posed by placing officers who subscribe to a religion or culture that promotes criminality – in the form of the use of dagga [marijuana] – in control of a high-regulation, quasi-military institution such as a prison'.[74] The Court was not convinced that the discrimination was justifiable on the grounds of its purpose being justifiable. Rather, it was found that the policy punished the practices of a religion and a culture, that it degraded and devalued the followers thereof, establishing 'a palpable invasion of their dignity which says their religion or culture is not worthy of protection'.[75] The facts of this case highlight the fact that the state with a religiously plural citizenry will constantly be confronted with seriously difficult choices relating to the religious preferences of its citizens – and that the making of those choices is unavoidable. In the end it is essential to have a sound and consistent basis for the making of the choices.

6.2.6 Conscientious Objection

The notion of conscientious objection is mostly associated with compulsory military service (and occasionally with compulsory attendance of public schools[76]), but it is also relevant in other contexts, for example medical personnel objecting to participation in procedures such as abortion or individuals refusing to undergo compulsory vaccination. What is usually at stake is essentially a refusal on religious (or similar) grounds to comply with a general legal obligation imposed by the state.

---

[74] *Department of Correctional Services v Police and Prisons Civil Rights Union (POPCRU)* 2013 (4) SA 176 (SCA) para. [19].

[75] *Department of Correctional Services v Police and Prisons Civil Rights Union (POPCRU)* 2013 (4) SA 176 (SCA) para. [22].

[76] See for example, the facts in the German case *BverfGE* 2 BvR 1693/04 of 31.5.2006 discussed above in section 6.2.1.3.

However, it does also crop up in situations where religious convictions prohibit the use of available medical remedies such as blood transfusion.[77] Whereas the latter category is not necessarily concerned with the exercise of the authority of the state, being called up for military service goes to the heart of citizenship, that is, individual membership of the state.

It would appear that the citizen's duty to serve as a soldier when called upon to do so[78] is based on notions of nationalism, patriotism and individual co-responsibility to defend a constitutionally defined society, that is, a particular state.[79] The idea of compulsory military service was institutionalized in modern times in Napoleonic France, where the concept of 'the nation' emerged after the French Revolution. This example was followed in the rest of Western Europe in the 19th Century and by the United Kingdom and the United States in the 20th. But compulsory military duty was attended from the outset by the need to deal with conscientious objection. Since the end of the Cold War and in conjunction with globalization, however, military conscription has declined sharply[80] but continues to be significant in countries such as Armenia, North and South Korea, Israel, Greece and Switzerland.

Around the world, members of the Jehovah's Witnesses have initiated cases of conscientious objection in different forms. The European Court of Human Rights was recently seized with two similar cases from Armenia, where objectors were imprisoned after having been convicted of draft evasion in 2001 and 2002.[81] Article 47 of the Armenian Constitution of 1995 provides that 'Every citizen shall participate in the defence of the Republic of Armenia in accordance with the procedure prescribed by law.'

As recently as 2006 the Court had not related imprisonment for draft evasion as an infringement of the freedom of religion, but rather as 'degrading treatment'.[82] In the *Bayatyan* case the Armenian government

---

[77] Cf. for example, Brugger and Karayanni (2007) 107.
[78] According to the UNHCR (2013): 'Every country has the right to ask its citizens to bear arms in periods of national emergency', subject, however, to an equal right to conscientious objection.
[79] The Constitution of Turkey of 1982 for example, provides in article 72: 'National service is the right and duty of every Turk.'
[80] Takemura (2009) 5–9.
[81] *Bayatyan v Armenia* (2011), paras 46–49 and *Bukharatyan* (2012).
[82] *Ülke v Turkey* (Application no. 39437/98) (Chamber judgment of 24 April 2006).

argued that it would violate the principle of equality if religious organizations were to be allowed to interpret the legislation relevant to conscription as they wished. The Court took note, however, of the trend among states in Europe and elsewhere towards the recognition of conscientious objection to justify a change of direction from its previous decisions[83] and therefore invoked the protection of freedom of religion by article 9 of the European Charter.

The Grand Chamber's finding was followed directly in the *Bukharatyan* judgment:[84]

> The Court reiterates that, as enshrined in Article 9, freedom of thought, conscience and religion is one of the foundations of a 'democratic society' within the meaning of the Convention. This freedom is, in its religious dimension, one of the most vital elements that go to make up the identity of believers and their conception of life, but it is also a precious asset for atheists, agnostics, sceptics and the unconcerned. The pluralism indissociable from a democratic society, which has been dearly won over the centuries, depends on it. That freedom entails, *inter alia*, freedom to hold or not to hold religious beliefs and to practise or not to practise a religion.

The position of the European Court of Human Rights therefore amounts in principle to a rejection of compulsion to do military service where the citizen concerned raises a conscientious objection, such being in accordance with the contemporary (European) notion of a democratic society.

6.2.7 Balancing Rights

Adjudication of fundamental rights quite often involves the balancing of competing rights of different parties.[85]

In 2006 both the Constitutional Court and Supreme Court of Uganda turned down an application by university students belonging to the Seventh Day Adventist Church to be allowed not to attend lectures or write exams on their Sabbath, Saturday.[86] The Supreme Court found that reasonable steps should be taken to accommodate religious beliefs, although not at the cost of undue interference or expense to the university whereby its ability to provide education to a diverse and multi-religious

---

[83] *Bayatyan* (2011) paras 100–109.
[84] *Bukharatyan* (2012) para. 46.
[85] See for example, the discussion above in section 6.2.4 of public disturbance by bells and calls to prayer.
[86] *Sharon v Makerere University*.

community would be affected negatively. Balancing diverse religious, social and legal interests is shown here not to be an easy matter.

A unanimous South African Constitutional Court decided in 2000 that corporal punishment of school children could not be sanctioned on religious grounds, even assuming that it would be administered without violation of the rights of the children concerned, since the responsibility of the state to protect people from violence weighed more than the religious conviction that corporal punishment was called for.[87] Here American examples were cited in aid of the argument that religion is intuitive and the law rational.

Citing Rutledge J in *Prince v Massachusetts*[88] Justice Sachs held:[89]

> [33] The most complex problem is that the competing interests to be balanced belong to completely different conceptual and existential orders. Religious conviction and practice are generally based on faith. Countervailing public or private concerns are usually not and are evaluated mainly according to their reasonableness. To the extent that the two orders can be separated, with the religious being sovereign in its domain and the state sovereign in its domain, the need to balance one interest against the other is avoided. However religion is not always merely a matter of private individual conscience or communal sectarian practice. ... [Religious bodies] are part of the fabric of public life, and constitute active elements of the diverse and pluralistic nation contemplated by the Constitution. Religion is not just a question of belief or doctrine. It is part of a way of life, of a people's temper and culture.
>
> [35] The answer cannot be found by seeking to categorise all practices as religious, and hence governed by the factors relied upon by the appellant, or secular, and therefore controlled by the factors advanced by the respondent. They are often simultaneously both. Nor can it always be secured by defining it either as private or else as public, when here, too, it is frequently both. The underlying problem in any open and democratic society based on human dignity, equality and freedom in which conscientious and religious freedom has to be regarded with appropriate seriousness, is how far such democracy can and must go in allowing members of religious communities to define for themselves which laws they will obey and which not. Such a society can cohere only if all its participants accept that certain basic norms and standards are binding.

The merit of this position taken by the Court is that it is impossible to confine religion to the private sphere, but acknowledging the overlap and

---

[87] *Christian Education South Africa v Minister of Education* 2000 (4) SA 757 (CC).
[88] *Prince v Massachusetts* 321 US 158 (1944) 165.
[89] *Christian Education* (2000) paras [33] and [35].

interaction between law and religion, as the Court does, is inconsistent with the statement that they 'belong to completely different conceptual and existential orders'. The manner in which law and religion have influenced one another through the ages and still do so makes it clear that they cannot be separated and preserved in hermetic reciprocal isolation.

Balancing dissimilar claims proportionally nevertheless seems to require more than mere logic: preferring dignity and bodily integrity above the religious convictions of a particular school community involves a moral choice. Courts do not often reveal the basis of such moral choices, except by presenting an argument intended to be understood to be rational and logical because it conforms to the provisions of the constitution.[90] A constitution has to be interpreted, and interpretation entails more than mathematical calculation producing certain results.

6.3 STATE-INITIATED ACTIONS HAVING DIRECT RELIGIOUS IMPLICATIONS

6.3.1 Religion-Related Funding, Subvention and Taxation

Due to the explicit constitutional secularism of France, often cited as the iconic instance of separatism between church and state, one might not expect the French to countenance official funding of church-related institutions and activities. This would be wrong, however, as is demonstrated by a remarkable decision of the French *Conseil Constitutionnel* in 2013.[91]

Since March 2010 the *Conseil* has had full concrete constitutional norm control jurisdiction over legislation already passed, and in this case it was seized with the question whether the fact that in three of the French eastern *départements* religious education in public schools was obligatory and clerics were being supported by the state was constitutionally tenable, given that article 2 of the 1958 Constitution provides that France is an indivisible, laic, democratic and social republic. Thus both

---

[90] See for example, *Christian Education* (2000) para. [51], where the sincerity of religious convictions of the concerned parties was not doubted, but the finding against them was described by the Court as not obliging the applicants 'to make an absolute and strenuous choice between obeying a law of the land or following their conscience'.

[91] *Alsace-Lorraine*, 21 February 2013. The discussion of this case and its background is based on the review of the judgment by Gross (2013).

the unitary form of the French Republic and its secularism came under consideration.

There are clear historical reasons for the exceptions to laicism in the eastern French regions, of which the most obvious is that Alsace-Lorraine was part of the German Empire between 1871 and 1918. Until the end of World War I the religious and cultural arrangements by laws adopted between 1784 and 1831 whereby local regulation of religious affairs was allowed were left intact under German rule and therefore the French law of 1905 in terms of which a strict separation between church and state and secularism was imposed did not apply in those parts of France. The current unitary and laic nature of the Republic entrenched in the 1946 and 1958 Constitutions contradicts the unchanged legal position in Alsace-Lorraine.

A belligerent society 'for the promotion and expansion of laicism', jointly opposed by Reformed, Lutheran, Catholic and Jewish institutions, contested these exceptional arrangements before the applicable lower courts, eventually ending before the *Conseil Constitutionnel*, which was challenged to resolve the discrepancy between the Constitution and the non-secularistic arrangements in the region.

The *Conseil* resolved the issue by means of three rulings:

- article 10 of the 1789 *Declaration of Human and Civic Rights*[92] means that the principle of laicity and the neutrality of the state is based upon the freedom of religion, and therefore the state may not support any religious education;
- the texts and adoption history of the 1946 and 1958 Constitutions must be understood to have established France as a 'laic Republic', which however does not mean that the legal arrangements of the relationship between state and church in the various regions of the state were questioned or amended;
- from this it follows that the pre-existing arrangements regarding state subvention of specific religious communities in Alsace-Lorraine were not affected by the adoption of the current Constitution and were therefore not unconstitutional.

The judgment of the *Conseil Constitutionnel* amounts to a finding that, in view of the fact that the exceptional arrangements of state support of religious institutions in the *départements* concerned were not specifically

---

[92] 'No one may be disturbed on account of his opinions, even religious ones, as long as the manifestation of such opinions does not interfere with the established Law and Order.'

on the agenda when the Constitution was drafted, they are not unconstitutional, although they are strictly speaking not in line with the Constitution! The exceptions therefore had to be left in place.

6.3.2 Labour Relations and Religion

The legal regulation of labour relations obtained its constitutional complexion relatively recently, mostly in the second half of the 20th Century.[93] Inevitably the legal demands of employers and employees will involve religious considerations, some having foundational implications for believers and religious institutions.

6.3.2.1 Germany
German constitutional law is unique when it comes to the legal disposition of churches. Section 140 of the 1949 *Grundgesetz* incorporated five articles of the Weimar Constitution of 1919. Article 136 guarantees religious freedom; article 137 precludes the establishment of a state church while ensuring a range of freedoms for 'religious communities' (*Religionsgesellschaften*), including the right to be recognized as a 'public corporation' (*Körperschaft des öffentlichen Rechtes*); article 138 allows state contributions to religious communities; article 139 protects Sundays and other religious holidays as 'days of rest from work and of spiritual elevation'; and article 141 allows religious communities to perform religious acts in public institutions. In 1977 the *Bundesverfassungsgericht* determined[94] that the Weimar article 137(3), which provides that a religious community is allowed to regulate and administer its affairs independently within the generally applicable limits of the law, applied also to foundations (*Stiftungen*) established by a church, for example for the operation of a hospital, school or orphanage. German churches have consequently established their own version of labour law for such foundations, known as the 'third way' (*dritter Weg*), which strives to be fair while not allowing for labour disputes, exclusions or strikes.[95]

6.3.2.2 The United Kingdom
Dealing with religion in labour relations was the focus of a judgment of the European Court of Human Rights in 2013 in a case dealing with four

---

[93] See for example, Hepple (2011) 37 *et seq* and also Chapter 4 of the same book 57–68 by Ruth Dukes.
[94] BverfGE 46, 73, the *Goch* decision.
[95] See for example, Evangelische Kirche in Deutschland (2013).

separate applications originating in the United Kingdom.[96] Reference to other parts of this judgment is made later,[97] but for present purposes the case of McFarlane is germane. Mr McFarlane was dismissed from his position in a private organization as a sex therapy and relationship counsellor after having been found in disciplinary proceedings to be refusing to provide counselling to same-sex couples on religious grounds. McFarlane engaged all available national legal remedies without success and then approached the European Court of Human Rights to determine if his right to freedom of religion (article 9 of the European Convention) had been breached. The Court did not doubt the sincerity of McFarlane's Christian belief that homosexual activity is sinful and that he should not do anything to endorse it. At issue was finding the balance between his employer's commitment not to discriminate on grounds of sexual orientation against persons seeking counselling and McFarlane's freedom of religion.

In its interpretation of article 9, the Court distinguished[98] between religious freedom being 'primarily a matter of individual thought and conscience' and the freedom to manifest one's religion or belief, which necessarily may have a public impact, may be limited, but in terms of article 9 § 2 only as 'prescribed by law and necessary in a democratic society in pursuit of ... legitimate aims'. Gauging the necessity of a limitation imposed by states party to the Convention or by laws regulating the conduct of private entities (in this case the private employer) engages 'a certain margin of appreciation' which leaves it to the state concerned to make provision for determining the outcome of a dispute about competing rights. The Court unanimously found that this margin was not exceeded in McFarlane's case.[99]

6.3.2.3 South Africa

Section 9(4) of the South African Constitution of 1996 proscribes 'unfair discrimination' by private persons against anyone. In pursuance of this provision the *Promotion of Equality and Prevention of Unfair Discrimination Act*, 4 of 2000 was adopted. One of the grounds upon which discrimination is rendered 'unfair' is sexual orientation. When a church that maintained a music academy discovered that one of the music teachers in its temporary employ was engaged in a homosexual relationship, the teacher's contract was terminated on the grounds that church

---

[96] *Eweida* (2013).
[97] See section 6.4.2 below.
[98] *Eweida* (2013) para. 80.
[99] *Eweida* (2013) paras 84 and 109.

doctrine discouraged same-sex relationships and the teacher was in a position to set a bad example to his pupils.

When the dispute was brought before the Equality Court, the judge dealt with the matter on the basis of having to balance the church's right to freedom of religion against 'the constitutional imperative that there must not be unfair discrimination on the basis of sexual orientation'.[100] Apart from pointing out the heavy emphasis placed by the Constitution on equality, also as a constitutional value, the Court decided for the teacher on the grounds that not granting the church exemption from the prohibition of discrimination would have a minimal impact on the church, whereas the dismissal of the teacher had an enormous impact on his right to equality and impinged upon his dignity.[101]

What is not clear from this judgment is what, if any, circumstances could exist that would allow a church to make distinctions between employees on religious grounds, or if such distinctions that would amount to unfair discrimination on any of the grounds listed in section 9(3) of the Constitution[102] would trump the church's religious rights.

6.3.3 Days of Rest

Often closely associated with labour relations are matters concerning the regulation of hours of business and the institution, recognition or toleration of religion-related days of worship or festivity and rest.

6.3.3.1 Israel

The State of Israel, which operates constitutionally not on a consolidated constitution, but on a combination of common law and a range of 'basic laws', adopted the *Basic Law: Freedom of Occupation* in 1992 (hereafter referred to as 'the Basic Law'), which serves with its equivalents as the normative framework for constitutional scrutiny. Thus the constitutionality of the *Hours of Work and Rest Law*, 5711–1951, providing for at least 36 consecutive hours of rest per week for workers, which, in terms of section 78(b):

---

[100] *Strydom v Nederduitse Gereformeerde Gemeente, Moreleta Park* 2009 (4) SA 510 (EqC), especially para. [14].
[101] *Strydom v Nederduitse Gereformeerde Gemeente, Moreleta Park* 2009 (4) SA 510 (EqC), para. [25].
[102] Race, gender, sex, pregnancy, marital status, ethnic or social origin, colour, sexual orientation, age, disability, religion, conscience, belief, culture, language and birth.

shall include –

(1) For a Jew – the Sabbath;
(2) For someone who is not a Jew – the Sabbath or Sunday or Friday, all of which in accordance with what is acceptable to him as his day of weekly rest.

had to be decided upon by the Israeli Supreme Court sitting as the High Court of Justice in 2005.[103] The petitioner challenged this provision as a violation of the freedom of occupation after it was fined for employing Jews to work in its shops on Saturdays.

In terms of section 2 of the Basic Law, its purpose is 'to protect freedom of occupation in order to enshrine in a Basic Law the values of the State of Israel as a Jewish and democratic state'.

The 'Jewish and democratic' nature of the State of Israel was explicated by the Court as having three elements:[104] Jewish, having two aspects, namely Zionist and traditional-religious, and democratic, being 'based on both the sovereignty of the people and the rule of values that characterize democracy'; and thirdly 'the constitutional interpreter should make an effort to achieve an accord and harmony between the values of the State of Israel as a Jewish state and its values as a democratic state'.

The Court found the provisions prescribing the days of rest, albeit restrictive, consistent with the Basic Law, *inter alia* since it conformed to the values of the State of Israel in that it served an important social purpose on the one hand ('the welfare of the employer and his family') and on the other, it accommodated various religious convictions without coercion.[105]

According to Kalman[106] the *Hours of Work and Rest Law*:

> is a conduit through which Israel's public, legislature, and court system debate religion in the public sphere, and it serves as a symbol of how Israelis attempt to define their society, their culture, and their identity as both a democratic and Jewish nation. Its interpretations are an opportunity to carve out precisely which Jewish and democratic values take precedence and which will prevail if they conflict.

---

[103] *Design 22 Shark Deluxe Furniture Ltd v Rosenzweig* 2005(1) Isr. L. Reps. 340 [2005].
[104] *Design 22 Shark Deluxe Furniture Ltd v Rosenzweig* 2005(1) Isr. L. Reps. 340 [2005] para. 15 of President Barak's judgment.
[105] *Design 22 Shark Deluxe Furniture Ltd v Rosenzweig* 2005(1) Isr. L. Reps. 340 [2005] paras 22 and 23 of President Barak's judgment. See also para. 2 of Justice Procaccia's supporting judgment.
[106] Kalman (2013) 147.

6.3.3.2 South Africa

The difficulty of dealing with the accommodation of different approaches to Sunday trading (distinct from labour issues) became apparent in South Africa when it was contended before the Constitutional Court that the legislation prohibiting the sale of wine on Sunday was unconstitutional:[107] the outcome – to the effect that the legislation was to be upheld – was supported by four of the nine sitting judges; two further members of the Court supported the outcome but on other grounds and three formulated an opposing position both regarding outcome and justification.

The majority considered the legislation not to promote or to interfere with the free exercise of trade; two construed it as marginal, but not fatal, state favouritism of the Christian faith, justifiable on the basis of the legitimate limitation of alcohol abuse; and the minority of three considered the legislation to be discriminatory against non-Christians. Although the Court expressly stated in the majority judgment[108] that the South African approach was essentially different from the American notion of non-establishment, to draw clear conclusions from the judgments in this case regarding the dominance or not of secularism and neutrality in South Africa is not possible.

6.3.3.3 France

Perhaps as an example of the expression of laicism in France, the *Conseil Constitutionnel* decided that legislation which reaffirmed 'the principle of Sunday rest' but provided for exceptions to be allowed administratively for voluntary Sunday labour was consistent with the Constitution.[109] What is remarkable about this judgment is that the Council could completely avoid reference to religious considerations because the members of the National Assembly and the senators that requested the constitutional review did not object to the legislation on religious grounds.

Ruth Gavison and Nahshon Perez[110] identified the problem of days of rest in multicultural societies and suggested guidelines for the solution of the problem. Their solution amounts to having the cultural preferences of the majority in the state reflected in the legal arrangements regarding days of rest, but with individual and communal accommodation of the

---

[107] *S v Lawrence; S v Negal; S v Solberg* 1997 (4) SA 1176 (CC).
[108] *S v Lawrence; S v Negal; S v Solberg* 1997 (4) SA 1176 (CC) para. [100].
[109] *Sunday Rest* 6 August 2009.
[110] Gavison and Perez (2008).

preferences of the minority cultures in the plural society.[111] The merits of the solution aside, their evaluation of the liberal approach to privatize religion as one of 'all non-civic affiliations' is revealing:[112]

> [N]eutral liberalism of this sort does not in fact treat all non-civic affiliations in the same way. The inability of political theory, and of liberal states, to remain neutral with regard either to conceptions of the good or to culture has been pointed out over and over again. Indeed ... the choice and meaning of the day of rest, far from being neutral, are grounded in thick cultural traditions. In this context it is perhaps preferable to use the term 'even-handedness', rather than neutrality. Neutrality suggests the possibility of a hands-off policy to culture, which is impossible. By contrast, even-handedness treats equally all existing cultural demands (that do not violate individual human rights).

6.4 GOVERNING ACTIVITIES INITIATED FROM RELIGIOUS PERSPECTIVES

6.4.1 Recognition of Religious Institutions

The range of institutions founded in religious belief, culture or ritual is very wide. It frequently involves aspects of family law such as polygamy, the right to obtain a divorce or being forced to divorce and the choice of one's spouse, as well as the law of succession (inheritance), the succession of tribal leaders, circumcision, religious rituals such as burial customs and the liturgical consumption of drugs, food codes, and so on. Here it must suffice to demonstrate the nature of the issues being brought before court and the judicial responses in a selection of only a few of these religious institutions.

6.4.1.1 Religious consumption of cannabis

In a case concerned with the religious consumption of cannabis,[113] the South African Constitutional Court handed down a divided judgment. The minority consisted of four justices, two of whom delivered a separate judgment, and a majority of five. The majority found the statutory prohibition of the possession and use of cannabis to be a reasonable and justifiable limitation on the religious freedom of Rastafari since the making of an exception on the prohibition was considered impracticable

---

[111] Gavison and Perez (2008) 209.
[112] Gavison and Perez (2008) 206–207.
[113] *Prince v President, Cape Law Society* 2002 (2) SA 794 (CC).

and would impair the state's ability to protect society against the abuse of harmful drugs. The minority found the prohibiting legislation to be unreasonable and overbroad since, in their opinion, an exception for the purposes of allowing and strictly regulating the harmless use of cannabis for religious purposes could be crafted by the legislature. In the additional minority judgment the need for tolerance and respect for diversity was emphasized, and the position was taken that the forcing of people to choose between their faith and respect for the law for the sake of easing the task of the maintenance of order should be avoided. This case demonstrates how religious practices that are unusual or even disruptive in the broader society concerned confront the constitutional state with policy decisions based on a spectrum of considerations.

6.4.1.2 Burial rites

When a Maori man who had lived and had two children with his (white) partner died in Christchurch, New Zealand in 2007, his extended family took the body against the wishes of the 'widow' (who was also legally his executor) for burial according to the Maori rites and in a grave situated in a ritually designated place. When the courts were called upon to deal with the dispute, questions arose about the lawfulness and place of Maori custom in the New Zealand common law.

The widow succeeded in her application to have the body exhumed and reburied in Christchurch. The New Zealand Supreme Court confirmed that the High Court properly used its inherent jurisdiction to settle the dispute according to the method of the common law since it could not be settled either in the usual manner through family processes nor through '*tikanga*' processes (Maori custom to which the common law gives effect) whereby 'disputes in respect of cultural claim may usually be resolved'.[114]

Although the Supreme Court acknowledged[115] that in cases of this nature '[h]uman rights are engaged because the disposal of human remains touches on matters of human identity, dignity, family, religion and culture', it did not take the matter of balancing religious values against the long-standing common-law rule that property does not exist in the dead body of a human being any further. In a separate, confirming judgment, three of the judges did, however, explain the position as follows:[116]

---

[114] *Takamore v Clarke* [2012] NZSC 116 para. [91].
[115] *Takamore v Clarke* [2012] NZSC 116 para. [82].
[116] *Takamore v Clarke* [2012] NZSC 116 para. [164].

[T]he common law of New Zealand requires reference to the tikanga, along with other important cultural, spiritual and religious values, and all other circumstances of the case as matters that must form part of the evaluation. Personal representatives are required to consider these values if they form part of the deceased's heritage, and, if the dispute is brought before the Court because someone is aggrieved with the personal representative's decision, Māori burial practice must be taken into account.

6.4.1.3 Circumcision

In a German case of 2012[117] the balancing of the religious rights of parents with the rights of their children was shown up as a matter of some complexity.[118] A Muslim couple in Köln approached a medical practitioner to circumcise their son, four-years-old. The prosecuting authority of Köln became aware of the operation when the child was taken back to the emergency ward about a week later for treatment of minor complications. The parents and doctor subsequently stood trial on a charge of infant genital mutilation and the court held that the procedure, which led to permanent and irreversible physical alteration, had also inhibited the child's freedom to choose its religious affiliation later on.

Both Muslims and Jews around the world were immediately up in arms. The German government reacted swiftly by introducing legislation in October 2012 in terms of which the conditions for lawful circumcision of infants were to be laid down.[119] The *Landesgericht* of Köln appears to have underestimated the strength of the symbolism of circumcision in the Islamic and Jewish religions when it allotted more weight to the individual child's rights to bodily integrity and religious freedom than to collective religious sentiment.

The legislation that was passed by the German *Bundestag* on 12 December 2012, not without controversy in the legislative debates, seeks to strike a satisfactory objective balance by not prohibiting the religious ritual but regulating its performance according to objectively acceptable standards.[120]

6.4.1.4 Solemnization of marriages

When a couple wished to be married in London in a meeting place of the Church of Scientology, the question arose before the United Kingdom

---

[117] See for example, Fateh-Moghadam (2012).
[118] See for example, Tagesschau (2012).
[119] See for example, Gesetz (2012).
[120] See Beschneidung (2012).

Supreme Court whether a decision of the Queen's Bench of 1970[121] should be upheld that a similar Scientology venue did not qualify for the purpose.[122] The question of whether or not Scientology should be recognized as a religion was at the heart of the matter.

Finding that Scientology did qualify as a religion, the Court overruled the 1970 decision in *Segerdal*, declared the chapel concerned to be 'a place of meeting for religious worship' and ordered it to be registered as a place for the solemnization of marriages. Lord Toulson, writing for the Court, emphasized that he did not wish to provide a definitive formula but nevertheless, finding guidance in judgments of courts in the United States and Australia, 'described' religion in summary:[123]

> as a spiritual or non-secular belief system, held by a group of adherents, which claims to explain mankind's place in the universe and relationship with the infinite, and to teach its adherents how they are to live their lives in conformity with the spiritual understanding associated with the belief system. By spiritual or non-secular I mean a belief system which goes beyond that which can be perceived by the senses or ascertained by the application of science.

6.4.2 Religious Dress and Symbols

Religious dress and symbols, such as distinctive attire, hair styles and jewellery, have often cropped up in diverse contexts of constitutional litigation. Thus for example German law has had various encounters with the question of whether or not teachers in the employ of the state should be allowed to demonstrate their religious affinities through their dress.

The manner in which the wearing of the Muslim headscarf by teachers was excluded but nuns' habits were allowed demonstrates how tenuous judicial neutrality can be. In 2007 the Bavarian Constitutional Court explained its perspective on state neutrality. In translation (by the author) the Court stated:[124]

---

[121] In *R v Registrar General, Ex p Segerdal* [1970] 2 QB 697.
[122] *Hodkin* (2013).
[123] *Hodkin* (2013) para. 57.
[124] *Islamische Religionsgemeinschaft* (2007) V.2 c), bb), second paragraph of the judgment:

> Der Begriff der religiös-weltanschaulichen Neutralität des Staates ist vielschichtig. Er umfasst verfassungsrechtliche Inhalte wie Toleranz und Nichtidentifikation sowie den Gleichbehandlungsgrundsatz gemäß Art. 118 Abs. 1 BV. Das Neutralitätsgebot ist nicht als Gebot zur Eliminierung des Religiösen

Religious and ideological neutrality of the state is a complex notion. It embraces elements of constitutional law such as tolerance and non-identification as well as the fundamental principle of equal treatment in terms of Article 118 of the Bavarian Constitution. The imperative of neutrality must not be understood to be a command to eliminate the religious from the public sphere; it does not indicate complete indifference in religious and ideological questions at all, nor a laic separation of state and church. The legislature may and must in its provisions abide by the system of values underpinning the Constitution.

Concerning the Bavarian legislation that was adopted to disallow the wearing of headscarfs by teachers, the Court explained that the constitutional values included Christian-occidental (*abendländische*) educational and cultural values, meaning the values of the Western world founded upon Humanism and the Enlightenment. Nuns' habits were not, according to the Court, in conflict with these values, whereas Muslim headscarfs were.

This judgment is obviously open to criticism from the proponents of secularism who maintain that neutrality demands complete indifference to religious considerations of any nature. The judgment, however, demonstrates the difficulty of neutralizing state conduct to the extent that religious considerations are completely eliminated. A legitimate question here is if the Court's qualified understanding of neutrality allowed for an objective consideration of the issues at hand and, if so, whether a truly objective weighing of the facts would have produced the same result.

Regarding the public wearing of religious symbols in other contexts, the *Eweida* case decided in 2013 by the European Court for Human Rights[125] dealt *inter alia* with policies concerning the display on a company uniform of a religious symbol. The first applicant, Ms Eweida, was a Coptic Christian in the employ of British Airways (a private company) whose uniform code first prohibited the display of a cross while working in its uniform, but later the code was amended to allow it. In the course of this process the applicant did not work for some time and claimed compensation for the earnings she lost in this period. The Court granted her compensation for non-pecuniary damages, costs and expenses.

---

aus dem öffentlichen Bereich zu verstehen; es bedeutet keine völlige Indifferenz in religiös-weltanschaulichen Fragen und keine laizistische Trennung von Staat und Kirche (VerfGH 50, 156/167). Der Gesetzgeber darf und muss sich bei seinen Regelungen an der Wertordnung orientieren, die der Verfassung zugrunde liegt (VerfGH 41, 44/49).

[125] *Eweida* (2013).

The second applicant in the same case, a nurse who was refused permission to wear a necklace with a cross as a manifestation of her faith, did not convince the Court that she was discriminated against, since the reasons for the refusal – clinical safety and hygiene – were found not to be disproportionate. An interesting component of the judgment is a brief comparative survey of the law of 26 member states of the Council of Europe, the USA and Canada relating to the wearing of religious clothing and symbols at work.[126]

The Court found that in the majority of states the matter is not regulated. In Ukraine, Turkey and Switzerland civil servants were prohibited from wearing religious symbols, but it was allowed in principle by private companies. In Belgium, Denmark and the Netherlands courts have granted employers the right to regulate the wearing of religious symbols in the absence of statutory regulation thereof, but in France and Germany employees of the state are strictly prohibited from wearing such symbols at work, and French legislation allows private employers to regulate it within specific parameters. In the United States, government employees have a constitutionally protected (First Amendment) right to wear religious symbols, only limitable under circumstances where an important 'Government interest' can be proven. However, private employers are not prevented constitutionally from imposing restrictions. In Canada limitations by the state are constitutionally required to impose the least restrictive limitations in the interest of a 'compelling government interest'. 'Reasonable accommodation' and the avoidance of a disproportionate impact on religious minorities are required.

In 2013 an interesting case concerning religious clothing was decided by the German Federal Administrative Court. At issue was the request of a Muslim schoolgirl to be excused from attending compulsory swimming classes at school, attended by both sexes. She contended that participation would offend against her religious convictions relating to physical contact with and exposure of the female form to the opposite sex. The school offered her a solution in the form of allowing her to wear a 'burkini' during swimming classes, a swimsuit known to be used in public and designed to cover all but the face, hands and feet, and not revealing body contours even when wet.

The Court found that the school could reasonably require the applicant to wear the burkini without offending against her freedom of religion, since it complied with Muslim clothing requirements. The Court reiterated the position that the right to freedom of religion and the state's right

---

[126] Contained in paras 47–49 of the judgment.

of determination (*Bestimmungsrecht*) of school education were of equal rank and that conflictual demands on these rights should be resolved in such a manner that both were realized optimally in accordance with the notion of *praktischer Konkordanz*. The Court pointed out that the demand for religious neutrality of education prohibited indoctrination by the state, which, however, did not require the accommodation of the religious rules of conduct applicable to everyone in the school. The school was not required in the (German) society characterized by pluralism and individualism, in addition to its educational function, to withhold the exposure of schoolgoers to current social habits, including those of the scant clothing styles current for swimming in public.[127]

6.4.3 Intra- and Inter-religious Disputes

Courts in constitutional states do not as a matter of course assume the jurisdiction to adjudicate on theological matters or religious dogma. Nevertheless, issues turning on intra- or inter-religious disputes do reach the courts. How courts deal with such matters in different jurisdictions is instructive. Two examples of intra-religious disputes respectively from Germany and Canada may be cited here.

German university professors are nominally civil servants, appointed and remunerated by the provincial (*Land*) authorities. Their academic independence is nonetheless entrenched very effectively. Professorial appointments are made in conjunction with the university concerned, and in the case of professors of theology, in consultation with the relevant clerical structures. In a book published in 1998, professor Gärditz of the Faculty of Theology of the University of Göttingen announced that he had lost his faith. In reaction to this pronouncement the university decided to modify professor Gärditz's teaching mandate from New Testament subjects to early Christian history and literature. The professor contested this decision through various courts, ending in the Federal Constitutional Court in 2008.

The courts weighed the professor's academic freedom against the right to self-determination of the church, the *Evangelische Landeskirche* in Niedersachsen, whose ministers are trained by the university in terms of an agreement between the church and the government of the *Land*. As has been indicated in the discussion of some German cases above, the Court's established interpretative approach, where competing fundamental rights, in this case the professor's academic freedom versus the

---

[127] *BVerwG* 6 C 25.12, delivered on 11 September 2013 paras 12, 15 and 30.

right of self-determination of the church and the Faculty's right to protect its identity, is known as 'practical concordance' (*praktische Konkordanz*), meaning the balancing of conflicting interests in such a manner that as much as possible of each is preserved.[128] The Court took pains to explain that it was not for the state, which is constitutionally 'neutral in religious and ideological matters', to determine whether the nature of the training provided on behalf of the denomination concerned was appropriate, but that the right of that particular religious community to make such decisions deserved protection.[129]

In 2004 the Canadian Supreme Court heard an appeal against an order to remove individual *succahs* (temporary huts erected by orthodox Jews for the Sukkot festival or 'feast of booths') from the balconies of certain buildings. The appellants were co-owners of units in luxury buildings in Montréal. A religious dispute existed within the Jewish community over the question of whether dogma required individual *succahs* to be erected, or if a communal construction on the grounds of the building would satisfy the particular religious demands. A majority of five against four of the judges decided that the by-laws, which, *inter alia*, prohibited decorations, alterations and constructions on balconies, therefore also prohibiting the erection of the *succahs*, infringed upon the appellants' Charter right to freedom of religion.

The majority judgment interestingly opened with a definition of religion:[130]

> Defined broadly, religion typically involves a particular and comprehensive system of faith and worship. In essence, religion is about freely and deeply held personal convictions or beliefs connected to an individual's spiritual faith and integrally linked to his or her selfdefinition and spiritual fulfilment, the practices of which allow individuals to foster a connection with the divine or with the subject or object of that spiritual faith.

An important reason for allowing the appeal was that the trial judge heard evidence on and made a choice between opposing religious interpretations of Jewish law instead of merely determining whether the appellants' belief that each had to build his own *succah* was sincerely

---

[128] Where Alexy (2002) discusses his 'Law of Balancing' (102 *et seq*), he puts *praktische Konkordanz* in the following perspective: 'The very idea of a principle means that balancing is not a matter of all or nothing but a requirement to optimize.'
[129] BVerfG, 1 BvR 462/06 vom 28.10.2008, for example, paras 47 and 61.
[130] *Syndicat Northcrest v Amselem*, 2004 553.

held.[131] Three dissenting judges, however, considered it necessary for the Court to weigh the sincerity of the appellants' belief against the expertly determined content of the dogma, and found that their right to freedom of religion did not outweigh other co-owners' rights to the property. The remaining dissenting judge assumed that the appellants should have considered their religious needs when they entered into the agreement of co-ownership and accepted that it did not outweigh regard for the rights of others.

Inter-religious disputes mostly involve the balancing of the rights to freedom of religion and freedom of expression and the determination of the boundaries between freedom of expression and religious hate speech.

In 2001 the Tanzanian Court of Appeal quashed the conviction by a lower court and the sentence of imprisonment of a member of an Islamic organization for urging non-Muslims to embrace the Islamic faith and stating that Jesus Christ was not the Son of God. The Court of Appeal found that the freedom of religion guaranteed the profession, practice and propagation of faith and belief and that sober and temperate criticisms of other religions are not prohibited by law.[132]

The European landmark decision dealing with the conflict between freedom of expression and religious rights dates back to 1994. At issue was the banning and confiscation by the Austrian government of the film 'Das Liebeskonzil', which contained material grossly offensive to Christians. The majority of the Court found that the exercise of the freedom of expression entailed certain duties and responsibilities, among which was 'an obligation to avoid as far as possible expressions that are gratuitously offensive to others and thus an infringement of their rights, and which therefore do not contribute to any form of public debate capable of furthering progress in human affairs'[133] and that the interference of the freedom of expression was therefore proportionally justified.

Conversely, the minority judgment held the freedom of expression, being a fundamental feature of a democratic society, not only allowed the distribution of information and inoffensive ideas, but that it applies 'particularly to those that shock, offend or disturb the State or any sector of the population'.[134]

---

[131] *Syndicat Northcrest v Amselem*, 2004 554.
[132] *Dibagula v Republic* (Court of Appeal 24/08/2001).
[133] *Otto-Preminger-Institut v Austria* EuCtHR Application no. 13470/87 20 September 1994 para. 49.
[134] Para. 3 of the minority judgment in *Otto-Preminger-Institut* (1994).

6.5 WHAT JUDGES HAVE IN COMMON IN RELIGIOUS ADJUDICATION

The foregoing review of cases that have been decided in various constitutional environments around the world reveals eclecticism rather than consistency. Although a widely supported coherent judicial approach would be too much to expect, especially given the immense (though waning) influence of liberal secularism and the historical and normative diversity of the jurisdictions from which the judgments were collected, adherence to true constitutionalism by the courts concerned might by now have given rise to indications of the development of a general approach in the ideal constitutional state of the 21st Century. It is not to be, however, a *lacuna* which gives one cause to consider what the reasons for its existence might be.

Should the logic of liberal secularism be drawn to its full conclusion, the state would not at all have had cause to be concerned with religious issues: this logic seeks to separate the public and private spheres in absolute terms, law and politics being a public matter, religion exclusively private. It is submitted that the cause for the inconsistencies and uncertainties characterizing adjudication where religion comes into play can largely be attributed to the attempts by many courts to put the flawed logic of secularism into practice. Such attempts have shown themselves repeatedly to be fruitless, the reasons therefor including the state's inability to acquit itself of its existential responsibility to maintain legal order without accounting for religion, and the fact that people (be they judges, politicians or bureaucrats) are incapable of religious neutrality: human beings are in their nature religious, and neutrality entails not being engaged.

From the survey of judgments one clear conclusion emerges: for judges there is nowhere to hide from religion. The range of religion-related legal issues is very broad, and judicial opinion on dealing with religious conflicts varies widely. The stream of legal controversies caused by religious pluralism is not diminishing. The nature and ubiquitousness of questions regarding the manner in which the state and its institutions should deal with issues pertaining to religious pluralism and the protection of the relevant rights and interests have global dimensions. Religion has returned with a vengeance to the public debate and scholarly consideration.[135]

---

[135] Cf. for example, Willems (2012) 131 *et seq.*

As a person, no judge has the ability to disengage from personally held convictions, nor can judges as the bearers of the judicial authority of the state disengage themselves 'neutrally' from the burning issues brought about by religious conflicts occurring in their societies, especially given the escalation of cultural pluralism characterizing the mobile population of the world, which is simultaneously increasingly also insisting on the benefits of constitutionalism. Ultimately the question should be if secularism can be a vehicle for the attainment of justice in conformity with the golden rule: granting others what you demand for yourself.

Malcolm Evans gives expression to the need for a different approach by the European Court of Human Rights where he concludes:[136]

> The difficulty with the Court's individual rights decisions is that language appropriately used in case law concerning State regulation of legal personality of religious entities has increasingly been used in situations concerning the individuals' manifestation of religion through clothing, symbols, buildings, etc. In such contexts, the call for 'impartiality' and 'neutrality' has increasingly been taken to mean that the State must present itself as neutral, i.e. non-religious, in all of its dealings. In this view, the mere presence of the religious is a threat to the demonstration of neutrality.

And:

> The Court has correctly argued that when exercising its regulatory powers with regard to religious communities the State should act impartially or 'neutrally.' But when the State addresses the freedom of individuals to express themselves on matters of religion or belief in words, in dress or in architecture, it is respect rather than neutrality that provides the better starting point.

To this must be added that impartiality and neutrality cannot and should not be considered to be the same. More on this in Chapter 9 below.

In similar vein Mark Witten, exploring the tension between the ideal of objective, rational, adjudication and the critique that neutral decision-making is a naive fiction in the Canadian context, found[137] that:

> Some arguments and beliefs will always be more tenable than others. Moreover, there will always be the need to judge, and judging will inevitably depend on the faculty of reason. However, to obscure that a judgement, and not merely a neutral adjudication is taking place, represents a blind faith in constitutionalism. Such a blind faith cripples the capacity to properly evaluate a religious claim, and to judge well.

---

[136] Evans (2010–2011) 370.
[137] Witten (2012) 115–116.

'A blind faith in constitutionalism' certainly does not present any solutions if by it is meant a mechanical application of a particular interpretation of a constitutional text. Constitutionalism understood as the carrier of universalized constitutional values, as described in Chapter 3, on the other hand, holds out the possibility of true objective judgement according to solid standards.

In his search for solutions to the state-and-religion predicament, Paul Horwitz[138] propounds the idea of 'constitutional agnosticism'. He demonstrates how the current American judicial and academic approach to law and religion tends to 'either sh[y] away from questions of religious truth altogether or smuggles in a set of conclusions that ultimately give an unfair advantage to secular interests'.[139] Horwitz's 'constitutional agnosticism' is 'an approach to religious liberty that reflects the spirit of our agnostic age', which builds on certain phenomena:[140]

> [T]he suspension of ontological commitments, and the capacity for negative capability that has become ingrained in modern thought. Unlike either openly secular or openly religious approaches to religious freedom, it does not stake its all on a positive claim about religious truth.
>
> At the same time, unlike the conventional liberal approach to religious liberty, it does not seek to avoid questions of religious truth. Instead ... it takes a positive and genuinely committed approach to these questions.

Although this notion of constitutional agnosticism is not obviously attractive as a solution to the difficulties of dealing with religious plurality, at least because it implies replacing the certain hostility to religion of secularism with agnostics' inherent insecurity about religion, I agree with him that courts tend to take refuge in concepts such as neutrality and secularism to hide their bias or their embarrassment at not finding accommodating answers to intractable problems.[141]

Although we are primarily concerned here with considerations of constitutional law, it is impossible to ignore the broader context of the debate on the relevance and impact of religion on the human condition. A prominent contemporary manifestation of this debate is the very public disputation among mostly natural scientists under the rubric 'new atheism'. Horwitz devotes a chapter in his book[142] – in which he addresses the unwillingness of 'today's leading theorists on freedom of

---

[138] Horwitz (2011).
[139] Horwitz (2011) xxix.
[140] Horwitz (2011) 150–151.
[141] Horwitz (2011) 155.
[142] Horwitz (2011) Chapter 4.

religion' to ask the question 'what is truth'[143] – to a discussion of the confrontation between the new atheists and their opponents. He finds that the debate is at a stalemate:[144] 'In significant ways, then, atheism and belief are at an impasse when it comes to offering a final answer to the ultimate questions of religious truth: the nature of the universe and the existence or nonexistence of God.'

These considerations are part and parcel of the problematics surrounding constitutionalism and religion. If state neutrality is called for in religion-related matters, there is no clarity regarding the meaning of such neutrality: it would appear from the jurisprudence that 'neutrality' has such an uncertain content that it can be employed to satisfy arguments ranging from justified state hostility to religion to the justification of cultural preference, much of which amounts to judicial escapism from the responsibility to confront the realities of religious pluralism.

---

[143] Horwitz (2011) xi.
[144] Horwitz (2011) 134.

PART III

Obligations of the constitutional state in religious matters

Given the nature of the state as the primary repository of governmental authority and the most productive generator of binding legal norms,[1] it bears the responsibility of maintaining public peace and order. Where 'authority' is understood as raw power, the maintenance of order tends to depend on forceful means and coercion to ensure compliance by the populace with the commands of the authorities. Where such circumstances prevail, it is hardly possible to speak of constitutionalism.

Conversely, where state authority is rooted in a sound constitution which prohibits the organs of the state from stepping beyond clearly defined limits to the extent and manner of the exercise of their constitutionally regulated powers, the means with which social peace and order can be maintained have a different character. Although compulsion will always be an ingredient of legal authority, in a constitutional state the application of force is a last resort to be used only when the doctrinal, normative and formal elements of constitutionalism[2] have failed to secure compliance with the law.

Religious plurality in the populace of a constitutional state presents the state with unique challenges. Some of the reasons for the existence of these challenges are to be found in realities such as beliefs being beyond the reach of legal regulation, while the existence and practice of religion requires not only legal recognition but also active protection, especially in societies where religion is a distinguishing characteristic of various

---

[1] Cf. section 1.5 in Chapter 1 above.
[2] Cf. section 3.5 in Chapter 3 above.

components of the society concerned and brings about competing demands and claims with legal implications.

In the following chapters the usual responses to these challenges and the appropriate responses called for by the nature of constitutionalism are considered. This is inevitably done against the background of the failures of contemporary constitutional states to respond appropriately to the growing need to do so.

7. The weaknesses of contemporary statehood in the face of religious pluralism

Remarkably, amidst the rhetorical expansion of secularism, the warranting of freedom of religion continues to be one of the important characteristics of the law of constitutional states such as the USA, Germany and South Africa. And yet, when dealing with the plurality of religion in their populations, the legislatures, executives and judiciaries of all three of these states have often stumbled inelegantly, as can be seen in some of the judgments discussed in Chapter 6 above. The reason for this must be sought in the conventional pre-programmed responses to the challenges of religious pluralism, and the continuing exposure of the shortcomings of the currently available constitutional instrumentation that was designed for the justification of liberal democracy.

This chapter reviews the crumbling foundations upon which the notions of sovereignty, citizenship, the social contract, *pouvoir constituant* and the counter-majoritarian dilemma, all central to the conventional understanding of the state as preserver of justice, are based. The weaknesses of the standard responses of states when called upon to maintain justice amidst religious pluralism in a post-secular world are thereby pointed out.

7.1 CURRENT FORTUNES OF STATEHOOD

The 'state', 'sovereignty', 'nation', 'citizenship' and similar terms belong to the daily fare of lawyers, and also of practitioners of disciplines such as political studies, economics and geography. The exact meaning of these concepts has never been settled, and this uncertainty has fuelled many a scholarly analysis.

The law, in particular international law and constitutional law, cannot function without the notion of the state. The state cannot exist without its citizens. Coercive legal authority (power) in the hands of the state and its organs is an essential ingredient of statehood. Closely associated with the notion of the state is sovereignty.

Here we will not endeavour to reiterate the extensive published learning concerning these key notions. We will instead briefly investigate doctrinal positions taken on these matters in order to facilitate the discussion of another point which has generally gained currency: despite the endurance of the terminology, the meaning of the terms 'state', 'sovereignty' and 'citizenship' is in flux.

7.1.1 State Sovereignty

Sovereignty is not founded upon a mystical social contract[1] or on popular sentiments inspiring a constitutional moment,[2] but on effective norms contained in constitutional and international law rooted in historical events. Constitutional law (and for that matter, also international law) has nevertheless evolved, and still operates on the assumption that the state is sovereign and that it exists for the benefit and protection of its 'nation' and the associated legal system. Key references for this assumption continue to be the famous opening words of the US Constitution of 1789 'We the People ...' and the French constitutional principle of 'government of the people, by the people, for the people',[3] both of which are often, and sometimes bizarrely, reiterated in modern constitutions where one is hard put to associate popular sovereignty or democracy with local reality.[4]

The assumption that a supreme constitution represents the binding ethos of a state to which a democratic majority and all the organs of state

---

[1] Glenn (2013) 133–134 makes short shrift with dispatching the social contract to the domain of the 'implausible' and having had some effect 'in those jurisdictions least in need of it and where common laws provided ongoing continuity of state structures'.

[2] The notion of 'constitutional moments', described as 'decisive moments at which deep changes in popular opinion gained authoritative constitutional recognition' (by means of constitutional jurisprudence) was first propounded by Ackerman (1991) 41. It represents an important theoretical construction because it enforces a theoretical consideration of the modalities of legitimate constitutional amendment. It is not beyond criticism, however: for example, Choudhry (2008).

[3] Article 2 of the current Constitution of the Vth Republic of 1958.

[4] Recent examples are to be found in for example, the preamble to the 2003 Constitution of the Islamic Republic of Afghanistan, 'We the people of Afghanistan', and the first sentence of the preamble to the 2013 Constitution of Zimbabwe, 'We the people of Zimbabwe.'

and the population are subject until it is amended in accordance with the provisions of the constitution is indeed a cornerstone of text-based constitutionalism – a widely accepted idea, given the proliferation in recent decades of written constitutions – but it is by no means beyond theoretical contestation. This is demonstrated in the division of 'monism' and 'dualism' in the oldest existing constitutional state, the United States of America. The division is explained by Ackerman with reference to British parliamentary practice:[5] having won a credible general election, the House of Commons routinely gives its majority support to the proposals of the government, and if the actions of the government lose majority popular support, the opposition will win the next election. In the meantime legislation passed by Parliament will not be undermined by the Crown, the House of Lords or the judiciary. The American system is fundamentally different, however, in that the popularly elected House of Representatives is constantly challenged by constitutional entities such as the Senate, and especially the Supreme Court. Monism considers this to be anti-democratic, as expressed in the notion of the 'countermajoritarian difficulty', but dualism distinguishes between decisions made by 'the people' and by the government. The Constitution as the 'higher law' expresses the will of the people, a change of which can be recorded only by means of an amendment in accordance with an onerous and inclusive process. The judiciary is charged with the responsibility to preserve 'the will of the people' by judging in accordance with the Constitution and not necessarily in accordance with the wishes of the current political majority. It is incidentally not unlikely that many of the difficulties that especially younger constitutional democracies experience are caused by a monistic confusion of the political preferences of the incumbent government with the imperatives of the constitution.

It is in the final instance a matter of the legitimacy of the constitution, however justified. Justification of the supremacy of the constitution may vest *inter alia* in the romantic notions held by the citizenry concerned of a social contract or in the presumed unimpeachable wisdom of the authors of the constitution (the USA comes to mind), or it may be founded upon an historic sense of the inevitability of negotiated compromise (South Africa), or it may be accepted as a prerequisite for universal recognition (Japan may be an example), and it may even be founded in

---

[5] Ackerman (1991) 8–10. Whether Ackerman's description of British democracy in the 1990s is still accurate today can be doubted, but this does not detract from its explanatory value for present purposes.

the involvement of the international community in the process of constitution-making.[6]

Noting the breathtakingly interesting discussions among political and legal philosophers like Giorgio Agamben,[7] Hans Lindahl,[8] Andrew Arato and Jean Cohen,[9] frequently contemplating the work of the likes of Carl Schmitt, Hannah Arendt, Hans Kelsen, Martin Heidegger, Jürgen Habermas, and so on on sovereignty and related notions concerned with the age-old difficulty of explaining the existence and sources of government authority, it is preferred for present purposes not to draw the details of those conversations into this exposition, other than to remark that the seemingly rising level of the debate should be seen as a sure indication of its growing topicality. To all readers of and participants in these debates it must be clear that a universal consensus is not achievable: the reason for this is that one's approach to the explanation of authority is profoundly determined by one's own ontological convictions. The current topicality of the matter nevertheless points directly at the need for the reconsideration of various constitutional axioms such as those discussed below in this chapter.

Sovereignty is conceptually integrated in the notion of statehood. It is possible to distinguish, as Vinx does,[10] between strong and weak popular sovereignty. The 'strong' concept of popular sovereignty (obviously imbued with social contract notions) locates 'the people' (or the 'nation') in the central position as the source of the original authority by which the constitution was called into existence and assumes the continued existence of the people and its constitutive power to be exclusively competent to replace the constitution. The 'weak' form of sovereignty places the emphasis on the authority of the democratically constituted structures endowed with the lawful (constitutional) power to amend or even replace the existing constitution in accordance with existing norms, thereby possibly even creating a new people or nation. One does not have to be a

---

[6] The role of international law in constitution-making processes which are undertaken under international supervision and stricture can be significant. Various historical examples like Germany and Namibia are apposite, and more recent instances seem to increase in number: see for example, Dann and Al-Ali (2006).

[7] Cf. Kistner (2009) and Johan van der Walt's response to her, Van der Walt (2009).

[8] For example, Chapter 1 in Loughlin and Walker (2007) 9–24 entitled 'Constituent Power and Reflexive Identity: Towards an Ontology of Collective Selfhood'.

[9] For example, Arato and Cohen (2009).

[10] Vinx (2013) 102–103.

positivist to consider Vinx's 'weak' version of sovereignty to be a more accurate description of the foundations of sovereignty, since the 'strong' conception is based on the erroneous idealistic fabrication of nationhood and the nation state.[11]

The political and related events that lead to the establishment of a sovereign state are crucial for an understanding of the nature of its constitutional law. How else could one explain the constitutional position of the British Crown in Canada, Australia and New Zealand, for example, or the state-managed church tax in Germany? The legal norms on which the sovereignty of a state is based (usually contained in a constitution, and enhanced by the state's status in international law) constitute the visible manifestation of sovereignty, but the impact and interpretation of those norms are almost always deeply embedded in the constitutional and political culture and history of the state concerned, and never based on any real form of a Hobbesian, Lockean or any other social contract.

Sovereign statehood in international law is usually described as the existence of conditions where, in a defined territory with a permanent population, a government has exclusive authority and the capacity to engage effectively with other states.[12] Failure to embrace the social contract theory does not preclude recognition of the exclusivity of the state's sovereignty within its territory (albeit subject to some qualifications), nor of the globalization-induced dispersal of authority for governance beyond the state. Neither constitutional law nor international law is incapable of accommodating qualifications on sovereignty, except if one insists on the personification of the imaginary constructs of peoples and nations (as distinct from populations or citizenries) as being substantive legal entities. Given the global, regional and local realities of the 21st Century, taking an extreme position on sovereignty has become indefensible.

In this regard Daniel Halberstam,[13] citing a wide range of topical authorities, analyses the differences between 'pluralists' and 'new sovereigntists'. The new sovereigntists deny that the state shares its sovereignty with global governance regimes such as the United Nations, the World Trade Organization and the International Labour Organization on the basis of subordinating international law to the authority of the state as the only legitimate source of authority. Globalists, on the other hand, award a share of governance authority to international and supra-national

---

[11] Cf. Glenn (2013) 100–101 and the authoritative writing which he cites that indicates that the nation state has always been merely an idealistic figment.
[12] Cf. for example, Beal (2012) 554–555.
[13] Halberstam (2012).

agencies, thereby qualifying the exclusivity of state sovereignty. Halberstam convincingly suggests an alternative, namely 'plural constitutionalism', which is manifested in 'partial autonomy' located respectively at the national, supra-national and international levels, an openness of the various sites of governance to one another and resorting to the values of constitutionalism (which provides 'a common grammar of legitimacy') to resolve competing claims to authority.

In his introductory chapter to a book on the future of international law Antonio Cassese states:[14]

> Another major problem is the current role of sovereignty. Although this old pillar of world society is far from waning, some traditional state prerogatives are being steadily eroded by the emerging universal values consecrated in peremptory international norms. Yet again, tensions between these two conflicting poles are not satisfactorily regulated by law. In addition, while globalization is gradually restricting state sovereignty, no legal regulatory mechanisms are replacing the void left behind as a result.

In the same book Luigi Condorelli (whose contribution was enhanced by Cassese)[15] identifies three major trends that are restraining the 'traditional sovereign prerogatives of states', viz. the spread of human rights doctrines, the effects of globalization, and increasing internal ethnic, religious or social tensions.

Eyal Benvenisti interestingly draws a picture of the contemporary responsibility of sovereigns to others.[16] Sovereigns, he says, should be understood to be 'trustees of humanity' since '[w]e live in a shrinking world where interdependence between countries and communities is increasing'. He draws a metaphorical picture that contrasts traditional notions of sovereignty as ownership of large estates with rivers and deserts as boundaries, as opposed to contemporary sovereignty represented by ownership of a small apartment in a huge high-rise building, housing many other families. The point that this picture brings home is that one sovereign inhabitant of 'our global apartment building' can no longer ignore the possibility that other stakeholders (not only other sovereigns but also foreign nationals) may be entitled to be heard when domestic decisions are taken.[17] His article reflects on the theoretical and

---

[14] Cassese (2012) xix.
[15] Condorelli (2012) 22–24.
[16] Benvenisti (2013).
[17] Benvenisti (2013) 295.

moral grounds for sovereign states to shoulder trusteeship responsibilities, and concludes with the following findings:[18]

> In an era of intense interdependency of the globe's diverse human communities, the private vision of sovereigns gives rise to three types of challenges: to the efficient and sustainable management of global resources, to equality of access to global goods and protection from global harms, and to democracy (specifically in relation to the diminishing opportunities for individuals to participate in shaping the policies that affect their lives). ... sovereigns should be regarded as trustees of humanity and therefore subjected to at least some minimal normative and procedural other-regarding obligations.

The relevance of the transformation of sovereignty for our consideration of the responsibilities of the constitutional state regarding religious pluralism is that religion, science and the economy are well-established global systems with which the state has to cope against the background that its sovereignty still tends to be primarily inward-looking.[19]

7.1.2 Citizenship

As the notion of the contemporary state emerged, particularly in the course of the 19th Century, the association of an identifiable population of individual persons with a particular state became important. From a legal perspective it can in fact be argued that the state as an entity is composed of its citizens as the collective substance of its national and international legal subjectivity. It is also possible to distinguish citizenship as a constitutional notion from nationality as one of international law. Recent decades have seen major shifts away from neat conceptual and theoretical categorizations of citizenship and nationality, however, leaving us with widely diversified applications of the terms. Nevertheless, citizenship remains a key component in the determination of the status of the individual, regarding both public privileges and obligations (for example, the franchise and compulsory service in the military) as well as a primary mechanism for identification both internally and internationally (for example, in the form of identity documents and passports). Changing

---

[18] Benvenisti (2013) 332.
[19] Teubner (2012) 72 for example, explains this by pointing out that religion, science and the economy are established as world systems, whereas politics and law continue to find their focus in the processes of the nation state.

concepts of citizenship provide us with a barometer for the assessment of the changing nature of statehood.[20]

In a remarkably compact but profoundly informative exposition of the development of citizenship over time, Patrick Glenn identifies citizenship as an invention without inherent, historically justified content, created by legislation in order to connect individuals' loyalty to a territorially defined state. He further argues that citizenship is incapable of expressing exclusive loyalty, given the realities within all states through the centuries of cultural, linguistic, religious and other forms of diversity.[21]

The continued relevance of citizenship and nationality is nevertheless graphically underscored whenever a traveller's status and authorization to enter a country is scrutinized by the immigration officials of a foreign state.[22] Migration management has become a major function of the contemporary state, and in view of the rising trend in global migration, immigration legislation and administration have become more stringent in popular migration destinations.[23] Demographic mobility is significantly increasing the diversification of state populations. Statistically the extent of migration can be expressed in terms of the number of inhabitants of a country who were not born there. Informed estimations of these statistics indicate a rapid growth of migration in this era, for example approximately 154.2 million people were migrants in 1990 (2.9 per cent of the global population), and in 2013 the estimated number of international migrants had grown to 231.5 million (3.2 per cent of the global population).[24]

---

[20] See for example, Venter (2010a) section 4.1 at 119–130.
[21] Glenn (2013) 187–193. Also Habermas (2008) 119, where he refers to personal identity being interwoven with collective linguistic, cultural and religious identities.
[22] It is also intriguing to observe the immense surge of patriotism that international sports events evoke, including the display of national symbols like flags and anthems: cf. the remarks in Venter (2010a) 119–120.
[23] See for example, Cox and Miles (2013), finding at 132 that 'it is clear that today there is an ongoing project to systematize and centralize the exercise of discretion within the immigration bureaucracy' in the United States; see also Tom (2006), who pointed out (at 462) that in 2006 immigration laws were being more strictly enforced, that new legislation was limiting immigration for employment and marriage, that police were cracking down on the hiring of and renting of housing to illegal immigrants, that asylum procedures had become harsher, and that immigrating unaccompanied minors were being disadvantaged. See also Tardif (2012).
[24] See for example, United Nations Department of Economic and Social Affairs, Population Division (2013).

The mobility of humanity, enhanced by globalization, is bringing about significant restrictions of the exclusivity of citizenship. Where dual citizenship was until not long ago seen by many states to be undesirable, it is no longer frowned upon if it is applied for duly.[25] In some contexts, of which the European Union is the prime example, citizenship has been regionalized: 'nationals' of EU member states automatically also acquire 'EU citizenship'.[26] In various other regions of the world, neighbouring countries allow citizens to move freely, or with minimal formalities, across common borders.[27]

Many contributors to scholarly literature on citizenship show a tendency to move away from reserving the concept only for the law and the state. Thus it is not unusual to encounter a variety of epithets attached to 'citizenship', such as 'equal', 'democratic', 'social' and 'multicultural' citizenship, and to read of civil society citizenship, workplace citizenship, corporate citizenship, post-national citizenship, quasi-citizenship and resident aliens with local voting rights.[28] There is even talk of 'a citizenization process in the United Nations'.[29]

As the nature of the state is steadily evolving, it is inevitable that a concept so intricately entwined in its conceptualization as citizenship should also change. It is hard to say which of these changes precedes or drives the others. That they are all subject to similar global influences is clear, however. In this regard, I have concluded elsewhere as follows:[30]

- Despite the indications that the rigidity of the status of citizenship may be dissipating, it is not citizenship as such whose survival is

---

[25] Spiro (2010) for example, opens with the following statement, which he elaborates upon in the following eight pages:

For most of modern history, dual citizenship was considered an anomaly, at best, and an abomination, at worst. It has since become a commonplace of globalization. The sequence has been from strong disfavor to toleration; indeed, some states have moved to embrace the status. Could plural citizenship now achieve the status of a right?

Also Pohlmann (2013) 59.

[26] See for example, Kochenov (2009) 171–172.

[27] The notion of 'integrated border management' has been developed by the EU and is being promoted strongly in other regions. See for example, the website of the International Organization for Migration at www.iom.int-ibm@iom.int (accessed 7 March 2014).

[28] Cf. Bosniak (2006) 1, Smith (2009) 912, and Glenn (2013) 200, who speaks of 'cosmopolitan citizenship'.

[29] Auvachez (2009).

[30] Venter (2010a) 129–130.

under pressure, but rather the established *terminology* of constitutional law as we know it.
- Citizenship, the state and national constitutional law can no longer be approached and utilized in scholarly and practical intercourse as they were a few decades ago, but to predict the demise of any of them is not only premature but also untenable: they are still indispensable and are growing in conceptual richness along with the shrinking of the spaces between jurisdictions and systems.
- As citizenship continues to be a key indicator in law of the individual's identity, it is becoming less essential and more easily acquired and disposed of by the increasingly autonomous individual, whose status as a 'subject' of the state continues to diminish in favour of the status of a 'client' of the state.
- The utility of citizenship as an indicator of the limits of the responsibilities of the state is fading in view of the growing need for and obligation of the state to provide social services to all under its jurisdiction, in addition to the provision of a protective order.

Citizenship, having become a relative identifier of members of the migrating human race, and always having been an abstract legislative artefact very seldom related to more than considerations of who the citizen's parents were and where the birth took place, cannot be understood to be a significant inhibiting factor in the process of the religious pluralization of state populations around the world. Sharing or not sharing the citizenship of a constitutional state with others has no or negligible implications for sharing religious solidarity, or for demanding recognition of lawful dissention from the prevailing religious ethos.

Citizenship is seldom dependent upon religious affiliation, but it stands to reason that civic mores that developed in a particular religious environment may come under pressure when the environment is changed in terms of the composition of the citizenry. Still being a constitutive notion of statehood, the acquisition of the citizenship of a state by significant numbers of people of 'different' origins who are adherents of 'different' religions thus becomes a serious consideration regarding the nature of the particular state and its legal regime.

7.1.3 The Need for the Doctrinal Liberation of Tired Constitutional Artefacts

Over the centuries constitutional law has (as most scholarly disciplines have) accumulated a number of idiosyncrasies generated by the influences of philosophy, political science, sociology, and so on. Many constitutional lawyers continue to operate with theoretical constructs and assumptions unquestioningly, simply because they provide the commonly used and readily available instrumentation. Some of these constitutional artefacts are so entwined in our constitutional discourse that it is almost unthinkable to replace or discard them. Thus constitutional law without the state as the key entity can obviously not be imagined, despite the existence of the many divergent views on the nature and definition of the state, its authority and its internal and external obligations. Similarly, the dominant liberal democratic approach to constitutional law inexorably operates upon certain assumptions concerning the foundations of state authority. These assumptions are often contradictory, illogical, indeterminate and founded on fictional constructs. A prime example is what Martin Loughlin and Neil Walker aptly labelled 'the paradox of constitutionalism'. They introduce the theme with a clear statement:[31] 'Modern constitutionalism is underpinned by two fundamental though antagonistic imperatives: that governmental power ultimately is generated from the "consent of the people" and that, to be sustained and effective, such power must be divided, constrained, and exercised through distinctive institutional forms.' The veracity of this statement is borne out fully by the work of the other prominent scholars contained in the collection of contributions to Loughlin and Walker's book, a reading of which leads to the conclusion that no rational resolution of the paradox is possible. The difficulty lies in the indefensibility of the hypotheses upon which the theories of power have been construed, especially the supposition that individual reason drives the acquisition by others of power over people.

Due to the broadness of its connotations, 'liberal democracy' does not indicate any single moral choice regarding the source of state authority, although some voices of liberalism tend to claim it for the cause of the supremacy of the individual. In fact its two components 'liberal' and 'democracy' can be perceived to be opposites, the first emphasizing the predominance of the free individual, the second the demand that the will of the collective majority should prevail. In her attempt 'to take liberalism back to its humanistic roots and once again bring out in the open the objectivistic values involved in the metaphysics of the positive concept of freedom', Hellsten clearly shows up the inherent duality of liberal democracy as its crisis:[32]

---

[31] Loughlin and Walker (2007), 1.
[32] Hellsten (1998) 321–322.

> By applying the concept of moral individualism I am trying to find a way to redefine the objectivistic humanistic moral foundations of Western democracy. ... I wish to emphasize that in modern liberal reasoning, too, we can find the human ideal which requires that individual citizens display an autonomous but still socially constructive moral and political will. This shows that the concept of democracy *per se*, even in its liberal definition, is not only descriptive but also contains normative and teleological elements, elements that are often forgotten in modern mechanical, procedural individualism. This is simply to state that the concept of democracy defined as the self-government of autonomous individuals clearly asserts in itself what is the good that is to be promoted within a democratic order, and that democratic process presupposes moral standards which do not derive their validity from the random preferences of atomistic individuals, but which serve as the basis for the moral evaluation of state policies.

It seems to be clear that liberal democracy, despite its perceived prevalence in contemporary constitutional discourse, offers little guidance for the making of moral choices since it purports to veer away from foundational questions regarding the sources of state authority. Historically liberal thought took refuge in fictitious social contract theories. There is some considerable irony in the fact that the originators of the social contract theory pointedly also engaged in questions relating to state and religion. A good example is the keystone work of Jean-Jacques Rousseau on the social contract, which closes with a chapter[33] on 'civil religion' in which the following (among other) telling statements appear:

> There is therefore a purely civil profession of faith of which the Sovereign should fix the articles, not exactly as religious dogmas, but as social sentiments without which a man cannot be a good citizen or a faithful subject. While it can compel no one to believe them, it can banish from the State whoever does not believe them – it can banish him, not for impiety, but as an anti-social being, incapable of truly loving the laws and justice, and of sacrificing, at need, his life to his duty. If any one, after publicly recognising these dogmas, behaves as if he does not believe them, let him be punished by death: he has committed the worst of all crimes, that of lying before the law.
>
> The dogmas of civil religion ought to be few, simple, and exactly worded, without explanation or commentary. The existence of a mighty, intelligent and beneficent Divinity, possessed of foresight and providence, the life to come, the happiness of the just, the punishment of the wicked, the sanctity of the social contract and the laws: these are its positive dogmas. Its negative dogmas I confine to one, intolerance, which is a part of the cults we have rejected.

---

[33] Rousseau (1762) Book IV, 8.

Is it not remarkable how Rousseau condemns to death those who do not embrace the 'dogmas of good citizenship' that he proposed, and then subsequently rejects intolerance? In stark contrast to Rousseau, Mirabeau, the French leader of the National Assembly, is reported[34] to have said in the constitutional debates of 1789:

> I have not come here to preach tolerance. ... In my eyes the freedom of conscience is such a holy right that the word tolerance, which is intended to signify the notion in itself appears to me to be tyrannical since the authority that has the power to tolerate is launching an attack on the freedom of thought exactly by tolerating, while it is at the same time capable of not tolerating.

Social contract theories have now lost their persuasive force. Loughlin and Walker, as editors of an insightful book in which 'the paradox of constitutionalism' is addressed,[35] make this clear in their introduction:[36]

> We might note that many of the great works of political philosophy from Hobbes to Rawls seek to identify the essential nature of collective authority and of the realm of the political by reference to the idea of a social contract. This device is widely used not only because it provides a mechanism that is able to 'account for' how the constitution of a state is founded, but also because it offers a device through which the claims of autonomy and authority associated with that founding may be reconciled. But let us be clear on one thing: the social contract is such a potent and versatile tool of political philosophy precisely because it is treated as being entirely an exercise of the imagination.

And further:[37]

---

[34] Cited in its German translation by Von Mangoldt, Klein and Stark (2010) 451, here freely translated by the author from the German.

[35] Loughlin and Walker (2007). They open (at 1) their introduction by describing the paradox as follows:

> Modern constitutionalism is underpinned by two fundamental though antagonistic imperatives: that governmental power ultimately is generated from the 'consent of the people' and that, to be sustained and effective, such power must be divided, constrained, and exercised through distinctive institutional forms. The people, in Maistre's words, 'are a sovereign that cannot exercise sovereignty'; the power they possess, it would appear, can only be exercised through constitutional forms already established or in the process of being established.

[36] Loughlin and Walker (2007) 2.
[37] Loughlin and Walker (2007) 4.

constitutions can be operationlized and compromised in ways that owe no consistent fidelity to the original compact, or which offer entirely new interpretations of the status and content of that original compact. It is in coming to terms with these realities of power in modern societies that constituent power insinuates itself into the discourse of constitutionalism, whether in the form of oppositional politics in their various guises and the (counter)constitutional visions they implicitly or explicitly espouse or, more generally, by ensuring that the intrinsic tension between the abstract rationalities of constitutional design and the quotidian rationalities of governing remains exposed.

It seems to be incongruous that, now that the world has generally come to adopt the same or similar constitutional vocabulary, the realization is also dawning upon us that many of our age-old constitutional artefacts need to be re-examined for their validity. Suffice it here to mention a few of these artefacts (without the intention of proposing cogent alternatives, since that would divert us too far from the present discussion): the social contract, constitution-writing through the exercise of the *pouvoir constituant* by a constituent assembly, and the counter-majoritarian dilemma linked to democracy.

The absence of concrete meaning attached to conceptions of this nature, and the change or relativization of others, raise the difficulty that one can no longer assume that employing them will ensure that one's real intentions will be understood. As discussed above, among these are sovereignty and citizenship. Under the influence of developments brought about by globalization, a terminological and conceptual tipping point may lie not too far in the future, where it may become unavoidable to recognize that established constitutional doctrine has become too vague to serve the needs of the 21st Century. When this happens, will constitutional lawyers, political scientists and constitution-makers be ready to produce alternatives? Let us briefly examine the nature of this problem in connection with the social contract, the *pouvoir constituant*, and the counter-majoritarian dilemma.

7.1.3.1 The social contract

Essentially the social contract theory served and continues to serve as the primary explanation or justification of the existence of coercive government authority. The theory probably represents the most influential historical foundation for the development of liberal democracy, and is still a cornerstone of modern and contemporary thinking about the state, the law and government. It is nevertheless merely a fictional construct originally founded upon John Hobbes' cynical view of human self-centredness balanced by rationality as the key factors in collectively granting a third party (the sovereign or a body of rulers) the imperative power to maintain the peace. John Locke's view of a meeker, essentially good humanity, morally entitled to defend its property even if it involves overthrowing a tyrannical government, allowed for an equally fictitious social contract entailing the voluntary transfer of power and subjection to the majority will. Jean-Jacques Rousseau, observant of the inequality of wealth in society, was strongly concerned with social class and the ideal of confirming the equality of all by means of equal access to civil decision-making in a system of (impracticable) direct democracy. Common to these 'classic' social contract theories is the construction of a 'state of nature' from which human society had to escape by common agreement in order to establish authoritative government structures.

The reality of constitutions and constitutional government in the 21st Century is far removed from any real or imagined state of nature or from any fictitious or real social contract. In fact, it would seem that the 'contracting citizens' are steadily losing interest in the democratic process,[38] while entities within the global community are increasing their involvement in the exercise of authority to the level of the individual regardless of the national institutions whereby government authority is allocated within the state. While recently arguing for a 'counterfactual' legitimization of nation state liberal constitutionalism, Michel Rosenfeld conceded that:[39]

> [F]actual legitimacy is impossible not only because of the temporal dimension of multi-generational constitutions, but also because of inevitable shortfalls regarding democracy. The social contract requires the unanimous consensus of all those bound by it, and no actual constitution-making or ratifying could possibly be unanimous or account for all relevant differences while maintaining a coincidence or full continuity between the constituent power (*pouvoir constituant*) and the constituted power (*pouvoir constitué*).

These considerations relegate the social contract theory to the status of a fairy tale involving medieval princes and master-archers wearing green tights. If it is to continue its presence in constitutional theory, it is in dire need of reconstruction. This is a task at least as difficult as the renovation of an ancient structure that was built on weak foundations. Patrick Glenn attaches words such as 'implausible' and 'otiose' to the notion and

---

[38] According to Ellis *et al.* (2006) 11, voter participation has declined worldwide from an average of 74.4 per cent in 1945 to 66.5 per cent in 2006.
[39] Rosenfeld (2014) 182.

reminds us that Immanuel Kant regarded it as 'an idea of reason', divested of all historical reality.[40]

7.1.3.2 The exercise of the *pouvoir constituant* by a constituent assembly

The priest-philosopher Sieyès claimed to have been the inventor of the expressions *pouvoir constituant* and *pouvoir constitué*.[41]

The idea of a constitution-making authority flows from the concept of the sovereignty of the nation in which the authority is assumed to vest. An institution that establishes a new state as the expression of the 'will of the nation', or which pushes the constitutionally established authority aside and replaces it, cannot, according to this approach, be conceptually bound by a constitutional framework.

Reality, however, consistently presents a challenge to the viability of the theory: for instance, a constituent assembly cannot be composed of all belonging to a nation, a large representative constitution-writing assembly cannot function without more compact expert or discussion groups, and the electorate is sometimes required merely to express a majority opinion by means of a referendum or a plebiscite regarding the acceptability of the constitution produced by a constituent assembly.[42] Nevertheless the notion of 'we the people' lives on, more often than not as a tool in the hands of politicians seeking popular power by persuading the multitudes that they have their interests at heart.

The preamble of the German *Grundgesetz* contains the phrase '*hat sich das Deutsche Volk kraft seiner verfassungsgebenden Gewalt dieses Grundgesetz gegeben*' (by virtue of its constituent power the German nation has given this Basic Law to itself). The text was formulated and adopted by the *Parlamentarischer Rat* in 1948 and 1949 in less than eight months, whereafter it was approved by the three military governors appointed by the Allies and submitted to the various *Landtage*, where it was also approved. After the holding of elections, new federal organs were constituted. Regarding the nature of this process it may be asked if the *Parlamentarischer Rat* did exercise the *pouvoir constituant* and, if so, how it could be bound by the instructions of the Allied Powers,[43] and how the preamble could state that the German nation gave itself the constitution in terms of its constituent authority?

---

[40] Glenn (2013) 133–134.
[41] Cf. Berber (1973) 292–293.
[42] Cf. Isensee and Kirchhof (1987) 781–783 and 890–891 and also Von Beyme (1968).
[43] Herzog (1987) 1204–1212 and Doehring (1984) 55–61.

In South Africa it may be said that CODESA,[44] the Multi-party Negotiating Process in which a constitution was negotiated in 1993, and the Parliament that adopted the negotiated document jointly exercised the *pouvoir constituant*. At the moment of the coming into effect of the new Constitution in 1994 it had elevated itself in terms of its own section 4 to the 'supreme law of the Republic'.[45] An appropriate description of this process might be 'constitutional bootstrapping'.[46] This was not, however, the end of the South African constitution-writing process, because the 1993 Constitution provided that a new constitutional text had to replace it within a few years. However, the content of the subsequent Constitution had been pre-programmed by the 1993 Constitution, which provided for the procedures and structures to be utilized in future constitution-writing, and Schedule 4, which prescribed in 34 detailed 'Constitutional Principles' the requirements that had to be satisfied by the next constitutional text. Under these circumstances, even assuming the defensibility of the notion of a 'South African nation', the question may be raised whether the existence of its sovereignty was relevant at all. And yet it would be frivolous to argue that the Constitution of 1996 was not legitimately adopted.

7.1.3.3 The counter-majoritarian dilemma and democracy

Under the rubric 'the counter-majoritarian difficulty/dilemma' much has been written on the simplistic assertion that it is democratically outrageous for a bench of unelected constitutional judges to destroy the work of a large, democratically elected legislative body by declaring a statute to be null and void on the grounds that it is inconsistent with the provisions of a constitution. This point of view is obviously premised on the notion of popular sovereignty, which implies that the will of the people is expressed through the ballot, whereby those elected represent the sovereign people who should not be countermanded.

---

[44] The *Convention for a Democratic South Africa* established in 1991.

[45] Section 4 of the *Constitution of the Republic of South Africa* 200 of 1993 provided as follows:

(1) This Constitution shall be the supreme law of the Republic and any law or act inconsistent with its provisions shall, unless otherwise provided expressly or by necessary implication in this Constitution, be of no force and effect to the extent of the inconsistency.

(2) This Constitution shall bind all legislative, executive and judicial organs of state at all levels of government.

[46] Cf. the remarks in this regard of Kriegler J in *Du Plessis v De Klerk* 1996 3 SA 850 (CC) para. [128].

Various difficulties attend this construction, which is solidly rooted in the history of the constitutional theory of Western civilization. The difficulties arise from the fact that constitutional reality has evolved significantly since the times when absolutism, monarchy, popular ignorance and church–state competition for power characterized the emergence of 'civilized' society. Stating that contemporary electoral democracy in whatever form is an ineffective means of giving expression to the popular will hardly requires justification. This is not to say that any better means of composing bodies and identifying individuals upon whom the authority of the state may be conferred has as yet been devised – the difficulty lies in the construction that other instruments of the constitutional state, such as the judiciary, that perform specialized and professional functions should be seen as inferior to the work of a large body of career politicians owing their positions to their ability to manipulate popular or partisan opinion in their favour at the time of their election.

On the other hand, asking if a constitutional judgment is representative of the popular will is simply asking the wrong question. Judicial decisions, be they of a constitutional nature or otherwise, are founded upon expert interpretation and application of the law. This unavoidably (and significantly) implies a measure of judicial discretion and subjective understanding, but the justificatory framework within which the decisions are taken is infinitely more discernable and predictable than the justifications with which politicians, ostensibly representing the electorate, serve themselves. A very civilized distinction is made in this regard by Jörn Ipsen.[47] Politics, he says kindly, may be understood as the free structuring of society within the context of the law, and it is therefore purpose-driven and normatively limited. Adjudication, on the other hand, is normatively determined in the first place and therefore founds its legitimacy on completely different grounds. The political decision wants to be the right one, that is, successful, determining the future; the legal decision, however, aims at being equitable, that is, in accordance with the law.

---

[47] Ipsen (2007) 277:

Politik ist freie Sozialgestaltung im Rahmen des Rechts, also *zweckgerichtet* und *normbegrenzt*. Rechtsentscheidungen sind hingegen in erste Linie normbestimmt, weisen also ganz andere Legitimationsgrundlagen auf. Die politische Entscheidung will richtig, d.h. erfolgreich, zukunftsweisend sein; die Rechtsentscheidung dagegen beansprucht, *gerecht* zu sein, d.h. mit dem Recht übereinzustimmen.

The challenge faced by the judiciary in constitutional cases is to distinguish between the application and development of the constitution on the one hand and subjective social engineering on the other: the concern here should not be counter-majoritarianism but judicial proficiency and ethics. Constitutional review is justified by the need in the contemporary world of established and new states, many of which are newcomers to constitutionalism, to qualify blind popular majoritarianism with reasonable and justificatory judicial argument.

7.1.3.4 The need for innovation

In summary, regarding the need for doctrinal liberation, many of the ensconced but irrational constitutional artefacts have lost their defensibility and utility for the local and global conversation over constitutional law. Considering the tattered and superannuated state of the constitutional terminology and doctrinal conceptions inherited from the past, it would seem to be clear that there is a need for innovative constitution-making (as opposed to constitution-writing) in the course of which guidelines gleaned comparatively from around the globe and from diverse concepts of constitutionalism may be employed. Judged from the ballooning volume and range of comparative constitutional literature that is being published, and the innovative theorizing contained in recent literature, no campaign is required to achieve innovation. The challenge is rather to find sufficient common terminological and theoretical ground to allow for a fruitful constitutional conversation while taking the effects of globalization into account.

7.2 RESPONSES TO MIGRATION

José Casanova, renowned scholar in the sociology of religion, provided an insightful overview of the contemporary trends in religion, secularism and multiculturalism in an essay published in 2009. In his contribution, which builds upon much broader research, he made a number of salient points useful in one's attempts at understanding the current state of affairs concerning constitutionalism and religion in the historically most established and therefore generally leading constitutional states of this era, those in the European Union and the United States.

Casanova points out[48] that whereas North America was a destination for emigration from Western Europe in past centuries, the United States

---

[48] Casanova (2009) 139–140.

and Europe have become prime destinations for emigrants since the 1960s, in the case of the United States, mainly from the Americas and Asia, and in the case of the core Western European countries first from Southern European countries and later from former colonies in Africa and the East, as well as from Eastern Europe. Whereas the United States has long had a self-understanding as an immigrant society, Western Europeans continue to perceive even permanent immigrants and their offspring not to be Europeans:[49]

> One of the most significant consequences of the new immigration has been a dramatic growth in religious diversity on both sides of the Atlantic. But while in the United States the new immigrant religions have mainly contributed to the further expansion of an already vibrant American religious pluralism, in the case of Europe, immigrant religions present a greater challenge to local patterns of limited religious pluralism and, even more importantly, to recent European trends of drastic secularisation.

The diverse previous approaches of Western European states to dealing with religion, French *laïcité*, British decentralization, German 'multi-establishment' and Dutch 'pillarization', tend to be perpetuated regarding immigrant religions, among which Islam is the most prominent. In contrast to the United States, where Muslims form a minor component of the immigrant population, in Western Europe the 'immigrant, the religious, the racial and the socioeconomically disprivileged Other all tend to coincide'.[50]

European secularization inclines to the privatization of religion, thus promoting dissociation from established churches ('believing without belonging'), but nevertheless Europeans continue to a significant extent to understand themselves as having a Christian cultural identity.[51] This provides the probable explanation for the European response to Islam ('an essentially un-European religion') and the expansion of the European Union. Europe is:[52]

> deeply divided over its cultural identity, unable to answer the question whether European unity, and therefore its external and internal boundaries, should be defined by the common heritage of Christianity and western

---

[49] Casanova (2009) 140–141.
[50] Casanova (2009) 142.
[51] See for example, the manner in which religious dress was dealt with by the Bavarian Constitutional Court discussed in section 6.4.2 in Chapter 6 above.
[52] Casanova (2009) 144–145.

civilisation or by its modern, secular values of liberalism, universal human rights, political democracy, and tolerant and inclusive multiculturalism.

Extremist and racist reactions apart, European liberal secularity purports to welcome diversity, but then on condition of everyone accepting secular standards such as the rejection of gender discrimination expressed in religious dress and symbols. In secular Europe the liberal view does not counterpose Christianity with Islam, but liberal secularism with conservative, pervasive Muslim religiosity:[53]

> What makes the intolerant tyranny of the secular, liberal majority justifiable in principle is not just the democratic principle of majority rule, but rather the secularist teleological assumption built into theories of modernisation that one set of norms is reactionary, fundamentalist and anti-modern, while the other set is progressive, liberal and modern.

Casanova reveals the essential nature of the problem of dealing with religious pluralism in Europe, and by analogy in many other parts of the world where constitutionalism is professed:[54]

> European societies tend to tolerate and respect individual religious freedom. But owing to the pressure towards the privatisation of religion, which among European societies has become a taken-for-granted characteristic of the self-definition of a modern, secular society, those societies have a much greater difficulty in recognising some legitimate role for religion in public life and in the organisation and mobilisation of collective group identities.

The United States, by definition the diversified immigrant country, has an established culture of plural religiosity and can therefore probably be described as the most religious country among present constitutional states. Immigrants therefore tend to grow in their religious engagement as part of the American way of life: 'Americans think that they are supposed to be religious, while Europeans think that they are supposed to be irreligious.'[55] The First Amendment protection of the state from religion and of religion against the state brought about 'a relatively free, pluralistic and voluntaristic religious market', distinguishing the American political community from the diverse denominational community, denominationalism being a 'great American religious invention'.[56]

---

[53] Casanova (2009) 147.
[54] Casanova (2009) 148.
[55] Casanova (2009) 150.
[56] Casanova (2009) 151–152.

No doubt Casanova's description of the respective European and American social responses to religious pluralism is accurate but, as we have seen in previous chapters, secularism and the concomitant privatization of religion is the common legal response in both contexts. Eric Tardif confirms this by concluding that the entire debate concerning the accommodation of religious pluralism in Western countries is founded on 'an irrefutable premise':[57] 'While in Western societies, religion is mostly a private matter, many immigrant communities consider the sheer idea of separating the private from the public dimensions of religion as a non-sense.'

7.3 SECULARISM AS THE 'NATURAL' RESPONSE

In the preceding chapters the notion of secularism (and derivatives such as 'secularity', 'secularization', etc.) was encountered repeatedly, and although reference to the meaning of 'secular' in different contexts was made in some cases, it is necessary here to seek more conceptual clarity on the matter.

The Canadian philosopher Charles Taylor opens his compact but analytically powerful foreword to Levey and Modood with the statement that '[i]t is generally agreed that modern democracies have to be "secular"' – and immediately goes on to speak of confusion over the 'multiple meanings of the term'.[58] Taylor discerns two different models of a secular regime, both involving 'some kind of separation of church and state'. The first model relies on timeless principles construed by the application of reason alone. These principles are, according to Taylor,[59]

- 'no one must be forced in the domain of religion, or basic belief' (liberty);
- 'no religious outlook or (religious or areligious) *Weltanschauung* can enjoy privileged status' (equality);
- 'all spiritual families should be heard' (fraternity); and
- as far as possible, 'relations of harmony and comity between the supporters of different religions and *Weltanschauungen*' must be maintained.

---

[57] Tardif (2012) 101.
[58] Taylor (2009) xi–xxii, xi.
[59] Taylor (2009) xii.

The second model that Taylor construes is one that depends on democratic negotiation: '[t]he actual principles are what we can come to agree on, as something we can all justify from our own point of view'.[60] Such agreement does not, according to Taylor, make the agreed principles 'right', but the desire for the 'fraternity' of all relevant groups (that all of them be heard) is satisfied thereby.

Taylor pinpoints[61] the roots of the notion of secularity as a product of Latin Christendom, where it emerged as a means of distinguishing between profane time and 'higher' time (eternity). This coincided with the dichotomy between the spiritual and the temporal, the church occupying the first and the state the second. Following the Reformation various functions, properties and institutions were transferred out of the control of the church to that of 'laymen' – a process of 'secularisation'. Taylor then succinctly summarizes the conceptual changes flowing from this distinction from the 17th Century on:[62]

> A new conception of social life came gradually to be defined, in which the 'secular' was all there was. Since 'secular' originally applied to a kind of time – profane or ordinary time, seen in relation to higher times – what was necessary was to come to understand profane time as all there is: to deny any relation to higher time. The word could go on being used, but the meaning was profoundly changed, because what it contrasted with was quite altered. The contrast was not another time-dimension, in which 'spiritual' institutions found their niche; rather the secular was in the new sense defined over and against claims on resources or allegiance made in the name of something transcendent to this world and its interests. Needless to say, those who imagined a 'secular' world in this sense saw these claims as ultimately unfounded, and only to be tolerated to the extent that they didn't challenge the interests of wordly power and well-being.

The (still dominant) Western thinking therefore ended up with the distinction between what is real, of 'this world', the immanent as the primary and exclusive consideration, and that which is irrelevant to the state and the law, the transcendent, those religious inventions in which individuals may be free to indulge, but strictly in a manner that does not interfere with what is real, which is the secular: in this concept

---

[60] Taylor (2009) xvi.
[61] Taylor (2009) xvii–xx.
[62] Taylor (2009) xviii.

of the world, the secular is real, the religious is false; secular reality is necessary, religion is superfluous.[63]

Against this background the positions taken on secularism by others can better be understood. Secular neutrality is closely and mainly associated with liberalism. Ironically, liberal notions of the state owe their emergence to religion, more particularly to the attitudes regarding the toleration of religious diversity, including a-religiosity, that took root following the Protestant Reformation in the 16th Century.[64]

Growing religious and legal pluralism[65] within states is challenging legal orders increasingly. Previously, as Pamela Slotte[66] also indicates, the coexistence of adherents to different religions in Europe was not complicated and high-profile cases involving freedom of religion were rare, but now the 'religious landscape' is changing and 'established notions of faith and society are being tested'.

A broad classification of constitutional approaches to religious pluralism may be drawn, following Adams,[67] who usefully distinguishes between active and passive pluralism: active pluralism indicates an approach that acknowledges, not merely tolerates, the convictions of the believer, as opposed to passive pluralism which occurs in a state that reduces religion to a private affair. Passive pluralism is an approach typically advanced by contemporary liberal secularists as represented for instance by Stefan Huster and Denise Meyerson,[68] following in the footsteps of John Rawls.[69]

Huster states the case of liberal secularism as follows:[70] it is an essential characteristic of modern political orders that they are, both in their existence and in their specific actions, principally bound to justify and explain themselves to everyone. Their legitimacy is based upon this, not on an appeal to the will of God, to the nature of a pre-existing society or to tradition. Political measures, regulations and institutions cannot be justified by such considerations, but only by the approval of those

---

[63] Taylor (2009) xx. He also points out – xix *et seq* – how different this Western notion is from what applies elsewhere on the globe, where neither Islam nor other religious systems had gone through the secularizing processes to which Latin Christendom was exposed.
[64] For example, Levey (2009) 4–5.
[65] For example, Davies (2008).
[66] Slotte (2010) 264.
[67] Adams (2009) 13–14.
[68] Meyerson (2009).
[69] Meyerson principally cites Rawls (1993) and Rawls (1997).
[70] Huster (2002) 85 and 633–634.

concerned. This, he says, represents the basic idea of the theoretical legitimation of the individualism of the construction of the social contract from Hobbes to Rawls. To enable the state to respect its citizens' claim to equal respect, it must relinquish all particular religious philosophical (*religiös-weltanschauliche*) and ethical justifications for its actions.

A (telling) American rendering of this position is provided by Kent Greenawalt:[71]

> Influenced by the writings of John Rawls, political philosophers have debated whether political decisions in liberal democracies should be based on public reasons, reasons accessible in the right way to all citizens. It is generally assumed that reasons grounded in religious premises fall outside the domain of public reasons. If citizens and officials improperly rely heavily on religious premises in advocating and adopting laws, we could think of that as a misguided 'establishment' of religion, although not one necessarily covered by the Establishment Clause.

Adams maintains that the notion of the separation of church and state is inappropriate, since the state can hardly have nothing to do with religious institutions. In some states (surprisingly, as we have seen in the preceding chapters, for example in the laic France and Belgium) the state is active in the religious domain through actions such as the subvention of clerics out of public funds, whereas others do their best to keep religion out of the public domain.[72] Adams usefully analysed the liberalist approach[73] with reference to Meyerson's 'three principles of public morality',[74] namely that:

- the government should not act on religious purposes;
- it should not assist religious groups to spread their religious beliefs; and
- arguments based solely on religious convictions should not be offered as reasons for laws and public policies.

In his critique of Meyerson's defence of the Rawlsean notion that the state should be governed in accordance with an overlapping consensus on what is good which is not dependent on arguments based on any religious convictions, Adams makes the following sound point:[75] judgement of

---

[71] Greenawalt (2009) 2392.
[72] Adams (2009) 7–11.
[73] Adams (2009) 14–17.
[74] Meyerson (2009) *passim*.
[75] Adams (2009) 22.

what is good is by definition made from a personal perspective on the good. If that were not the case, one would have had nothing on which to base one's judgement. Liberalism's ambition to relegate religion to a private affair from which the state should withdraw fully thus flounders in its own logic.

Ian Hunter also considers liberal theory on sovereignty, democracy and secularism to suffer from 'philosophical shallowness':[76]

> In the rationales that the proto-liberals elaborated for political authority, sovereignty cannot be popular, because it is uncoupled from the expression of a common moral will – whether God's, the people's or reason's – and is tied instead to the achievement of a particular end, civil peace, for which the state is brought into existence.

This is not an unknown problem among liberal thinkers. Sirkku Hellsten has for example argued for 'moral individualism' to counter the 'degeneration of modern welfare liberal democracy'. Such moral liberalism should according to her be constructed upon the 'actualization' of human dignity which implies self-restraint and 'human universality'.[77] The problem of the liberal state, according to Hellsten, lies in the fact that where sectional values in a plural society clash, or are in conflict with the liberal ethos itself, neutrality is incapable of providing an overarching measure according to which such conflicts may be mediated and resolved.[78]

Beyond liberalism's attempts to lift itself by its own bootstraps, a more generalized explanation for the shallowness of liberal philosophy was provided by the Dutch legal philosopher Herman Dooyeweerd:[79]

> Philosophy is theoretical, and in its constitution it remains bound to the relativity of all human thought. As such, philosophy itself needs an absolute starting point. It derives this exclusively from religion. Religion grants stability and anchorage even to theoretical thought. Those who think they find an absolute starting point in theoretical thought itself come to this belief through an essentially religious drive. Because of a lack of true self-knowledge, however, they remain oblivious to their own religious motivation.

By its own confession, liberal thinking is devoid of an 'absolute starting point': its banning of religion from the public domain renders it bland,

---

[76] Hunter (2009) 54.
[77] Hellsten (1998) 344.
[78] Hellsten (1998) 329.
[79] Dooyeweerd (2012) 8.

bloodless, requiring all, including the state, to be neutral. Australian legal philosopher John Finnis captures it neatly where he refers to 'The Philosophers' Brief' on assisted suicide, authored as *amici curiae* to the US Supreme Court in 1997 by six 'moral philosophers', including Ronald Dworkin and John Rawls:[80]

> Of course, a group of philosophers such as these brief-writers ... will deny that they are advancing an emotivist, subjectivist, perspectivalist, or any other meta-ethical scepticism. They will say that their claim about neutrality is purely about political rights and the proper competence of the state's rulers, and the value or dignity of individual autonomy. And so, on its face, it is. But the weakness of all the arguments which these philosophers have put forward to justify their claim about individual rights and state competence is good reason to conclude that their position's real foundation is the concern to be 'let alone' to *do what one really feels like*.

The 'secularization' of the state is indeed routinely presented by many as merely indicating the historical withdrawal of ecclesiastical domination over the state.[81] The origins and application of the term are, however, not so readily sanitized. John Finnis, for example, points out,[82] as Taylor does,[83] that 'secular' is a word minted by Latin Christians as a translation for Greek words 'signifying the affairs of this world, sometimes neutrally the world of time rather than eternity, and the daily life of any human society, sometimes pejoratively as matters which distract us from realities and dispositions of lasting worth'. Aquinas used the term to point out a distinction of competencies between the political and ecclesiastical authorities. Finnis takes the position[84] that secularism induces 'the withering away of reverence for God' and (following Maritain) that it is 'a kind of deficiency detectable to a greater or lesser degree in every human soul'.

Secularization bears the connotation that religious conviction has no role to play in public affairs, while non-religious considerations must steer the conduct of the state and its organs, as though only religion

---

[80] Finnis (1997–1998) 507.
[81] Cf. for example, Böckenförde (1967) 76 n. 5.
[82] Finnis (1997–1998) 491–493.
[83] Taylor (2009) xvii–xx.
[84] This he does with reference to the modern parallel to Plato's distinction between the propositions: there is no God; no God has any concern with human affairs; or that any divine concern with the human is easily appeased by a superficial piety not requiring human reform, viz. atheism; a deistic assumption that human history knows no divine intervention; and a 'liberal' religiosity unconcerned with immorality. Finnis (1997–1998) at 493.

engenders prejudice and only rational decision-making guarantees justice. Being 'secular' is far from being neutral, however, and scarcely conducive to being objective. It is therefore unavoidable that secularism, properly understood, itself essentially expresses a religious stance. Not surprisingly, for those not subscribing to secularism, the notion bears a negative meaning.[85]

Bill Marshall identifies three limits to the secular ideal in the United States: first its 'unavoidable internal inconsistencies', which lie in the fact that secularism is itself 'not completely secular' since, in an allegedly secular state it amounts to a 'competing faith system';[86] secondly its clash with the demand of equality due to its failure to be neutral between religion and non-religion, for example secular support by the state of a range of institutions or interests except those that are religious, obviously amounts to unequal, and therefore discriminatory, treatment;[87] and thirdly its clash (in the US) with 'a public culture that is replete with religious symbols, names, and references'.[88]

Regarding the role of religion in public life, secularism is quite evidently losing its pre-eminence. As De Been and Taekema[89] put it: '[T]he secular nature of liberal democracy is losing its artless, self-evident quality. Secularism is coming under increased scrutiny.'

7.4 THE RETURN OF RELIGION

There is much evidence that global society is experiencing a renewed prominence of religion in the public discourse. Anders Berg-Sørensen opened his introduction to a collection of comparative contributions on the state of secularism with the following statement:[90] 'The start of the twenty-first century has witnessed a growing awareness that modern societies are not becoming straightforwardly secular and that religion is playing a significant and ever-changing role in public life.' Rajeev Bhargava points out that secularism is not being contested only by religious groupings in Western societies, but by almost everyone in non-Western societies.[91] According to De Been and Taekema:[92] '[E]ven

---

[85] Cf. also Henrard (2001) 54.
[86] Marshall (2009) 235–236.
[87] Marshall (2009) 236–237.
[88] Marshall (2009) 237–238.
[89] De Been and Taekema (2012) 1.
[90] Berg-Sørensen (2013) 1.
[91] Bhargava (2013) 17.

the devoutly secular theorist Jürgen Habermas has retreated from his previous secularism, and has started talking about the rise of the "post-secular" society, that needs to adjust to the enduring presence of religion, even under conditions of continuing modernisation.'

The German weekly news magazine *Der Spiegel*, known for its investigative journalism, published a comprehensive overview of the growing influence of the major world religions on culture, politics and social values in 2006 in its series *Spiegel Special*.[93] In the opening article to this edition, Rainer Traub makes the point that the expectation that the triumphal ascendency of modernity would inevitably cause religion to lose its significance has been shattered. He wrote[94] (freely translated): 'At the beginning of the 21st Century religion appears as a capricious, chameleon-like world power – a development that was inconceivable only a generation ago in the public opinion and for the leading social scientists of the Western world.'

Some of the causes behind the recognition of the phenomenon that religion is being re-established as a social force to be reckoned with in matters of state are obvious, others less so.

Some of the obvious causes concern the reality of the raised levels of religious, cultural and technological interwovenness, most especially of historically Christian populations and Muslims. Although Christians and Muslims have a long and even bloody history of conflict and competition associated with the dominance of territory and symbolic places, reciprocal influences are currently pronounced: whereas a significant component of the population and even the citizenry of Western Europe are now adherents of the Islamic faith, the Arabic and Eastern nations that are traditionally Islamic are relentlessly exposed to American and European culture and technology (for example, social media played an important role in the 'Arab Spring' and American links with the Egyptian military are well known).

The crusades of the middle ages lie far back in history, but European colonialism in Muslim countries is relatively recent: France in the Maghreb, Syria and Lebanon; Britain in Egypt, Palestine, Iraq, India and Malaysia; Italy in Libya; Spain in Morocco and Mauretania; and the Netherlands in Indonesia.

Violence seems to characterize the relationship between Christians and Muslims, not only historically but also currently, of which the destruction

---

[92] De Been and Taekema (2012) 2.
[93] The series provides in-depth expositions (richly enhanced with photographs and graphics) of facts and analyses of specific themes.
[94] Traub (2006) 8.

of the World Trade Center in New York on '9/11' and the subsequent declaration of the 'war on terrorism' are prominent examples, despite the rejection of terrorism by moderate Muslims. Other violent incidents relate not only to fundamentalist actions but result also from incidents such as the publication of insulting caricatures and policy decisions regarding religious garb.[95]

Various other phenomena may be understood to have had and continue to have an invigorating influence on the renewed awareness of the significance of religion in public affairs. The fall of communism in the USSR and the rise of capitalism in China have opened or reopened the potential of especially Christian religion to expand among millions of people in many parts of the world.[96] Furthermore, the increased accessibility of global travel has for obvious reasons brought about intensified contact between divergent religions at all levels of social life. Add to this the awe regarding its own powers that humanity has to assimilate in the process of the unceasing discovery and implementation of technological and scientific wonders that seem to follow one another with increased frequency.[97]

Traub closes his article in *Spiegel Special* with reference to the public dialogue on reason and religion in München in January 2004 between Joseph Cardinal Ratzinger (who became Pope Benedict XVI little more than a year later) and Jürgen Habermas, from which he concludes that belief, reason and doubt will continue to have to get along.[98] These forceful contributions from essentially opposing positions were published and also translated into English.[99] The degree of congruence in the papers of the two discussants surprised many.

The views of Habermas, who popularized the concept of the 'postsecular age', are notable for our present purposes not only because he is an influential thinker and masterful writer in the liberal mode both in Europe and the United States, but more particularly because the gradual shift in his thinking about religion coincides with the phenomenon of the return of religion to the public agenda. In his work he has sought to infuse credible ethics and morality into liberalism. In the 1970s and 1980s he pointed out the value of religion as a means for rescuing 'the substance of the human'. A decade later he emphasized the need for reflection on the religious in order to gain an understanding of the history

---

[95] See for example, Krämer (2006).
[96] See for example, Phillips (2014).
[97] According to Schilling (2013).
[98] Traub (2006) 15.
[99] Schuller (2006).

of ideas and also stressed as a given that in contrast to philosophy, religions contain semantic elements crucial to a just social order.

More recently, since 2001, Habermas has propounded the position that the secularization hypothesis can no longer explain social reality and that, although faith and knowledge constantly stand in opposition to one another, religion represents a valuable moral resource.[100] In 2005 he published his book *Zwischen Naturalismus und Religion*, in which his ideas about religion and its contemporary place were brought together. Towards the end of his chapter on the equal treatment of cultures and the limits of postmodern liberalism, he offers the following insight:[101]

> If we conceive of the modernization of public consciousness in Europe as a learning process that affects and changes religious and secular mentalities alike by forcing the tradition of the Enlightenment, as well as religious doctrines, to reflect on their respective limits, then the international tensions between major cultures and world religions also appear in a different light. The globalization of markets, the media, and other networks no longer leaves nations any realistic prospect of opting out of capitalist modernization. Neither can non-Western cultures evade the challenges of secularization and a pluralism of worldviews generated by an inadequately regulated process of modernization that they also actively pursue.

These understandings of where states find themselves in the globalized world of the early 21st Century – powerfully shaped by liberal constitutionalism, but confronted with the inadequacies of the concomitant ideas of secularism when dealing with a resurgent wave of religiosity – may prove to be useful for the development of solutions to problems that may otherwise continue to be perplexing dilemmas.

---

[100] Cf. the excellent synopsis of Habermas' work by Reder and Schmidt (2010) 3–7.
[101] Habermas (2008) 310.

8. The demands of constitutionalism regarding religion

As can be seen from the previous chapters, the 'secular' reaction is widely considered to be an appropriate response to the difficulties facing the state, religious communities and individuals, caused by the growing religious pluralism of the citizens and denizens of many countries around the globe. Pamela Slotte for example identifies 'the principle of secularism' as a duty of states, groups and individuals in European human rights law.[1]

Jeroen Temperman presents an argued apologia for 'religiously neutral governance'. He casts the secular 'solution' in the form of everyone's right that the state should be prohibited by law (constitutional and international) from discriminating directly or indirectly on grounds of religion or belief.[2] However, Temperman's impressive comparative study of the manner in which states across the globe deal in theory and practice with religion and related matters shows how deeply intermingled law and religion are and the extent to which historical and contemporary predilections will have to be overcome if religious neutrality is to be achieved in governance. In fact, religious neutrality appears to be beyond the reach of humanity, and where it is propounded it does not produce the desired results. Nevertheless Temperman concludes:[3]

> [I]f we do allow a role for religion to be played within the political discourse we must make sure that constitutional safeguards are in place to prevent human rights abuses. In the latter respect, it has been submitted that the combined principles of state neutrality and non-establishmentarianism allow for a political discourse in which religion can play a role but these maxims, at the same time, regulate that role by identifying certain boundaries that may not be crossed.

From the examples described in Chapter 6 it indeed appears that neutrality does not provide a consistent balance between the state's

---

[1] Slotte (2010) 255–259.
[2] Temperman (2010a) *passim*, but see especially Chapter 8 at 171–201.
[3] Temperman (2010a) 348.

responsibility for maintaining social order, religious preferences and legal certainty. On the other hand, a simple formula that would provide a universal solution for balancing religious interests in diverse societies is inconceivable. What the individual, regardless of opinion or creed, might reasonably require of the state may be a direction in which one might seek greater consistency. Naturally, national and the international human rights regimes and the nuances of various constitutional approaches purporting to promote justice for all, regardless of religion and entrenched constitutional ideologies, are relevant. However, these are clearly not sufficient, since they have produced such scattered results.

A precondition for the suggested approach that might satisfy the reasonable expectations regarding state conduct that the individual believer within a religiously pluralistic society might entertain is the acceptance by such a person of the precepts of constitutionalism. The logic is simple: a person subject to a constitutional regime operating on the assumptions of constitutionalism can only expect state conduct that conforms to those assumptions. The rejection of constitutionalism therefore disqualifies one from demanding its benefits. For those whose beliefs clash with constitutionalist principles, the benefits of constitutionalism cannot apply without qualification. This naturally cannot mean that the constitutional state should be excused from honouring its own constitutionalist foundations when confronted with the demands of those who reject those foundations, but it does mean, for example, that the protection of the fibre of constitutionalism must be given precedence. Were that not the case, the state would lack a consistent frame of reference for the determination of its actions.

A crucial question in this regard is if constitutionalism as such is capable of a more universal understanding than one which depends only on its historic roots – incontestably the Western liberalism that accompanied the emergence of constitutional statehood.

8.1 ASSUMPTIONS ABOUT CONSTITUTIONALISM AND RELIGION

Constitutionalism is not holy. It is not the foundation of a faith. It is a widely endorsed, value-laden conceptual framework for the structuring of a state and for a balanced mode of exercising state authority. The notion of 'liberal democracy' is routinely associated with constitutionalism, but this should not be taken to mean that the appropriate nature of such democracy requires approval or subscription to doctrinal liberalism. The elements of constitutionalism described above in Chapter 3 and considered in the context of religion in the next section have achieved acceptance in different parts of the world as desirable objective attributes of good and just governance – shaped not necessarily by local conditions but accepted most likely due to the political and economic success of Western democracies. It may therefore be assumed that constitutionalism (sometimes insufficiently condensed into expressions such as the 'rule of law', *Rechtsstaat* or even simply 'democracy') has developed into a common global standard useful as a touchstone for laudable state structuring and conduct.

All cultural and constitutional notions have their own histories. As was argued above in section 7.1.3, constitutional law continues to operate with various conceptual artefacts from the past, such as the social contract and constituent power, that have outgrown or outlived rational defensibility as reflections of actual occurrences – but they can hardly simply be discarded before they are sensibly replaced. Despite its deep historical roots in Western culture, however, constitutionalism does not fall into the category of 'tired constitutional artefacts'. Its various elements have gained their own legitimacy, free from the constraints of sectional philosophical preference. To illustrate this with reference to some of the widely accepted elements of constitutionalism: only illogical prejudice can support an argument against judicial independence; the legal balancing of interests in aid of the maintenance of social order is capable of justification from various points of departure; the accountability of organs of state to the electorate is considered desirable not only in one line of political philosophy but by all except authoritarian power-mongers.

Given the comprehensive acceptance of constitutionalism, claiming it to be defensible only from a single approach would be to impoverish it and endanger its viability. Not to put too fine a point on it, constitutionalism does not require liberalism and does not need secularism when confronted with religious affairs. Liberal and secular claims to the parenthood of constitutionalism endanger the chances of its global proliferation and acceptance in environments where world and life views are not imbued with liberalism or where religion, albeit pluralistically, performs an increasingly important social function.

8.2 ELEMENTS OF CONSTITUTIONALISM GERMANE TO RELIGION

From the analyses and discussion in the foregoing chapters, it follows that a solution to the difficulties that states encounter regarding religion among their populations might be sought in the merits of constitutionalism as composed of the elements identified in Chapter 3. How this might be realized can be indicated in broad terms.

For this purpose, that distinguishing characteristic of states in general, sovereignty, and especially the understanding of sovereignty from a constitutionalist perspective, is a useful starting point for a consideration of the impact of constitutionalism on an appropriate attitude of the state to religion.

As was pointed out in section 7.1.1, consensus on the source of state sovereignty or on the identity of its possessor(s) is not achievable, because any opinion on the primary source of authority is inevitably built upon profound subjective ontological views. Nevertheless, state sovereignty is a crucial ingredient in the exercise of the authority of the state, whatever its perceived or assumed source might be – including religious matters.

Like economics and science, religion is globally dispersed and globally relevant. These are social systems with which the sovereign state cannot avoid dealing. Among constitutional states the manner in which state sovereignty is employed in affairs of religion varies according to differing conceptions of sovereignty, or confusion over the notion itself. Where 'the people' are considered to express their 'sovereign will' in perpetuity in a supreme constitution, the interpretation of relevant constitutional provisions will take precedence. Where the democratically elected representatives of the 'sovereign people' are considered to bear the responsibilities of sovereignty for the time being, popular acceptance of government policy and legislation will determine the justification of sovereign state conduct. Where there are confused or unformed ideas regarding the precedence of constitutional or electoral sovereignty, the justification of sovereign state conduct concerning religion is bound to be erratic or opportunistic. Unfortunately this situation of inconsistency is quite common, and in fact appears to be predominant in the world of the early 21st Century.

Regardless of the degree of clarity or confusion over the nature and source of sovereignty, it is indisputable that the state has the power, due to its sovereignty, to decide how it and its various organs will respond to the social challenges of religious pluralism. Constitutionalism demands just responses, justifiable in terms of fairness and state responsibility for good social order. Retreating behind conceptual barricades of secularism and unconcerned neutrality when dealing with such a profound human attribute as religion therefore would not reflect an honest commitment to constitutionalism.

Liberal concessions to the effect that religion may, under the pressures of the return to public religiosity, be allowed by the neutral state to play some role in providing morality to law and politics do not succeed in infusing morality into neutrality. True neutrality essentially implies a moral void. If secular neutrality is therefore to be enriched somehow by religious morality, the question arises which one of the religions present in the religiously plural society should provide the morals to fill the neutral void.

In the constitutional state arbitrary decision-making and conduct are anathema, but the availability and constitutional empowerment of a final arbiter to determine the tenability of state conduct are crucial. In well-developed and balanced democracies a legislative or parliamentary institution can contribute much in this regard, but the judicial capacity, that is, the jurisdiction, to serve as the authoritative arbiter in such matters is recognized to be a prime element of constitutionalism.

Implied herein is more than judicial authority; judicial independence is essential, and creativity may also be called for. There is unfortunately compelling evidence that courts often tend to avoid their constitutionalist responsibilities in matters involving religion by taking refuge in secular neutrality. Under the current circumstances of increasing religious pluralism and the growing social significance of religion, judges are not justified in claiming to arbitrate justly and objectively on sensitive religious issues when they subscribe to neutrality, thus explicitly confessing to one essentially religious or at least metaphysical stance labelled 'secular'.

Questions concerning the constitutional legality of state conduct affecting religious concerns are bound to arise frequently, especially because the protection of freedom of religion as a fundamental constitutional right is relevant in a great number of cases of this nature. The effectiveness of the constitutional guarantee of the relevant religious interests by means of fundamental rights is in itself a standard by which the prevalence of constitutionalism can be measured. Determining the lawfulness of both religious actions of individuals or religious institutions and that of the state requires the organs of a constitutional state to interpret and apply the constitutional and other legal protections rendered to religious litigants.

Given the reality that most constitutions contain such protections but the outcomes vary greatly across the different legal orders and also often over time within a specific constitutional dispensation, the determination of what is lawful and what the limits and the nature of the qualifications on religious rights are is of crucial importance. Consistency of outcome, that is, legal certainty in religious matters that are brought before the courts, is hard to find. This points to the importance of the role that the acceptance and effective internalization of constitutionalism, including legality as one of its elements, plays in any legal order in which sound and consistent justice can be expected in religious affairs.

If one assumes that a key function of the law is to establish and maintain social order as a characteristic of constitutionalism, the test of the measure of constitutionalism prevailing in a state is the quality of peace and order that legislation, administration and jurisprudence maintain in a religiously pluralistic populace. Constitutionalism would suffer where state-made or state-sponsored norms and conduct are effective due to the suppression or severe limitation of religious behaviour within its borders. Should the measures taken by the state, however, satisfy legitimate religious interests to the extent that only conscionable limitations are imposed, causing those affected to recognize the justification of the limitations according to the principle of reciprocity, constitutionalism will have triumphed. Secular neutrality, being essentially focused on the suppression of religion in the public sphere, cannot achieve such a result.

Another prominent element of constitutionalism is democracy, which does not at first glance display any religious connotations. However, the 'paradox of constitutionalism'[4] includes the real potential of majoritarian dominance to the detriment of religious minorities if the nature of the democracy that is being practised does not prevent it. Although not necessarily as a component of the electoral system, democracy in a balanced constitutional state demands that all legitimate religious concerns be heard and fairly treated in a manner that holds all other actors, including the state, to a standard of fair accountability. This would include unbiased and non-arbitrary conduct that reflects the recognition of the dignity of all concerned.

Constitutionalism must not be understood merely to be a burden on the state and its organs. Its viability depends greatly on popular respect for the legitimacy and understanding of the constitution and the law. This can be problematic, especially in new and pseudo democracies, that is, in states that have recently or only apparently 'converted' to constitutionalism by the adoption of constitutions containing the 'right' elements and that apply to governments and citizenries that have a shallow or recent history of constitutionalist sentiment.[5] Where contentious religious issues especially concerning minorities arise under such circumstances, the

---

[4] Cf. section 7.1.3 in Chapter 7 above.

[5] Despite the accolades for the democratizing process and the adoption of an excellent Constitution two decades ago, South Africa is an example in this category. See for example, Venter (2010b). See also Landau (2013) 195:

quality and depth of constitutionalist sentiments are likely to be severely tested. Thus, for example, Mira Lulic and Nives Kumric conclude at the end of an article dealing with the role of the media in the promotion of the interests of religious minorities in Croatia[6] that:

> [t]he question of faith and religion is a personal choice and [a] human right, but respecting the faith and religion of all people is [a] question of the society and its civil maturity to acknowledge the difference, to promote it and use it as a means to accelerate building and sustaining ... democracy as the highest human and social value.

In the end it must also be asked if the constitutional state would be justified in defending itself against religious assault. It is not uncommon for political causes to be supported or even inspired by religious fervour, whether justified by state conduct or not. Under those circumstances the boundary between politics and religion usually blurs, raising difficult ethical questions.

Pitching the integrity of the state against religious convictions can bring up hard questions such as the need to infringe upon religious freedom in order to defend the constitution. To resolve such questions it remains important to distinguish between the nature of the law and religion: whereas the constitutional state is not to function as a religious institution (to accept this does not require the endorsement of liberal secularism), it is equally important to acknowledge that religion should not perform the role of a political vehicle (acceptance of which should not be understood to preclude religion from providing the justification for political opinion). Thus a religiously motivated campaign to undermine or overthrow a constitutional state calls for the application of legitimate state authority to protect the constitutional integrity of the state. Whereas religious conviction should be allowed by law to contest the legitimacy of state conduct that runs counter to those convictions, religious people and institutions must acknowledge the sovereign authority of the state to

---

> In contrast to past practice, where authoritarian regimes were generally formed through military coup or other unconstitutional practices, would-be autocrats now have significant incentives to appear to be playing by the constitutional rules. Thus they are increasingly turning towards constitutional amendment and replacement as tools to help them construct a more authoritarian order. ... The end result of these practices is not likely to be full-fledged authoritarianism, but rather a hybrid regime where elections continue to be held but opposition forces face severe disadvantages in seeking to win election.

[6] Lulic and Kumric (2014) 111.

protect itself and its constitution against attrition, whatever its source might be. Under conditions of significant religiously motivated assault on the integrity of the state, religious rights and interests may not be allowed to take precedence over constitutionalism. However, state responses to religious issues will be justifiable only if those responses themselves correspond with the principles of constitutionalism.

8.3 THE NEED FOR THE CONSTITUTIONAL STATE TO RECOGNIZE THE SOCIAL RELEVANCE OF RELIGION

Sociologists consider the affirmation of the 'return of religion' to modern society to be trite and the designation of this era as 'post-secular' to be apposite.[7] More often than not this is ascribed to the recent rise of Islamic fundamentalism in international politics and within some countries around the world. There is no doubt that this tendency, highlighted by highly publicized occurrences like '9/11' in New York, various other acts of terrorism and various wars, is a major contributing factor, but there is much more, as is illustrated by Bryan Turner,[8] who mentions as examples of the 'vitality of religion' in various parts of the world modern pilgrimage, religious revivalism in Southeast Asia, Pentecostal and charismatic movements in South America and Africa, religious reformism in Indonesia and Malaysia, the restoration of Confucianism and Daoism in China, the reinstatement of spirit-possession cults in Vietnam with the Renovation Period, shamanistic religions in South Korea, the spread of Buddhism from Taiwan to the USA, the mobilization of Tibetan Buddhism as a global model of meditation, and the transformation of Hinduism outside India. With reference to Europe, Peter Cumper and Tom Lewis add:[9]

> [T]he revival of religious belief in some European states; a growth in 'alternative' forms of spirituality; the proliferation of new religious movements; the influence of religion in domestic political discourse; the centrality of religion in the identity of many European minority faith communities; and a rejection by some faith groups (particularly Muslims) of rigid public/private classifications in relation to the manifestation of religious belief.

---

[7] Cf. for example, Turner (2011) Chapter 7, especially at 146–150 and the range of sociological authorities cited there.
[8] Turner (2011) 147–148.
[9] Cumper and Lewis (2012) 2–3.

Turner furthermore puts his finger on the nature of the challenge faced by constitutional states when confronted with post-secularism where he concludes an article with the statement:[10] 'The modern liberal paradox is that while a secular liberal state is committed to regarding religion as a matter of private conscience, the liberal state constantly intervenes to manage religions in the name of civil harmony and political security.' The existence of this paradox can be explained by the incompatibility of the basic liberal thesis with the unavoidable demands of the reality of state practice. Put differently, the liberal theory that the ideal nature of the state is secular holds the threat of depriving the state of its capacity to perform its constitutional obligation to establish and maintain a peaceful social balance in its religiously plural polity.

Italy emerged at the time of its unification in 1861 from being a Catholic state, was influenced by liberalism until 1922 and by Fascism until 1943, and adopted a Constitution in 1948 that was neither Catholic nor secular. It poses a topical example of the modern liberal paradox.[11]

In 1989 the Italian Constitutional Court declared Italy to be a secular state,[12] finding that *laicità* was a 'supreme principle deduced from the Constitution', which should, however, not be understood to be 'synonymous with indifference towards the experience of religion' but represented 'the state's guarantee that religious freedom will be safeguarded, in a framework of denominational and cultural pluralism'.[13]

The attitudes of Italian governments to secularism and religious pluralism, driven by vacillating political impulses, brought about the notion of a 'Catholic secular Italy' coexisting with the notion of a 'pluralistic secular Italy', leaving Ventura to conclude:[14] 'Against the background of a heavily secularised and increasingly multi-religious Italian society, Italy is indisputably a *stato laico*. But *laicità* remains a deeply contradictory principle.'

The paradox and contradictions may also be described in terms of a clash between values. Cumper and Lewis describe the paradox[15] in terms of the 'values of European liberal democracies in the twenty-first century' that:

---

[10] Turner (2012) 1070.
[11] Cf. Ventura (2012), and on the 'liberal paradox', see also section 6.2.2 in Chapter 6 above.
[12] Ventura (2012) 135, who cites the case at 127 and 135 as 'C cost 11 April 1989'.
[13] Ventura (2012) 135–136.
[14] Ventura (2012) 146.
[15] Cumper and Lewis (2012) 5–6.

often lead to religious and social pluralism, as individuals and groups exercise their liberty and pursue their own paths in matters of faith. Yet, ironically, it appears that these paths are often at odds with the secular liberal values that have facilitated their very existence.

The paradoxes, clashes and contradictions characteristic of the liberal secular state obviously cannot be resolved by ignoring them and steadfastly maintaining that their merits are indisputable. The circumstances demand of the constitutional state a principled response commensurate with its responsibility to maintain social stability and peaceful acceptance by the populace that the state's efforts are not prejudiced under the influence of an anti-religious stance, but that they are optimally just.

8.4 DIRECTIVE CONSIDERATIONS OF CONSTITUTIONALISM REGARDING RELIGION

From the consideration described above of the difficulties the liberal secular state experiences in dealing adequately with the challenges of religious pluralism, the nature of constitutionalism and the need for direction in these matters, some directive considerations can be gleaned. These are construed and submitted here without further elaboration and in the acknowledgement of the fact that they are debatable:

- A constitutional state properly so called must guarantee the right of all individuals to freely give expression to their religious convictions, subject however to the need to uphold the law and to protect the rights of others.[16]
- In a constitutional state the explicit favouring of a religion or religious institution amidst religious pluralism cannot be defended as just, for the obvious reason that such favouring will be discriminatory against the unfavoured religions and their institutions. It is equally indefensible, however, for the state to ignore the historical and social ethos, as well as the religious pluralism of its population and to act as though religious convictions are irrelevant.[17]

---

[16] Cf. section 3.4 in Chapter 3 above.

[17] This is supported by the argument of Ladeur and Augsberg (2007a) 16–18, who call for a recognition in law of the valuable social products (*Leistungen*) of religion in the functioning of society and the acknowledgment of the relative extent of influence of the different religious views in a society.

- It is realistic not to expect judges to divorce themselves from their personal convictions when they are called upon to adjudicate upon the beliefs of others. The adjudication of issues of religious freedom may on the other hand not be determined by the dogmatic considerations of a specific church or religious movement, or for that matter by the judge's subjective predilections. Judges should nonetheless not pretend to be able to adjudicate in a super-human vacuum of neutrality while they are actually imposing their personal convictions in the name of secularism.[18]
- Striving to achieve justice by means of the proportional limitation and balancing of rights is laudable, but more thought needs to be given in most legal orders to the manner in which proportional results can be achieved with greater consistency and less subjectivity. The German mechanism of *praktische Konkordanz* is attractive as a means of facilitating an optimized result,[19] but relegating religion to the merely private, 'irrational' and individual spheres without recognizing its social, cultural and moral value amounts to avoiding a confrontation with the reality that religion is foundational to humanity, and that it has recently steadily grown in social significance.

Debate on these and similar considerations, especially among lawyers, it is submitted, is sorely needed in the interests of the consolidation and global proliferation of constitutionalism.

---

[18] Cf. section 6.5 in Chapter 6 above.
[19] Cf. the discussion of the nature of *praktische Konkordanz* towards the end of section 6.2.1.3 in Chapter 6 above.

9. A post-secular approach to religious pluralism

In this concluding chapter consideration is given to the possible benefits of employing constitutionalism as it is characterized in Chapter 3 above for dealing with religious pluralism against the background of the expositions and analyses of all the previous chapters.

There is a problem in this regard, on the nature of which it is necessary to reflect. Whether or not constitutionalism provides the solution must first be asked, followed by the identification of the shortcomings of common notions regarding constitutionalism. Finally an approach that may provide a foundation for an escape from the barrenness of secularist solutions will be suggested.

9.1 SUPPLANTING SECULARISM WITH CONSTITUTIONALISM

Human society is complex – a truism that is easily set aside due to the impossibility of comprehending the full or even the partial extent of the complexity. The limitations of the human mind necessitate that in any systematic investigation of reality – scientific, scholarly, educational, or simply for the purposes of making sense of one's place in life – it is necessary to break down one's observations into fractions small enough to be dealt with intellectually and emotionally. This brings about the need in scholarship and science to specialize, to limit one's focus to a field that is manageable within the rigour of a specific discipline. Inevitably, however, it also causes observers and scholars to develop intellectual blind spots, that is, areas of knowledge and research outside one's field that may be highly relevant to one's work, but which are ignored as a field of specialization of others.

Contemporary scholarship is being challenged severely, however, as is ordinary personal life experience in our globalized social environment with its knowledge economy, which provides and often demands access to a spectrum of information of unimaginable dimensions. Obviously unfairly, there is in principle no excuse in scholarship and science for being ignorant of all the readily accessible information produced in various other fields of intellectual investigation potentially relevant to one's own. In addition to the historical, conceptual and normative commonalities of the disciplines of law and those that are concerned with religion, this is part of the background to the fact that the knot between them is one that cannot be untied.[1] And yet, when we look closer at the manner in which many (if not most) Western lawyers, be they practitioners, academics, judges, politicians or administrators, go about their professional business, we find an established tradition of conscious effort to isolate law from religion.

Due to a discernable shift taking place in social attitudes towards religion as a dimension of human existence that cannot be separated from public life, including in the context of the state, it is becoming increasingly clear that the notion of legal neutrality in matters of religious concern is losing traction.

However, a return to an undifferentiated society where state and 'church', law and religion are not distinguished is simply no longer possible because, among other reasons, whereas contemporary states tend to be understood in increasingly similar constitutional terms, when it comes to religion societies are unstoppably becoming pluralistic. Governors, justices and lawyers ignore these developments at their own cost, at the cost of social justice, and potentially at the cost of stability.

The impact on and importance of religion for contemporary society naturally does not manifest itself only where law meets religion. It is arguable that the raging and often acerbic battle between naturalists and theists, evolutionists and creationists, cosmological 'big-bangers' and 'intelligent designers' in the natural sciences is evidence of the same social phenomenon: a battle of beliefs, ranging from atheism and agnosticism manifested as state secularism to the various mono-theistic and other religions and life views that produce constitutional configurations such as Islamic theocracies and selective church establishment.

But it is not only the changes in religious attitudes around the world that are relevant to the challenges to the state brought about by pluralism. The nature of the state itself and of its foundational law, constitutional law, is evolving. Being subject to the same factors that drive globalization, a common constitutional vocabulary has taken root that facilitates the need for and utility of constitutional comparison as a burgeoning and indispensable discipline.

---

[1] Cf. Chapter 1 above.

However, the meanings of various key terms in constitutional law, long-established elements of the common vocabulary, have become moving targets. These include sovereignty, citizenship, democratic majoritarianism, the social contract and the *pouvoir constituant*. Add to this the internationalization of constitutional law, the constitutionalization of international law and the continued variation of national constitutional preferences, and it becomes evident that stock responses to the problem of state responsibilities and appropriate reactions to the religious pluralization of populations are not to be had.[2]

Despite its not being a monolithic doctrine, it is fair to say that liberalist constitutional thinking still rules supreme when religious questions arise in law, especially in Western constitutional states, but also in international law. The adequacy of the liberal response is increasingly being challenged, however. Thus, for example, Peter Danchin performed a thorough analysis of the difficulties arising from value pluralism when it comes to conflicts of religious claims, and then pointed out that:[3]

> [T]he case of proselytism presents a series of individual and collective interests that are 'inherently rivalrous, and often constitutively uncombinable, and sometimes incommensurable, or rationally incomparable.' At the same time, the fundamental rights and liberties of liberal thought allow no escape from the need to make radical choices in which 'reason leaves us in the lurch and in which, whatever we do, there is a wrong or an irreparable loss of value.' What would it mean to take these deep conflicts of value more seriously? What are the implications of a moral theory of value pluralism that recognizes an irreducible diversity of ultimate values while at the same time denying the availability of any overarching standard or Archimedean point to resolve conflicts both within and between them?

Where should we then turn to find comparative constitutional direction regarding the appropriate state responses to the demands of post-secular society? A reasonable answer would be to look to a commonly respected constitutional standard or notion that is understood to give expression to that which is good in constitutional thinking: constitutionalism.

It emerges that constitutionalism is widely used to express or emphasize various desired attributes of the constitutional state. When these features that are variously attributed to constitutionalism are compiled, an interesting picture composed of coherent, mutually supportive elements, structural, substantive and doctrinal, comes to light. A widely supported image can be drawn of how 21st Century states should be structured and

---

[2] Cf. Chapter 2 above.
[3] Danchin (2008) 307 quoting from Gray (1995).

should function in order to conform to the requirements of constitutionalism and to be acknowledged as respected members of the community of constitutional states.[4] Should constitutionalism, viewed comprehensively, indeed be a credible standard for 'good' statehood, it may also serve the purpose of presenting us with a measure for acceptable legal resolution of matters concerning religion, especially insofar as it may be understood to evoke the ethical norm of reciprocity.

Confirming the relevance of religion to (constitutional) law, it is remarkable how ubiquitous references to religion in constitutions around the world are, at least in the form of the real or pretended protection of religious freedom, but also quite often as invocations of moral authority (sometimes referred to as 'ceremonial deism'). State-specific arrangements regarding religious institutions and even religious doctrines are frequently encountered in constitutional texts, in some cases to affirm an injunction on the 'establishment' of churches, in others to regulate the recognition of and even support for specific denominations or religious institutions in general.[5] It is useful to conceive of a continuum ranging from no protection of religious freedom to optimal protection thereof, and to project this continuum on constitutional attitudes in a loop from theocracy, passing through secularity to religious abolition.[6] To the extent that such a representation may be understood to promote the merits of secular state neutrality, it raises the question of whether impartial constitutionalist state engagement would not offer a better means for the achievement of justice in a plural society.

Due to the increasing interaction between constitutional law and international law, the manner in which religion features in international law is of interest in a consideration of state responses to religious issues. Religion performed an essential role in the emergence of international law, and even today it is said to be capable of serving the purpose of infusing international affairs with morality, although this is not often highlighted.

As is the case in other fields, international law is not helpful in resolving the difficulties surrounding the definition of religion. Notwithstanding the difficulty of clarifying what exactly is to be understood under the concept, ample provision is made in various international instruments for the protection of religion, especially for the purposes of

---

[4] Cf. Chapter 3 above.
[5] Cf. Chapter 4 above.
[6] See Figure 4.1 above.

expounding religious freedom and related individual claims, most particularly related to education, in the form of human rights.

Furthermore, international and supra-national institutions are constantly engaged in operationalizing the international legal norms dealing with religion. International diplomacy and politics frequently serve as religious battlefields and religious institutions are often engaged in creating or solving conflicts founded in religious differences, which are easily translated into political terms. International discourse on religion is, as is the case in constitutional law, infused with liberal conceptions such as the privatization of religion.[7]

A perusal of examples from various jurisdictions of jurisprudence concerning religion reveals on the one hand the enormous range of issues that are brought before the courts, and on the other the inconsistencies among jurisdictions, and often also within jurisdictions, regarding the judicial approach to matters of this nature.

State engagement with religion can be classified into three categories: general functions of the state that incidentally impact on religion; state-initiated activity concerning religion; and matters inspired by religion requiring the attention of the state authorities.

From the examples of the cases brought before courts[8] it is clear that a great deal of the activities of members of society that may call for adjudication can and often do involve the religious beliefs or interests of the parties. The impact of the law on religious life that calls for resolution by judges is caused not only by constitutional norms but also by legislation, administrative action and policies imposed on sensitive and sometimes controversial matters ranging from education and labour relations to religious symbolism and much more. In the process of adjudication the courts have developed volumes filled with precedent, interpretation and dogmatics.

However, consistency in judicial guidance for the development of a conscionable and predictable approach of the state to religion is rare. A noteworthy phenomenon is that multi-member benches are very often divided when they adjudicate about religion, even if all the judges concerned purport to hold similar or even the same liberal views of secularism and state neutrality. The reasons for the discordance among the judges are usually unclear, but perhaps they may be found in the impossibility for people of flesh and blood to achieve neutrality, especially where such a patently subjective matter as religion is involved.

---

[7] Cf. Chapter 5 above.
[8] Cf. Chapter 6 above.

Judicial neutrality in religious matters has nevertheless been identified as an abused route of escape from the challenges that such cases pose, but there can be no doubt that the state and all its institutions, the judiciary included, have nowhere to hide from the implications of growing religious pluralism. Ways must be found to ensure improved hopes for justice for believers of all stripes coming before the courts. What, then, it must be asked again, are the appropriate responsibilities and obligations of the contemporary constitutional state in this regard?

In view of the fact that the complex legal entity we call the 'state', despite being subject to evolution, continues to be the major bearer of legal authority in society and the most authoritative legislator, adjudicator, administrator, policy-maker and locus of citizenship and nationality, not many will contest the assertion that it must take responsibility for the establishment and maintenance of peaceful order within its sovereign territory.

Against the backdrop of age-old histories of various forms of nation-forming being a prominent characteristic of contemporary society, the fact of global migration evokes divergent responses. North American and Western European countries, in recent years the destinations of choice (if not of desire) for migrants from many other parts of the world, each also with its own older patterns of immigration and emigration, display dissimilar responses to the inevitable cultural and religious pluralism that has wrought significant societal change within their borders. These countries nevertheless are not the only destinations for people in lower economic brackets seeking a better life elsewhere, or for the economically mobile participants in the global economy. Examples are Australia for the Chinese, Indians, Vietnamese, Filipinos and Malaysians; South Africa for Africans from north of its borders; Ecuador, Chile and Guyana for other South Americans; the migrant labour in the Gulf States; and 'internal migration' within China.

As the demography of states shifts away from what was conceived to be culturally 'comfortable', it seems that social tensions rise and political backlashes become evident. And what is the standard response where organs of state are called upon to maintain public order? It is a notionally neutral indifference to religion, which is categorized as being not a matter for the public sphere (where reason is assumed to reign) but one for the private sphere, where the irrational beliefs of individuals properly resort. Reaction to the secularism that was primarily a product of 19th Century liberalism is on the ascendant, however, even from some liberal quarters, where the idea of the dawning of a 'post-secular' era has gained a foothold, although proposals for an appropriate response to the global return of religiosity are not readily on offer.[9]

In this context it is conceivable that constitutionalism can survive critical scrutiny from divergent perspectives because its characteristic elements have the flavour of universal 'constitutional good'. When related to the problems presented by religious pluralism, the elements of constitutionalism emerge as the need for the just exercise of state sovereignty; the exercise of judicial authority in a manner that mediates religious conflict and contention fairly; consistent legal protection of frequently divergent religious interests that speak for constitutional legality; the conscionable imposition of limitations on or the balancing of religious interests capable of reasonable acceptance by those affected as respectful of their dignity; the popular internalization of the tenets of constitutionalism; and the acceptance that religious undermining of the constitutional state is to be condemned.[10]

Constitutionalism calls for the recognition of the relevance of religion for all the citizens of and denizens in the state. However, can constitutionalism provide us with the ultimate solution?

9.2 THE POTENTIAL WEAKNESS OF CONSTITUTIONALISM

In the foregoing chapters it was suggested that constitutionalism could provide contemporary states with the means to do justice to diverse and sometimes conflictual demands within a pluralized society. Such a contention is not self-evident, though, especially due to the malleability of the notion of constitutionalism itself on the one hand, and on the other the tendency to view it through the lenses of the entrenched concepts of constitutional liberalism. It is suggested above, in Chapter 3, that it should be possible to stabilize the meaning of constitutionalism by means of the identification of elements properly associated with it. The remaining difficulty is that each of those elements, some more than others, can be and is viewed differently by different observers. Thus, for example, an exponent of secularism would assume that religious neutrality of the judiciary is characteristic of constitutionalism, whereas judicial engagement with religious sentiments is expected in legal orders in which a

---

[9] Cf. Chapter 7 above.
[10] Cf. Chapter 8 above.

specific religion (or religions) is a prominent constitutional feature. A further examination of these divergent positions is called for.

9.2.1 Liberal Constitutionalism

Liberal thinking about state and religion relies on powerful logic. Denise Meyerson offers a clear exposition of this logic, which can be summarized as follows:[11]

- inevitably (even reasonable) people will disagree on religious matters;
- in a society which strives to treat everyone with mutual respect, shared reasons must be found to justify the exercise of state power;
- to honour the demand for mutual respect, religious disagreements must either be put aside or the state must be neutral in respect of the disagreements;
- to achieve this, the state must not be allowed to prefer one religion above the other, nor religion over non-religion.

The power of this logic lies in the self-evident truth that religious preferentialism cannot be fair or just in a religiously plural society. Its weakness lies in the notion of neutrality. Nevertheless, proponents of secularism consider neutrality to be its most important virtue. Arguing that the 'non-secular' alternatives to secularism, which she identifies as 'religious diversity, pluralism or theo-democracy', are undesirable, and that neutrality towards religion is essential to human rights, Frances Raday extols the merits of 'secular constitutionalism' in the following terms:[12]

> It is a system which allows pluralism of thought and conscience to thrive. It is a system which allows individuals and groups to express themselves freely, not coerced by a prevailing creed. Under secular democracies, this may be achieved either by guaranteeing non-interventionist neutralism or of permitting promotion of religion in accordance with constitutional principles.

There would have been merit in promoting state secularism if, as Raday seems to assume, the only alternative would be the promotion of a constitutional system operating within some other religious or denominational framework, because it must be conceded that religious minorities

---

[11] Meyerson (2009) 67–71.
[12] Raday (2009) 2770.

in for example Catholic states, Muslim theocracies and communist regimes have to appeal to the tolerance of the authorities – and tolerance implies leniency without the guarantee of continuity. But a rejection of secularism cannot so simply be equated with factional sectarianism. If constitutionalism is complied with by any state, regardless of the religious composition of its population, sectarian preferentialism cannot prevail.

The shortcomings of the neutrality that characterizes secularism have not gone unnoticed around the world. Recognizing the trend referred to in Chapter 7, that religiosity is returning to the public sphere, Karl-Heinz Ladeur and Ino Augsberg[13] speak from a German perspective of 'a global revitalisation of religion' including 'a re-politicisation of religion' and describe the approach of Western democratic states to religion as something that does not allow the favouring of or discrimination against specific professions of faith. However, they maintain that the 'equidistance to religion', expressed as the 'principle of state neutrality', requires more:

> It commits the state to generally withdraw from religious issues, especially the political act of defining what can legitimately be classified as religion and religious behaviour. The leeway given to the selfconception of religious groups by the German Federal Constitutional Court and its wide understanding of what kind of behaviour has a direct relationship to faith and therefore deserves protection by the freedom of religion, is to be understood against the context of this general principle.

They then go on to describe the approach of judiciaries as follows:

> The courts use it [neutrality] as an exit-option in order to avoid addressing problems which appear to be too complex for the law relegating religion to sociological study. In this context, state neutrality merely functions as a *chiffre* for indifference. But this strategy of avoidance, though understandable in the light of the complexity of religious pluralism, undermines the law's function of conflict resolution. Furthermore, it neither corresponds to the historical development nor to the functional aspects of the idea of religious freedom.

Considering rationalism to be the 'epistemology of liberalism', Mark Witten[14] makes the following finding regarding Canadian jurisprudence:[15]

---

[13] Ladeur and Augsberg (2007b) 143–144.
[14] Witten (2012) 120.
[15] See also Von Heyking (1999–2000) 663–697.

> Some justices seemingly believe ... that constitutional adjudication's legitimacy depends on the superiority and neutrality of reason. As a result, despite relentless critique, many amongst the judiciary's ranks maintain a false confidence in neutrality. This failure to appreciate that law processes religion from a rationalist vantage point is problematic. It represents a blind faith in rationalism that thwarts much needed awareness and self-examination. It prevents awareness that rationalism construes and understands religion uniquely, and can be defensive when threatened. It prevents acknowledgement of the scepticism towards the metaphysical and the tendency to gravitate towards the universal. Ultimately, by perpetuating the mythical neutrality of judicial rationalism, courts may remain oblivious to the harshness with which they treat religion.

Regarding 'the principle of neutrality' in 'establishment clause cases' in the United States, Frank Ravitch concluded in 2004:[16]

> The principle sounds good in theory, but there is no neutral baseline from which we can gauge claims of neutrality. Thus, neutrality is an empty concept. Yet the Court has been increasingly gravitating toward neutrality, specifically formal neutrality, as the centerpiece of its Establishment Clause doctrine. ... This move is dangerous, not because of its results, but because the Court has gone from using neutrality as a broad and vague principle that needs other principles such as separation or accommodation in order to function, to using it as both the means and ends of Establishment Clause analysis. It is deeply troubling that the Court has placed such great weight on such weak footing.

Against the background of the travails of judges in the cases discussed in Chapter 6, Ladeur and Augsberg's European understanding of judicial neutrality as a code for indifferent avoidance of intractable religious issues is convincing, and is supported by the North American views of Witten, Von Heyking and Ravitch.

It is clear that liberalism-induced secularism fails to offer solutions to multi-religious tensions in a plural society: secularism is after all, despite the protestations of its adherents to the contrary, not neutral, because it amounts to a specific religious (or religion-like) stance that should be taken account of in the same way as other religious beliefs when dealing with conflicting religious interests. An exclusive preference for secularism is therefore patently discriminatory, indeed comparable to 'establishment', if not more comprehensively unjust, since it promotes, contrary to the reality that religion is the key to moral choices, the idea that religion is irrelevant as a factor in public life.

---

[16] Ravitch (2004) 573.

Secularism assumes, in a manner typical of a religious stance, that only its morality of assumed rationality is valid. Ansah captures this well:[17] 'The elimination of religion from the juridical discourse of morality means, in effect, that the concepts of good and evil have likewise been secularized, in the sense that they are defined by external contingency rather than internal imperative.'

The dilemma of liberalism was concisely characterized in 2008 by Peter Danchin when he wrote,[18] with reference to the resolution of different, culturally inspired understandings of values and virtues:

> The liberal algebra is intended to resolve these different types of conflict by specifying a scheme of basic rights (or a public–private divide, or both) satisfying the two conditions of compossibility and adequacy. One of the ways it appears to achieve this is simply by removing from the scheme of liberties those rights that make obviously incompatible claims. This strategy is evident in the evolution of Rawls's notion of basic rights. In *A Theory of Justice*, Rawls defended the priority of liberty over other values by advancing the 'Greatest Equal Liberty Principle,' according to which each individual has the most extensive liberty subject to others having the same, restrictable only for the sake of liberty. But as HLA Hart famously demonstrated, this principle suffers from a disabling indeterminacy. Claims about the greatest liberty are not freestanding and depend on judgments concerning the relative value of the human interests that different liberties protect. Different views of human goods will therefore generate competing judgments about what constitutes the greatest liberty (or the meaning of 'equality' or the Millian 'harm' principle, for example). If this is correct, then there can be no perfect way to protect all liberties, and compromises between rival ideals involving conflicts of value are inevitable.

Given the centrality of liberal rationalism to both secularism and the development of constitutionalism, it must be asked if constitutionalism – which continues to be seen primarily through the lens of liberalism despite the dawning of the post-secular era – is rendered useless as a standard according to which state conduct regarding religion can be guided. Put differently: can constitutionalism be saved from secularism? And if it should be possible, are the alternatives inevitably religious fundamentalism, establishment or preferentialism?

---

[17] Ansah (2005) 24.
[18] Danchin (2008) 309.

9.2.2 Constitutional Engagement with Religion

In dealing with religious pluralism, the essential conceptual problem of constitutionalism is that it is itself embedded in a particular theoretical or philosophical history and foundation – constitutionalism itself is not neutral but has evolved over centuries into a coherent and globally accepted and supported complex of norms. Thus, the correctness of state conduct under constitutionalism is measurable against coherent norms that are widely known and understood. Interestingly the global striving to conform to those norms is not consistently driven by the theoretical and philosophical foundations upon which they grew. They seem to have developed a life of their own.

Accepting that liberalism gave birth to constitutionalism while simultaneously rejecting the precepts of liberalism as such does not preclude one from acknowledging the merits of constitutionalism. It can in fact be shown that the key conceptions upon which constitutionalism is built are founded at a deeper level on religion.[19] Liberal rationalism has produced constitutional constructs with a remarkable universal appeal, obviously absorbing intellectual and social products of ages of Western political culture such as democracy, legality, balanced power distribution and the recognition of human dignity. In constitutional law and politics, the elements of constitutionalism have achieved the same degree of inevitability as the culpability of murder and theft has in criminal law.

When it comes to religion and law, the liberal emphasis demands secularism, but other *Weltanschauungen* that subscribe, with equal fervour, to the crystallized elements of constitutionalism do not. In some of the alternative approaches lurk the danger of fundamentalist imbalances and selective support for constitutionalism. Ladeur and Augsburg capture this point as follows:[20]

> Th[e] rejection of a solely individualist understanding of religion oversimplifying its societal function, which is the dominant perspective within legal practice, also marks the contrast to currently observable extremistic forms of religion. ... [T]he fundamentalist attempt to de-privatise religion on the one hand strives to disengage religion from its cultural surrounding and the mutual exchange connected with it, for the benefit of a one-dimensional hegemony of religion.

---

[19] Cf. for example, Stein (2007).
[20] Ladeur and Augsburg (2007b) 150.

A post-liberal approach will, however, of necessity also reflect the realities of the post-secular era. These include the need to live with religious pluralism, to maintain public order justly, to recognize unbalanced fundamentalism for what it is and to counter it where necessary in the interests of good governance, and to recognize the shortcomings of liberalism and the inadequate solutions offered by secular neutrality – and the urgent need to develop alternative responses to questions concerning the interchange between law and religion.

In this era we have come to understand that public life cannot be rid of religion by 'neutrally' attempting to marginalize it and by relegating it to the *forum internum*.

9.2.3 The Challenge: Engaging Religion without Compromising Justice

Why can't religion be removed from the public sphere? Referring to the truism that structured religious activity is more than individual activity – that it is 'a collective phenomenon' – Ladeur and Augsburg offer the following explanation:[21]

> Since religions in general are 'extra-personal mechanisms for the perception, understanding, judgment and manipulation of the world, ... for the *organisation* of social and psychological processes,' the subjectivation of religion as a historical process is itself a product of transsubjective procedures of religious changes. And in these processes, religion still remains connected to its surrounding society by structural couplings and operations of exchange. Because of their intensive interaction with culture as a collective phenomenon (and not just as an individual choice), and because of their contribution to structuring and specifying cultural identities, religions generate orienting criteria for the selection of attentiveness and 'collective relevance.' In this respect, religions, as a part of the postmodern culture, are the memory of society challenged by the necessity to interpret reality under the condition of uncertainty. Without a 'common point of reference' underlying all explicit (however complex it might be in a liberal democracy) communications, societal reproduction is not possible.

It is precisely in the search for this 'common point of reference' that the challenges for 21st Century religiously plural society lie: legal escapism in the form of neutral disengagement has proven to be inadequate and to have been overtaken by rising levels of religiosity. Also recognizing the problems attending neutrality, and taking issue with the range of tests for

---

[21] Ladeur and Augsburg (2007b) 149–150.

constitutionality in American First Amendment jurisprudence in which neutrality was canvassed in attempts to balance separation and accommodation, Ravitch proposed a 'facilitation test',[22] essentially determining that government action that substantially facilitates or discourages religion is unconstitutional: government should avoid the encouragement of religion without unduly discouraging it. While Ravitch's diagnosis of the problem is sound, the proposed solution is hard to extrapolate beyond constitutional orders that share the built-in tensions of the American First Amendment.

Ladeur and Augsburg seem to suggest that the solution lies in recognizing the proportional importance of religions in a society, leading to the relative benefiting of the 'prevalent religion' dominant in that society without allowing the state to determine the 'rightness' of a religion.[23]

Although it must be conceded that it is problematic (to say the least) if the state ignores or even undermines the predominant religious sentiments among its citizens (the non-establishment approach in the USA comes to mind), it is submitted that there is more potential for justice in accepting the tried and proven elements of constitutionalism as a point of reference common to all beliefs that do not entail the subversion of the constitutional state.

This submission assumes that the norms of constitutionalism have achieved global acceptance without any remaining dependence on constitutionalism's historical humanistic and liberal roots. If that were not the case, secular liberalism would have had to be the constitutional creed of all states whose constitutional law allows for the juridical (especially the judicial) limitation of state authority, constitutional supremacy, human dignity as a core constitutional value, and the entrenchment and protection of fundamental rights. These are also key premises that are reflected in international law, whether in treaties, *ius cogens* or customary international law.

A focused articulation of the essence of constitutionalism is to be found in the universally supported principle of reciprocity.[24]

---

[22] Ravitch (2004) 544 *et seq.*
[23] Ladeur and Augsburg (2007b) 151.
[24] See section 3.5 in Chapter 3 above.

9.3 MOVING FROM NEUTRALITY TO OBJECTIVITY

It has become clear that the complexity of the interface between law and religion has escalated and continues to do so as religious pluralism spreads across the globe amidst a pronounced trend towards heightened levels of public religiosity. It is also clear that the standard liberal and secular approach for dealing with these complexities is no longer effective and can no longer reasonably be maintained – if it ever could. Developing alternatives is therefore essential, and calls for much thought and effort. A simple, one-off solution is not possible, but as a point of departure for the purpose, it is suggested that the notion of state/legal neutrality towards religion within the context of liberal constitutionalism should be replaced with *objectivity*, applied in the context of *constitutionalism*, understood as a standard for the just exercise of the authority of the state as it has crystallized over centuries of human experience with the allocation and limitation of public authority.

It is submitted that the trap in which various states have landed themselves under the influence of Western liberalism by subscribing to secular neutrality when dealing with such a profoundly human attribute as religion (including anti- or non-religious stances) is caused by the deliberate blandness of the notions of secularity and neutrality. The law and its authors and practitioners are generally required to act fairly and in an even-handed manner.

Legal artefacts such as constitutions and fundamental rights are not bland, however. They are based on concepts and values inspired by profound philosophical and religious presuppositions. For judges, governments and legislatures, fairness does not require neutrality. On the contrary, neutrality implies detachment, disinterest, non-engagement, an attitude that one might associate with cybernetics, not with jurisprudence, politics, good governance or constitutional scholarship.

In most cases where law meets religion, objective legal standards are rightly sought in the text of a supreme constitution. However, this unavoidably calls for interpretation of the text, and interpretation is notoriously subjective. To cite the constitution as a neutral 'common point of reference' is therefore problematic: it amounts to the elevation of a particular, value-free interpretation of the constitutional text to the level of moral authority. Constitutional interpretation should therefore not be an attempt at neutrality but an exercise in objectivity.

It is impossible to ignore the growing difficulties that constitutional states are facing due to the global increase of the multiculturalism that characterizes contemporary society. To remain true to the need to be impartial when dealing with the unavoidable tensions arising from religious pluralism, the state must find a better means of conceiving and applying the law fairly to all.

Attempts at neutrality confronting these difficulties are not convincing. They cause confusion and unnecessary inconsistencies. Secularism simply is not neutral. Religion cannot arbitrarily be set aside at will. Neutrality is a cop-out. Neutrality means not taking sides, which implies that a neutral arbiter cannot resolve a dispute. It is easily confused with objectivity, which means not being prejudiced. Put differently, neutrality is bland, colourless, not engaged. Neutrality entails the supposition that subjectivity can be avoided, or worse, it supposes indifference.

A more fruitful channel that warrants further investigation is one that acknowledges the human inability to be neutral and then to seek solutions *objectively*. Some will object to this approach by assuming that neutrality is synonymous with objectivity and impartiality.

It is suggested, however, that whereas neutrality requires a personal ability to be completely detached from a legal question, objectivity involves the express acknowledgement of anyone's inability to be robotically detached in such a manner, followed by recognition of the responsibility to find objectively fair solutions. Where neutrality assumes the disengagement of feeling, objectivity switches on the desire to be even-handed, despite one's own predilections. This is, for example, what good judges routinely do in cases not involving religion. Neutrality is bleak, bloodless, evasive – objectivity is warm, alive and calls for conscious effort to do unto others as you desire to be done to.

Although the judicial constructs of *praktische Konkordanz*[25] and the balance of convenience[26] have not been motivated in terms of objectivity, and employing them may not always guarantee an outcome considered by all to be fair, they may be examples of a means of achieving justice objectively as opposed to neutrally, since they involve judicial engagement with the subjective realities of the conflicting claims of the parties to a dispute.

Aulis Aarnio strikingly depicts the distinction between neutrality and objectivity in the following manner:[27]

> As is well-known, the goddess of justice is usually described with her eyes covered with a bandage. Her impartiality is a kind of neutrality that does not glance around. The symbol is, however, simultaneously a sign of danger. The

---

[25] See section 6.2.1.3 in Chapter 6 above.
[26] See section 6.2.3. in Chapter 6 above.
[27] Aarnio (1997) 16–17.

goddess of justice can never see the course of her sword. Her dispensing justice is blind. And to blind action is always connected, whether we want it or not, the danger of sporadicality, ultimately of despotism. Only the kind of dispensation of justice that with an open look – fearing no justification – takes into consideration all circumstances, produces simultaneously both justice and reasonableness. For this reason one should, considering the challenges of modern society, presumably take off the bandage covering the eyes of the goddess of justice. It is then that the administration of justice has the courage to accept the entire enormous challenge that the future seems to unroll before man.

Being objective requires acknowledgement of one's natural subjectivity, followed by a consciously impartial engagement and the weighing of a matter in terms of clearly determined, external non-subjective standards. Constitutionalism properly construed can provide us with standards of this nature. It also requires justification according to disclosed, objective criteria.

No state or its organs can hope to succeed in their institutional tasks in the 21st Century by presuming that engagement with religion can be eliminated from their constitutional function of maintaining good and just social peace and order. It is not the function of the constitutional state to defend or maintain any specific religion, but it must promote religious patience amidst pluralism and search for a fair balancing of the religious interests of all, even where such balancing requires adherents of contending religions to forfeit some privileges.

In summary:

- Where church–state relations were an historical constitutional dichotomy as the nation state developed and became established, the contemporary challenge facing the constitutional state which is subjected to the effects of globalization is balancing the interests of the adherents of a plurality of diverse and often competing religions within its population.
- The notion that a 'secular state' can provide neutral solutions to this challenge is misleading, since secularism is in itself a value-laden and subjective stance with strong assumptive or even religion-like undertones.
- Although constitutional diversity around the globe can be expected to prevail indefinitely, it does not mean that persuasive guidelines for dealing with religious pluralism may not be gleaned from the expanding impact of the notion of constitutionalism as a general standard.

- Replacing neutrality, being an unachievable and justice-defeating goal, with objectivity in religious matters, does not mean either that authorities should be permitted in law to conduct themselves in a religiously prejudiced manner, nor does it mean that they are incapable of dealing justly with religious issues should they, as organs of a constitutional state, wish to perform their essential function of establishing and maintaining social peace and order.
- The universally accepted golden rule of reciprocity,[28] foundational to the rule of law and constitutionalism, contains the promise of the achievability of objective justice in religious matters.

---

[28] See section 1.5 in Chapter 1 and section 3.5 in Chapter 3 above.

Bibliography

Aarnio A. (1997) Reason and Authority – A Treatise on the Dynamic Paradigm of Legal Dogmatics. Ashgate, Dartmouth.
Ackerman B.A. (1991) We the People – Foundations. Harvard University Press, Cambridge, Mass.
Adams M. (2009) Religie in de publieke ruimte: constitutionele contouren en politieke theorie. In: Nieuwenhuis A.J. and Zoethout C.M. (eds) Rechtsstaat en religie. Wolf Legal Publishers, Nijmegen, pp. 5–29.
Alexy R. (2002) A Theory of Constitutional Rights. Oxford University Press, Oxford.
Ansah T. (2005) A Terrible Purity: International Law, Morality, Religion, Exclusion. Cornell International Law Journal 38:9–70.
Arato A. and Cohen J. (2009) Banishing the Sovereign? Internal and External Sovereignty in Arendt. Constellations 16(2):307–330.
Arnáson A.T. (2008) The Good State or the Constitutional Innocents of the Nordic Societies. In: Nergelius J. (ed.) Constitutionalism – New Challenges: European Law from a Nordic Perspective. Martinus Nijhoff, Leiden, pp. 155–160.
Auvachez E. (2009) Supranational Citizenship Building and the United Nations: Is the UN Engaged in a 'Citizenization' Process? Global Governance 15:43–66.
Backer L.C. (2007–2008) God(s) Over Constitutions: International and Religious Transnational Constitutionalism in the 21st Century. Mississippi College Law Review 27:11–65.
Backer L.C. (2009) The Ocratic Constitutionalism: An Introduction to a New Global Legal Ordering. Indiana Journal of Global Legal Studies 16:85–172.
Balme S. (2009) Ordinary Justice and Popular Constitutionalism in China. In: Balme S. and Dowdle M.W. (eds) Building Constitutionalism in China. Palgrave Macmillan, Basingstoke, pp. 179–198.
Balme S. and Dowdle M.W. (eds) (2009) Building Constitutionalism in China. Palgrave Macmillan, Basingstoke.
Basson A. (2012) Zuma Exposed. Jonathan Ball Publishers, Johannesburg.
Beal N. (2012) Defending State Sovereignty. Transnational Law and Contemporary Problems 21:549–570.

Bederman D. (1991) Religion and the Sources of International Law in Antiquity. In: Janis M.W. (ed.) The Influence of Religion on the Development of International Law. Martinus Nijhoff, Dordrecht, pp. 3–29.

Beer L.W. (2009) Human Rights Constitutionalism in Japan and Asia. BRILL/Global Oriental, Leiden.

Benvenisti E. (2013) Sovereigns as Trustees of Humanity: On the Accountability of States to Foreign Stakeholders. American Journal of International Law 107(2):295–333.

Benvenisti E. and Downs G.W. (2012) The Democratizing Effects of Transjudicial Coordination. Utrecht Law Review 8(2):158–171.

Berber F. (1973) Das Staatsideal im Wandel der Weltgeschichte. Beck, München.

Berg-Sørensen A. (ed.) (2013) Contesting Secularism – Comparative Perspectives. Ashgate, Farnham.

Berman H. (1974) The Interaction of Law and Religion. Abington Press, Nashville.

Beschneidung (2012) http://www.bmjv.de/SharedDocs/Archiv/DE/Kurzmeldungen/2012/20121212_Verabschiedung_des_Gesetzes_zu_Beschneidung.html;jsessionid=E651C453BDBF4DB6167612387F1D5AF9.1_cid297. Accessed 12 June 2015.

Bhargava R. (2013) Multiple Secularisms and Multiple Secular States. In: Berg-Sørensen A. (ed.) Contesting Secularism – Comparative Perspectives. Ashgate, Farnham, pp. 17–41.

Billias G.A. (2009) American Constitutionalism Heard Round the World, 1776–1989 – A Global Perspective. New York University Press, New York.

Blackburn S. (2005) The Oxford Dictionary of Philosophy, 2nd ed. Oxford University Press, Oxford.

Bobek M. (2010) The Administration of Courts in the Czech Republic: In Search of a Constitutional Balance. European Public Law 16(2):251–270.

Böckenförde E.-W. (1967) Die Entstehung des Staates als Vorgang der Säkularisation. In: Säkularistion und Utopie Ebracher Studien Ernst Forsthoff zum 65. Geburtstag. Kohlhammer Verlag, Stuttgart, pp. 75–94.

Bogdanor V. (2009) The New British Constitution. Hart, Oxford.

Bohlander M. (2012) 'There is No Compulsion in Religion' – Freedom of Religion, Responsibility to Protect (R2P) and Crimes against Humanity at the Example of the Islamic Blasphemy Laws of Pakistan. Journal of Islamic State Practices in International Law 8:42–43.

Boozari A. (2011) Shi'i Jurisprudence and Constitution. Palgrave Macmillan, Basingstoke.

Bosniak L. (2006) The Citizen and the Alien. Princeton University Press, Princeton.

Bruening M.W. (2005) Calvinism's First Battleground – Conflict and Reform in the Pays de Vaud, 1528–1559. Springer, Heidelberg.

Brugger W. and Karayanni M. (eds) (2007) Religion in the Public Sphere: A Comparative Analysis of German, Israeli, American and International Law. Springer, Berlin.

Brugger W. and Sarlet I.W. (2008) Moderner Konstitutionalismus am Beispiel der US-Verfassung, des Grundgesetzes und der brasilianischen Verfassung: eine rechtsvergleichende Perspektive. In: Jahrbuch des Öffentlichen Rechts der Gegenwart, Neue Folge, Band 56. Mohr Siebeck, Tübingen, pp. 613–638.

Casanova J. (2009) Immigration and the New Religious Pluralism: A European Union–United States Comparison. In: Levey G.B. and Modood T. (eds) Secularism, Religion and Multicultural Citizenship. Cambridge University Press, Cambridge, pp. 139–163.

Cassese A. (ed.) (2012) Realizing Utopia – the Future of International Law. Oxford University Press, Oxford.

Chen A.H.Y. (2010) Emergency Powers, Constitutionalism and Legal Transplants: The East Asian Experience. In: Ramraj V.V. and Thiruvengadam A.K. (eds) Emergency Powers in Asia – Exploring the Limits of Legality. Cambridge University Press, Cambridge, pp. 56–88.

Choudhry S. (2008) Ackerman's Higher Lawmaking in Comparative Constitutional Perspective: Constitutional Moments as Constitutional Failures? International Journal of Constitutional Law 2:193–230.

Christenson G.A. (2013) 'Liberty of the Exercise of Religion' in the Peace of Westphalia. Transnational Law and Contemporary Problems 21:721–761.

Cohen M. (2010) The Rule of Law as the Rule of Reasons. Archiv für Rechts- und Sozialphilosophie 96(1):1–16.

Cordorelli L. (2012) Is Leviathan Still Holding Sway over International Dealings. In: Cassese A. (ed.) Realizing Utopia – The Future of International Law. Oxford University Press, Oxford, pp. 22–24.

Cox A.B. and Miles T.J. (2013) Policing Immigration. University of Chicago Law Review 80:87–136.

Croxton D. and Tischer A. (2002) The Peace of Westphalia. Greenwood Press, Westport.

Cumper P. and Lewis T. (eds) (2012) Religion, Rights and Secular Society – European Perspectives. Edward Elgar, Cheltenham and Northampton.

Dabestani A., Sevinclidir P. and Erol E. (2012) Is Turkey's Secular System in Danger? BBC News Europe. http://www.bbc.com/news/world-europe-20028295. Accessed 19 March 2014.

Danchin P.G. (2008) Of Prophets and Proselytes: Freedom of Religion and the Conflict of Rights in International Law. Harvard International Law Journal 49:249–321.

Dann P. and Al-Ali Z. (2006) The Internationalized *Pouvour Constituant* – Constitution-Making under External Influence in Iraq, Sudan and East Timor. In: Von Bogdandy A. and Wolfrum R. (eds) Max Planck Yearbook of United Nations Law. Nijhoff, Leiden, Vol. 10, pp. 423–463.

Davies M. (2008) Pluralism in Law and Religion. In: Cane P., Evans C. and Robinson Z. (eds) Law and Religion in Theoretical and Historical Context. Cambridge University Press, Cambridge, pp. 76–99.

Davis A.P. (2011) International Civil Religion: Respecting Religious Diversity While Promoting International Cooperation. Hastings International and Comparative Law Review 34:87–126.

Davis M.C. (1998) The Price of Rights: Constitutionalism and East Asian Economic Development. Human Rights Quarterly 20:303–337.

Dawkins R. (2006) The God Delusion. Bantam, London.

De Been W. and Taekema S. (2012) Religion in the 21st Century – Debating the Post-secular Turn. Erasmus Law Review 5(1):1.

De Búrca G. and Weiler J.H.H. (eds) (2012) The Worlds of European Constitutionalism. Cambridge University Press, Cambridge.

De Wet, E. (2006) The International Constitutional Order. International and Comparative Law Quarterly 55:51–76.

Dicey A.V. (1885) Introduction to the Study of the Law of the Constitution. Macmillan, London.

Diggelmann O. and Altwicker T. (2008) Is There Something Like a Constitution of International Law? Zeitschrift für ausländisches öffentliches Recht und Völkerrecht. 68(3):623–650.

Doehring K. (1984) Das Staatsrecht der Bundesrepublik Deutschland, 3 ed. Metzner, Frankfurt a.M.

Dolnick E. (2011) The Clockwork Universe. HarperCollins Ebook.

Donahue C. (2006) Comparative Law Before the *Code Napoléon*. In: Reimann M. and Zimmermann R. (eds) The Oxford Handbook of Comparative Law. Oxford University Press, Oxford, pp. 3–34.

Dooyeweerd H. (2012) Roots of Western Culture: Pagan, Secular, and Christian Options. In: Strauss D.F.M. (gen. ed.) The Collected Works of Herman Dooyeweerd, Series B, Volume 15. Paideia Press, Grand Rapids, 1959 edition translated by John Kraay.

Duijnstee F.X. (1930) St. Aurelius Augustinus over kerk en staat. Het Nederlands Boekhuis, Tilburg.

Dukes R. (2011) Hugo Sinzheimer and the Constitutional Function of Labour Law. In: Davidov G. and Langille B. (eds) The Idea of Labour Law. Oxford University Press, Oxford, pp. 57–68.

Ehlers, D. (1996) Art 140. In: Sachs M. (ed.) Grundgesetz Kommentar. C.H. Beck, München, pp. 1910–1940.

Ellis A., Gratschew M., Pammett J.H. and Thiessen E. (eds) (2006) Engaging the Electorate: Initiatives to Promote Voter Turnout from Around the World. International Institute for Democracy and Electoral Assistance, Stockholm.

European Commission for Democracy Through Law (2013) Opinion on the Fourth Amendment to the Fundamental Law of Hungary. CDL-AD(2013)012, Strasbourg, 17 June.

Evangelische Kirche in Deutschland (2013) Dritter Weg. http://www.caritas.de/glossare/kirchlichesarbeitsrecht and http://www.diakonie.de/arbeitsrecht-in-kirche-und-diakonie-9452.html. Accessed 13 November 2013.

Evans E.C. (2008) Religious Education in Public Schools: An International Human Rights Perspective. Human Rights Law Review 8(3):449–473.

Evans M.D. (2010–2011) From Cartoons to Crucifixes: Current Controversies Concerning the Freedom of Religion and the Freedom of Expression Before the European Court of Human Rights. Journal of Law and Religion 26:345–370.

Falana F. (2010) Constitutionalism, Rule of Law, and Human Rights. In: Adejumobi S. (ed.) Governance and Politics in Post-military Nigeria – Changes and Challenges. Palgrave Macmillan, Basingstoke, pp. 125–143.

Fassbender B. (2007) 'We the Peoples of the United Nations' – Constituent Power and Constitutional Form in International Law. In: Loughlin M. and Walker N. (eds) The Paradox of Constitutionalism – Constituent Power and Constitutional Form. Oxford University Press, Oxford, pp. 269–290.

Fateh-Moghadam B. (2012) Criminalizing Male Circumcision? Case Note: Landgericht Cologne, Judgment of 7 May 2012 – No. 151 Ns 169/11. German Law Journal 13:1131–1145.

Favoreu L. (1990) Constitutional Review in Europe. In: Henkin L. and Rosenthal A.J. (eds) Constitutionalism and Rights. Columbia University Press, New York, pp. 38–62.

Finnis J. (1997–1998) On the Practical Meaning of Secularism. Notre Dame Law Review 73:491–516.

Flores I.B. (2013) Law, Liberty and the Rule of Law (in a Constitutional Democracy). In: Flores I.B. and Himma K.E. (eds) Law, Liberty, and the Rule of Law. Springer, Dordrecht, Chapter 6.

Fombad C.M. (2012) Internationalization of Constitutional Law and Constitutionalism in Africa. American Journal of Comparative Law 60:439–473.

Franck T.M. and Thiruvengadam A.K. (2003) International Law and Constitution-Making. Chinese Journal of International Law 2(2):467–518.

Friedrich C.J. (1964) Transcendent Justice/The Religious Dimension of Constitutionalism. Duke University Press, Durham.

Frishman M. and Muller S. (2010) Introduction. In: Frishman M. and Muller S. (eds) The Dynamics of Constitutionalism in the Age of Globalisation. Asser Press, The Hague, pp. 1–14.

Gavison R. and Perez N. (2008) Days of Rest in Multicultural Societies: Private, Public, Separate? In: Cane P., Evans C. and Robinson Z. (eds) Law and Religion in Theoretical and Historical Context. Cambridge University Press, Cambridge, Chapter 9.

Gesetz (2012) http://www.sueddeutsche.de/politik/gesetzentwurf-kabinett-bringt-gesetz-zur-beschneidung-auf-weg-1.1491979. Accessed 10 November 2012.

Ghai Y. (1990–1991) The Theory of the State in the Third World and the Problem of Constitutionalism. Connecticut Journal of International Law 6:411–423.

Glenn H.P. (2013) The Cosmopolitan State. Oxford University Press, Oxford.

Gray J. (1995) Enlightenment's Wake: Politics and Culture at the Close of the Modern Age. Routledge, London.

Greenawalt K. (2009) Secularism, Religion, and Liberal Democracy in the United States. Cardozo Law Review 30:2383–2400.

Greenberg D., Katz S.N., Wheatley S.C. and Oliviero M.B. (eds) (1993) Constitutionalism and Democracy – Transitions in the Contemporary World. Oxford University Press, Oxford.

Griffen S.M. (1990) Constitutionalism in the United States: From Theory to Politics. Oxford Journal of Legal Studies 10(2):200–220.

Grimm D. (2008) The Constitution in the Process of Denationalization. In: Nergelius J. (ed.) Constitutionalism – New Challenges: European Law from a Nordic Perspective. Martinus Nijhoff, Leiden, pp. 71–92.

Grimm D. (2009) Conflicts Between General Laws and Religious Norms. Cardozo Law Review 30(6):2369–2382.

Groh K. (2009) Staatlicher Schutz der Religionsfreiheit und das Problem der Definition von Religion. In: Bielefeldt H. *et al.* (eds) Jahrbuch Menschenrechte 2009, Böhlau Verlag, Wien, pp. 76–88.

Gross N. (2013) Frankreich ein kraft Verfassung laïzistischer Staat – mit regionalen Ausnahmen. Juristenzeitung 18:881–884.

Gunn J.T. (2003) The Complexity of Religion and the Definition of 'Religion' in International Law. Harvard Human Rights Journal 16:189–215.

Habermas J. (2008) Between Naturalism and Religion – Philosophical Essays (translated from the German by Ciaran Cronin). Polity Press, Cambridge.

Habermas J. (2012) The Crisis of the European Union in the Light of a Constitutionalization of International Law. European Journal of International Law 23(2):335–348.

Halberstam D. (2012) Local, Global and Plural Constitutionalism: Europe Meets the World. In: De Búrca G. and Weiler J.H.H. (eds) The Worlds of European Constitutionalism. Cambridge University Press, Cambridge, pp. 150–202.

Hallaq W.B. (2003) 'Muslim Rage' and Islamic Law. Hastings Law Journal 54:1705–1719.

Harding A. and Leyland P. (2007) Comparative Law in Constitutional Contexts. In: Örücü E. and Nelken D. (eds) Comparative Law – A Handbook. Hart Publishing, Oxford, pp. 313–338.

Hardt H. and Negri A. (2000) Empire. Harvard University Press, Cambridge, Mass.

Hassan F. (2002) Religious Liberty in Pakistan: Law, Reality, and Perception (A Brief Synopsis). Brigham Young University Law Review 2002(2):283–299.

Heckel M. (2013) Gesammelte Schriften – Staat Kirche Recht Geschichte, Band VI. Mohr Siebeck, Tübingen.

Hellsten S.K. (1998) Moral Individualism and the Justification of Liberal Democracy. Ratio Juris 11(4):320–345.

Henkin L. (1994) A New Birth of Constitutionalism: Genetic Influences and Genetic Defects. In: Rosenfeld M. (ed.) Constitutionalism, Identity, Difference, and Legitimacy – Theoretical Perspectives. Duke University Press, Durham, pp. 39–53.

Henrard K. (2001) The Accommodation of Religious Diversity in South Africa against the Background of the Centrality of the Equality Principle in the New Constitutional Dispensation. Journal of African Law 45(1):51–72.

Hepple B. (2011) Factors Influencing the Making and Transformation of Labour Law in Europe. In: Davidov G. and Langille B. (eds) The Idea of Labour Law. Oxford University Press, Oxford, pp. 30–42.

Herzog R. (1987) Grundgesetz. In: Kunst H., Herzog R., Schlaich K. and Schneemelcher W. (eds) Evangelisches Staatslexikon, 3 ed. Kreuz-Verlag, Stuttgart, pp. 1204–1212.

Hirschl R. (2011) Comparative Constitutional Law and Religion. In: Ginsburg T. and Dixon R. (eds) Comparative Constitutional Law. Edward Elgar, Cheltenham and Northampton, pp. 422–440.

Hirschl R. (2013) Editorial. International Journal of Constitutional Law 11(1):1–12.

Hirschl R. and Eisgruber C.L. (2006) Prologue: North American Constitutionalism? International Journal of Constitutional Law 4(2):203–212.

Höffe O. (2007) Democracy in an Age of Globalisation. Springer, Dordrecht.

Hoffman J. (1995) Beyond the State. Polity Press, Cambridge.

Horwitz P. (2011) The Agnostic Age – Law, Religion, and the Constitution. Oxford University Press, Oxford.

House H.W. (1999) A Tale of Two Kingdoms: Can There be Peaceful Coexistence of Religion within the Secular State? Brigham Young University Journal of Public Law 13:203–292.

Hunter I. (2009) The Shallow Legitimacy of Secular Liberal Orders: The Case of Early Modern Brandenburg-Prussia. In: Levey G.B. and Modood T. (eds) Secularism, Religion and Multicultural Citizenship. Cambridge University Press, Cambridge, pp. 27–55.

Huster S. (2002) Die ethische Neutralität des Staates – Eine liberale Interpretation der Verfassung. Mohr Siebeck, Tübingen.

Ipsen J. (2007) Staatsrecht I Staatsorganisationsrecht, 19 ed. Carl Heymanns Verlag, Köln.

Isensee J. and Kirchhof P. (1987) Handbuch des Staatsrechts, Vol I. Müller, Heidelberg.

Israel J. (2008) A Church in Saudi Arabia. *Time* 19 March. http://content.time.com/time/world/article/0,8599,1723715,00.html. Accessed 16 June 2015.

Janis M.W. (1991) Religion and the Literature of International Law: Some Standard Texts. In: Janis M.W. (ed.) The Influence of Religion on the Development of International Law. Martinus Nijhoff, Dordrecht, pp. 61–84.

Jennings I. (1938) Administrative Law and Administrative Jurisdiction. Journal of Comparative Legislation and International Law 20(1):99–104.

Kalman Y. (2013) Thou Shalt Accommodate the Secular: Sabbath Laws' Evolution from 'Day of Rest' to 'Day of Leisure'. Temple International and Comparative Law Journal 27:111–147.

Kellogg T.E. (2009) Constitutionalism with Chinese Characteristics? Constitutional Development and Civil Litigation. International Journal of Constitutional Law 7(2):215–246.

Kennedy D. (1991) Images of Religion in International Legal Theory. In: Janis M.W. (ed.) The Influence of Religion on the Development of International Law. Martinus Nijhoff, Dordrecht, pp. 137–146.

Kiiver P. (2010) The Impact of Internationalisation on Constitutional Law: Some Reflections. In: Frishman M. and Muller S. (eds) The Dynamics of Constitutionalism in the Age of Globalisation. Asser Press, The Hague, pp. 111–123.

Kirchhof G., Magen S. and Schneider K. (eds) (2012) Was weiß Dogmatik? Mohr Siebeck, Tübingen.

Kistner U. (2009) Sovereignty in Question: Agamben, Schmitt, and Some Consequences. SA Publiekreg/Public Law 24(2):240–268.

Kochenov D. (2009) European Citizenship and the Difficult Relationship between Status and Rights. Columbia Journal of European Law 15:169–237.

Kokott J. (1996) Art 4. In: Sachs M. (ed.) Grundgesetz Kommentar, C.H. Beck, München, pp. 249–275.

Krämer G. (2006) Der Islam und der Westen. In: Spiegel Special – Das Magazin zum Thema. Weltmacht Religion: Wie der Glaube Politik und Gesellschaft beeinflusst. 9:70–74.

Krisch N. (2010) Beyond Constitutionalism: The Pluralist Structure of Postnational Law. Oxford University Press, Oxford.

Kyriazopoulos K.N. (2001) The 'Prevailing Religion' in Greece: Its Meaning and Implications. Journal of Church and State 43:511–538.

Laczko F. and Appave G. (eds) (2013) World Migration Report 2013. International Organization for Migration. http://publications.iom.int/bookstore/free/WMR2013_EN.pdf. Accessed 11 March 2014.

Ladeur K.-H. and Augsberg I. (2007a) Der Mythos vom neutralen Staat. Juristen Zeitung 62:12–18. Ladeur K.-H. and Augsberg I. (2007b) The Myth of the Neutral State: The Relationship between State and Religion in the Face of New Challenges. German Law Journal 8(2):143–152.

Landau D. (2013) Abusive Constitutionalism. University of California, Davis Law Review 47:189–260.

Law D. (2004–2005) Generic Constitutional Law. Minnesota Law Review 89:652–742.

Lawrence E. (1970) The Origins and Growth of Modern Education. Penguin, Harmondsworth.

Laycock D. (2010) Religious Liberty Vol. 1. Eerdmans, Grand Rapids.

Le Roux C.S. (2011) European Foundations Shaping Schooling in South Africa: Early Dutch and British Colonial Influence at the Cape. In: Booyse J.J., Le Roux C.S., Seroto J. and Wolhuter C.C. (eds) A History of Schooling in South Africa. Van Schaik, Pretoria, pp. 57–86.

Lennox J.C. (2011) Gunning for God: Why the New Atheists are Missing the Target. Lion Hudson, Oxford.
Levey G.B. (2009) Secularism and Religion in a Multicultural Age. In: Levey G.B. and Modood T. (eds) Secularism, Religion and Multicultural Citizenship. Cambridge University Press, Cambridge, pp. 4–5.
Levey G.B. and Modood T. (2009) Secularism, Religion and Multicultural Citizenship. Cambridge University Press, Cambridge.
Levine S.J. (2012) A Look at the Establishment Clause Through the Prism of Religious Perspectives: Religious Majorities, Religious Minorities, and Nonbelievers. Chicago-Kent Law Review 87(3):775–810.
Lodge T. (1998) Political Corruption in South Africa. African Affairs 97:157–187.
Löhr I. and Wenzlhuemer R. (eds) (2013) The Nation State and Beyond – Governing Globalization Processes in the Nineteenth and Early Twentieth Centuries. Springer, Berlin.
Loth M. (2007) Limits of Private Law: Enriching Legal Dogmatics. Hofstra Law Review 35:1725–1751.
Loughlin M. and Walker N. (eds) (2007) The Paradox of Constitutionalism – Constituent Power and Constitutional Form. Oxford University Press, Oxford.
Lulic M. and Kumric N.M. (2014) Religious Minorities in the Media Space of the Republic of Croatia. US–China Law Review 11:94–111.
Madeley J.T.S. and Haynes J. (2011) Transnational Religious Actors. In: Reinalda R. (ed.) The Ashgate Research Companion to Non-State Actors. Ashgate, Dartmouth, pp. 63–74.
Mancini S. and Rosenfeld M. (eds) (2014) Constitutional Secularism in an Age of Religious Revival. Oxford University Press, Oxford.
Marshall W.P. (2009) Progressives, the Religion Clauses, and the Limits of Secularism. In: Balkin J.M. and Siegel R.B. (eds) The Constitution in 2020. Oxford University Press, New York, pp. 231–242.
Martínez-Torrón J. and Durham W.C. (2010) Interim General Report. In: Martínez-Torrón J. and Durham W.C. (eds) Religion and the Secular State – Interim National Reports. Brigham Young University, Provo, pp. 1–56.
Martínez-Torrón, J. and Durham W.C. (2012) Religion and the Secular State. In: Brown K.B. and Snyder D.V. (eds) General Reports of the XVIIIth Congress of the International Academy of Comparative Law/ Rapports Généraux du XVIIIème Congrès de l'Académie Internationale de Droit Comparé. Springer, Dordrecht, pp. 1–28.
McConnell M.W. (2009) The Influence of Cultural Conflict on the Jurisprudence of the Religion Clauses of the First Amendment. In: Cane P., Evans C. and Robinson Z. (eds) Law and Religion in

Theoretical and Historical Context. Cambridge University Press, Cambridge, pp. 100–122.
McIlwain C.H. (1947) Constitutionalism Ancient and Modern, revised edition. Cornell University Press, Ithaca.
Meyerson D. (2009) Why Religion Belongs in the Private Sphere, Not the Public Square. In: Cane P., Evans C. and Robinson Z. (eds) Law and Religion in Theoretical and Historical Context. Cambridge University Press, Cambridge, pp. 44–71.
Mirow M.C. (2004) International Law and Religion in Latin America: The Beagle Channel Dispute. Suffolk Transnational Law Review 28(1):1–29.
Mnyongani F. (2012) The Status of Animals in African Cosmology: A Non-legal Perspective. SA Public Law 27:88–102.
Möllers C. (2007) 'We are (Afraid of) the People': Constituent Power in German Constitutionalism. In: Loughlin M. and Walker N. (eds) The Paradox of Constitutionalism – Constituent Power and Constitutional Form. Oxford University Press, Oxford, Chapter 5.
Moon R. (2008) Government Support for Religious Practice. In: Moon R. (ed.) Law and Religious Pluralism in Canada. University of British Columbia Press, Vancouver, pp. 217–238.
Moon R. (2012) Freedom of Religion under the *Charter of Rights*: The Limits of State Neutrality. UBC Law Review 45(2):497–549.
Moore K. and Lewis D. (2009a) The Origins of Globalization. Routledge, New York.
Moore K. and Lewis D. (2009b) The Origins of Globalization: A Canadian Perspective. Ivey Business Journal 73(3):4.
Nafziger J. (1991) The Functions of Religion in the International Legal System. In: Janis M.W. (ed.) The Influence of Religion on the Development of International Law. Martinus Nijhoff, Dordrecht, pp. 147–169.
Nergelius J. (2008) Between Collectivism and Constitutionalism: The Nordic Countries and Constitutionalism – A 'Final Frontier' or a Period of Transition? In: Nergelius J. (ed.) Constitutionalism – New Challenges: European Law from a Nordic Perspective. Martinus Nijhoff, Leiden, pp. 119–133.
Nirenberg S. (2013) The Resurgence of Secularism: Hostility towards Religion in the United States and France. Washington University Jurisprudence Review 5:131–161.
Oliva J.G. (2010) Church, State and Establishment in the United Kingdom in the 21st Century: Anachronism or Idiosyncrasy? Public Law July:482–504.

Peté S.A. and Crocker A.D. (2012) Ancient Rituals and their Place in the Modern World: Culture, Masculinity and the Killing of Bulls. Obiter 33(2):278–296, 580–599.

Peters A. (2009) The Merits of Global Constitutionalism. Indiana Journal of Global Legal Studies 16(2):397–411.

Pew Research Center (2012) Rising Tide of Restrictions on Religion. http://www.pewforum.org/files/2012/09/RisingTideofRestrictions-full report.pdf. Accessed 20 August 2013.

Phillips T. (2014) China on Course to Become 'World's Most Christian Nation' Within 15 Years. The Telegraph, 19 April 2014. http://www.telegraph.co.uk/news/worldnews/asia/china/10776023/China-on-course-to-become-worlds-most-Christian-nation-within-15-years.html. Accessed 23 June 2014.

Pierard R.V. (1986) The Lutheran Two-Kingdoms Doctrine and Subservience to the State in Modern Germany. Journal of the Evangelical Theological Society 29(2):193–203.

Pohlmann M. (2013) The Migration of Elites in a Borderless World: Citizenship as an Incentive for Professionals and Managers? In: Pohlmann M., Yang J. and Lee J.-H. (eds) Citizenship and Migration in the Era of Globalization – The Flow of Migrants and the Perception of Citizenship in Asia and Europe. Springer, Heidelberg, pp. 59–70.

Pollis A. (1996) Cultural Relativism Revisited: Through a State Prism. Human Rights Quarterly 18:316–344.

Przeworski A., Alvarez M., Cheibub J.A. and Limongi F. (1996) What Makes Democracies Endure? Journal of Democracy 7(1):39–55.

Raday F. (2009) Secular Constitutionalism Vindicated. Cardozo Law Review 30(6):2769–2798.

Ramcharan B.M. (2010) Constitutionalism in an Age of Globalisation and Global Threats. In: Frishman M. and Muller S. (eds) The Dynamics of Constitutionalism in the Age of Globalisation. Asser Press, The Hague, pp. 15–47.

Randall M.H. and McGregor E. (2010) Reconciling Direct Democracy and Fundamental Rights: The Case of the Swiss Minaret Initiative. Tijdschrift voor Constitutioneel Recht 2010(4):428–436.

Rautenbach C. (2011) Umkhosi Ukweshwama: Revival of a Zulu Festival in Celebration of the Universe's Rites of Passage. In: Bennett T.W. (ed.) Traditional African Religions in South African Law. Juta, Cape Town, Chapter 4.

Ravitch F.S. (2004) A Funny Thing Happened on the Way to Neutrality: Broad Principles, Formalism, and the Establishment Clause. Georgia Law Review 38(2):489–573.

Ravitch F.S. (2012) Law, Religion and Science – Determining the Role Religion Plays in Shaping Scientific Inquiry in Constitutional Democracies – the Case of Intelligent Design. Contemporary Readings in Law and Social Justice 4(1):191–204.

Rawls J. (1993) Political Liberalism. Columbia University Press, New York.

Rawls J. (1997) The Idea of Public Reason Revisited. University of Chicago Law Review 64:765–807.

Reder M. and Schmidt J. (2010) Habermas and Religion. In: Habermas J. et al. An Awareness of What is Missing – Faith and Reason in a Post-secular Age (translated from the German by Ciaran Cronin). Polity Press, Cambridge, pp. 3–7.

Reisman M.H.A. (1991) Islamic Fundamentalism and Its Impact on International Law and Politics. In: Janis M.W. (ed.) The Influence of Religion on the Development of International Law. Martinus Nijhoff, Dordrecht, pp. 107–134.

Ritsert J. (2012) Gerechtigkeit, Gleichheit, Freiheit und Vernunft – Über vier Grundbegriffe der politischen Philosophie. Springer, Wiesbaden.

Roberts A. (2011) Comparative International Law? The Role of National Courts in Creating and Enforcing International Law. International Comparative Law Quarterly 60:57–92.

Robinson J.A. (2003) On the Sharpest Horns of Dilemma: What Does the Court Do Now? Tydskrif vir Hedendaagse Romeins-Hollandse Reg 66:131–138.

Robinson J.A. (2004) Children and the Right to Freedom of Religion. Tydskrif vir die Suid-Afrikaanse Reg 15(1):202–208.

Rommen H. (1935) Der Staat in der katholischen Gedankenwelt. Verlag der Bonifacius-Druckerei, Paderborn.

Rosenfeld M. (2014) Is Global Constitutionalism Meaningful or Desirable? European Journal of International Law 25(1):177–199.

Rousseau J.J. (1762) The Social Contract or Principles of Political Rights. Translated 1782 by G.D.H. Cole, public domain, rendered into HTML and text by Jon Roland. Available at http://www.constitution.org/jjr/socon.htm. Accessed 9 August 2013.

Sadurski W., Czarnota A. and Krygier M. (eds) (2006) Spreading Democracy and the Rule of Law? – The Impact of EU Enlargement on the Rule of Law, Democracy and Constitutionalism in Post-Communist Legal Orders. Springer, Dordrecht.

Sajó A. (2006) Becoming 'Europeans': The Impact of EU 'Constitutionalism' on Post-Communist Pre-modernity. In: Sadurski W., Czarnota A. and Krygier M. (eds) Spreading Democracy and the Rule of Law? – The Impact of EU Enlargement on the Rule of Law, Democracy and

Constitutionalism in Post-Communist Legal Orders. Springer, Dordrecht, pp. 175–192.

Schilling D.R. (2013) Knowledge Doubling Every 12 Months, Soon to be Every 12 Hours. In: Industry Tap Into News, 19 April 2013 http://www.industrytap.com/knowledge-doubling-every-12-months-soon-to-be-every-12-hours/3950. Accessed 23 June 2014.

Schuller F. (ed.) (2006) Joseph Cardinal Ratzinger (Pope Benedict XVI) and Jürgen Habermas, Dialectics of Secularization – On Reason and Religion. Ignatius Press, San Francisco.

Schwöbel C.E.J. (2010) Organic Global Constitutionalism. Leiden Journal of International Law 23:529–553.

Seiple R. (2012) Religion and International Law: Matching Mission to Vision. Santa Clara Journal of International Law 10:171–178.

Sexton J. (2012) State of the World's Science. Scientific American 307(4):28–32.

Shermer M. (2014) Skeptic. Scientific American 310(3):65.

Slotte P. (2010) The Religious and the Secular in European Human Rights Discourse. Finnish Yearbook of International Law 21:231–286.

Smith C. (2009) A Very English Affair: Establishment and Human Rights in an Organic Constitution. In: Cane P., Evans C. and Robinson Z. (eds) Law and Religion in Theoretical and Historical Context. Cambridge University Press, Cambridge, Chapter 8.

Smith R.M. (2009) Beyond Sovereignty and Uniformity: The Challenges for Equal Citizenship in the Twenty-first Century (Book Review). Harvard Law Review 122:907–936.

Spadijer S. (2012) A Hardcore Case Against (Strong) Judicial Review of Direct Democracy. University of Queensland Law Journal 31:55–99.

Spiro P.J. (2010) Dual Citizenship as Human Right. International Journal of Constitutional Law 8:111–130.

Stein T. (2007) Himmlische Quellen und Irdisches Rect – Religiöse Voraussetzungen des freiheitlichen Verfassungsstaates. Campus Verlag, Frankfurt.

Stern K. (1984) Das Staatsrecht der Bundesrepublik Deutschland, Vol. 1, 2d ed. C.H. Beck, München.

Supreme Court of Canada (2012) Scheduled Hearings. http://www.scc-csc.gc.ca/case-dossier/info/hear-aud-eng.aspx?ya=2014&ses=02&submit=Search. Accessed 29 November 2013.

Tagesschau (2012) http://www.tagesschau.de/inland/beschneidung152.html. Accessed 22 October 2012.

Takemura H. (2009) International Human Right to Conscientious Objection to Military Service and Individual Duties to Disobey Manifestly Illegal Orders. Springer, Berlin.

Tardif E. (2012) Immigration, Religion and Human Rights – State Policy Challenges in Balancing Public and Private Interests. European Journal of Law Reform 14:85–103.

Taylor C. (2009) Foreword – What is Secularism? In: Levey G.B. and Modood T. (eds) Secularism, Religion and Multicultural Citizenship. Cambridge University Press, Cambridge, pp. xi–xxii, xi.

Taylor P.M. (2005) Freedom of Religion – UN and European Human Rights Law and Practice. Cambridge University Press, Cambridge.

Temperman J. (2010a) State–Religion Relationships and Human Rights Law – Towards a Right to Religiously Neutral Governance. Martinus Nijhoff, Dordrecht.

Temperman J. (2010b) State Neutrality in Public School Education: An Analysis of the Interplay Between the Neutrality Principle, the Right to Adequate Education, Children's Right to Freedom of Religion or Belief, Parental Liberties, and the Position of Teachers. Human Rights Quarterly 32:865–897.

Temperman J. (ed.) (2012) The Lautsi Papers: Multidisciplinary Reflections on Religious Symbols in the Public School Classroom. Martinus Nijhoff, Dordrecht.

Teubner G. (2012) Verfassungsfragmente – Gesellschaftlicher Konstitutionalismus in der Globalisierung. Suhrkamp Verlag, Berlin.

Tiedemann P. (2012) Religionsfreiheit – Menschenrecht oder Toleranzgebot? Springer, Heidelberg.

Tierney B. (1996) Religious Rights: A Historical Perspective. In: Reynolds N.B. and Durham W.C. (eds) Religious Liberty in Western Thought. Emory University, Atlanta, pp. 29–57.

Tom A. (2006) How Stricter Dutch Immigration Policies are Contributing to Rising Islamic Fundamentalism in the Netherlands and Europe. Washington University Global Studies Law Review 5:451–468.

Traub R. (2006) Der Einfluss der Religionen auf Politik und Gesellschaft. In: Spiegel Special – Das Magazin zum Thema. Weltmacht Religion: Wie der Glaube Politik und Gesellschaft beeinflusst. 9:6–15.

Turner B.S. (2011) Religion and Modern Society – Citizenship, Secularisation and the State. Cambridge University Press, Cambridge.

Turner B.S. (2012) Managing Religions, Citizenship and the Liberal Paradox. Citizenship Studies 16(8):1059–1072.

UNHCR (2013) Protecting Refugees – Q&A. http://www.unhcr.se/en/who-we-help/refugees/protecting-refugees-qa.html. Accessed 29 November 2013.

United Nations Department of Economic and Social Affairs, Population Division (2013) World Migration in Figures. http://www.oecd.org/els/mig/World-Migration-in-Figures.pdf. Accessed 11 March 2014.

Van Bijsterveld S. (2002) The Empty Throne – Democracy and the Rule of Law in Transition. Lemma Publishers, Utrecht.

Van den Brink T. (2010) Fit for All Practical Purposes? Constitutionalism as a Legitimising Strategy for the European Union. In: Frishman M. and Muller S. (eds) The Dynamics of Constitutionalism in the Age of Globalisation. Asser Press, The Hague, pp. 125–143.

Van der Vyver J.D. (2005) Limitations of Freedom of Religion or Belief: International Law Perspectives. Emory International Law Review 19:499–537.

Van der Walt J. (2009) The Shadow and Its Shade: A Response to Ulrike Kistner's Paper 'Sovereignty in Question'. SA Publiekreg/Public Law 24(2):269–296.

Venter F. (2000) Constitutional Comparison – Japan, Germany, Canada and South Africa as Constitutional States. Juta/Kluwer, Cape Town, Dordrecht.

Venter F. (2010a) Global Features of Constitutional Law. Wolf Legal Publishers, Nijmegen.

Venter F. (2010b) Liberal Democracy: The Unintended Consequence – South African Constitution-Writing Propelled by the Winds of Globalisation. South African Journal on Human Rights 26:43–63.

Venter F. (2012a) Religion in the Classroom: Comparative Observations. SA Public Law 27:433–453.

Venter F. (2012b) South Africa: A Diceyan *Rechtsstaat*? McGill Law Journal 57(4):721–747.

Venter F. (2014) The 'Rule of Law' as a Global Norm for Constitutionalism. In: Silkenat J.R., Hickey J.E. and Barenboim P.D. (eds) The Legal Doctrines of the Rule of Law and the Legal State (Rechtsstaat). Springer, Cham, pp. 91–104.

Ventura M. (2012) The Rise and Contradictions of Italy as a Secular State. In: Cumper P. and Lewis T. (eds) Religion, Rights and Secular Society – European Perspectives. Edward Elgar, Cheltenham and Northampton, pp. 126–146.

Vinx L. (2013) The Incoherence of Strong Popular Sovereignty. International Journal of Constitutional Law 11:101–124.

Von Beyme K. (1968) Die verfassunggebende Gewalt des Volkes. Mohr, Tübingen.

Von Heyking J. (1999–2000) The Harmonization of Heaven and Earth? Religion, Politics and Law in Canada. University of British Columbia Law Review 33:663–697.

Von Mangoldt H., Klein F. and Stark C. (2010) Das Bonner Grundgesetz Band 1. 6 ed. Verlag Franz Vahlen, München.

Vorländer H. (2012) Die Verfassung vor, nach, über und unter dem Staat. Die Konstitutionalismusdebatte in der Suche nach einem anderen

Verfassungsbegriff. In: Lindemann H., Malaviya N., Hanebeck A., Hanschmann F., Nickel R. and Tohidipur T. (eds) Erzählungen vom Konstitutionalismus. Nomos, Baden-Baden, pp. 23–42.
Voßkuhle A. (2012) Was leistet Rechtsdogmatik? In: Kirchhof G., Magen S. and Schneider K. (eds) Was weiß Dogmatik? Mohr Siebeck, Tübingen, pp. 111–116.
Walker N. (2002) The Idea of Constitutional Pluralism. Modern Law Review 65:317–359.
Ward S. and Eden C. (2009) Key Issues in Education Policy. Sage Publications, London.
Wattles J. (1996) The Golden Rule. Oxford University Press, New York.
Webber J. (2009) Understanding the Religion in Freedom of Religion. In: Cane P., Evans C. and Robinson Z. (eds) Law and Religion in Theoretical and Historical Context. Cambridge University Press, Cambridge, pp. 26–43.
Weber M. (2010) Politik als Beruf. 11th ed. Duncker & Humblot, Berlin.
Whitman J.Q. (2008) Separating Church and State: The Atlantic Divide. Historical Reflections 34(3):86–104.
Wiener A., Lang A.F., Tully J., Maduro M.P. and Kumm M. (2012) Editorial – Global Constitutionalism: Human Rights, Democracy and the Rule of Law. Global Constitutionalism 1(1):1–15.
Wieser B. (2005) Vergleichendes Verfassungsrecht. Springer, Vienna.
Willems U. (2012) Religionsfreiheit und Religionspolitik im Zeitalter relgiöser und kulturelle Pluralität. In: Bogner D. and Heimbach-Steins M. (eds) Freiheit – Gleichheit – Religion. Ergon Verlag, Würzburg, p. 131 *et seq*.
Witte J. (1996) Moderate Religious Liberty in the Theology of John Calvin. In: Reynolds N.B. and Durham W.C. (eds) Religious Liberty in Western Thought. Emory University, Atlanta, pp. 83–122.
Witte J. (2006) God's Joust, God's Justice – Law and Religion in the Western Tradition. Wm B. Eerdemans Publishing Co., Grand Rapids.
Witten M. (2012) Rationalist Influences in the Adjudication of Religious Freedoms in Canada. Windsor Review of Legal and Social Issues 32:91–122.
Woodhead L. (2013) Neither Religious nor Secular: The British Situation and its Implications for Religion–State Relations. In: Berg-Sørensen A. (ed.) Contesting Secularism – Comparative Perspectives. Ashgate, Farnham, pp. 137–161.
Zafirovski M. (2011) The Enlightenment and Its Effects on Modern Society. Springer, New York.
Zeit Online (2009) Schweizer stimmen gegen Bau neuer Minarette, http://www.zeit.de/politik/ausland/2009-11/schweiz-minarett-wahl, 29 November. Accessed 9 August 2014.

Zucca L. (2009) Montesquieu, Methodological Pluralism and Comparative Constitutional Law. European Constitutional Law Review 5(3):481–500.

Zumbansen P. (2012) Comparative, Global and Transnational Constitutionalism: The Emergence of a Transnational Legal-Pluralist Order. Global Constitutionalism 1(1):16–52.

Zweigert K. and Kötz H. (1998) Introduction to Comparative Law. 3rd edn, translated by Tony Weir. Oxford University Press, Oxford.

Index

Aarnio 15–16, 238
academic freedom 172
Ackerman 182–183
Adams 24, 89–91, 204–5
adjudication 11, 32, 35, 45, 79, 82, 85, 114, 141, 157, 175–6, 198, 222, 227, 232
Afghanistan 54, 182
Africa 14, 37, 39, 54, 57, 60–63, 67, 70, 104, 127, 151, 200, 219, 228
agnosticism 14–15, 18, 28, 48, 87, 104, 139, 140–41, 147, 157, 177, 224
Alexy 15, 173
Alsace-Lorraine 159–60
Althusius 76
Altwicker 41
Anglo-American 92, 151
animal protection 131, 150
Ansah 127, 233
Apostasy 18
Aquinas 16, 76, 207
Arab Spring 127, 209
Arabic 105, 209
Arato 184
arbitrary 61, 65, 69, 82–3, 148, 216–7
Argentina 37, 102, 126
Aristotle 33, 67
Armenia 156
Arnáson 63
Aston 97
Atatürk 89
atheism 1, 14, 18, 28, 47–8, 87, 104, 139–41, 157, 177–8, 207, 224
Augsberg 221, 231–2
Augustine 10, 20, 76
Aurelius 20
Austin 112
Australia 114, 143, 169, 185, 207, 228
Austria 174

authoritarianism 54–5, 57, 61–2, 214, 218
authority 9, 19–22, 26–8, 30–31, 39–40, 42–5, 48, 54–6, 60, 64, 66, 68–9, 71–2, 75, 78, 80, 82–3, 97–9, 102, 108, 113, 115, 120, 126, 128, 132–3, 143, 148, 150–51, 153, 156, 172, 176, 179, 181, 184–6, 191–6, 198, 206–7, 213, 215–6, 218–9, 226–9, 231, 236–7, 240
autonomy 19, 59, 61, 63, 75, 186, 190, 192–3, 207
Auvachez 189

Backer 42, 54, 75
Baha'ism 103
Bahrain 43
balance of convenience 151, 238
Balme 55–6
Banjul 122
Basson 62
Bavaria 145, 147, 169–70, 200
Bayatyan 156–7
Beal 185
Bederman 112
Beer 58–9
Belgium 88, 90–91, 171, 205
belief 1–3, 9–16, 18, 27–8, 50, 75, 88, 90, 92, 94, 97, 104, 108–9, 112–8, 121–4, 132, 134–42, 144–9, 154, 157–8, 161–3, 166, 169, 173–4, 176, 178–9, 200, 202, 204–6, 210, 212–3, 219, 222, 224, 227–8, 232, 236
Benvenisti 70, 186–7
Berber 196
Berman 113
Beyme 196
Bible 21, 134

259

Bijsterveld 40–41
Billias 67
Blackburn 15
blasphemy 94
Bobek 60
Böckenförde 207
Bogdanor 77, 80
Bohlander 94
Boozari 53–4
Bosniak 105, 189
Brahmanic 59
Brownlie 112
Bruening 21
Brugger 67, 156
Buddhism 59, 90, 103, 126, 219
burial 166–8
burkini 171
  see also burqua, clothing, dress, headscarf, jewellery, religious dress
burqa 91
  see also burkini, clothing, dress, headscarf, jewellery, religious dress

Calvin 20, 38, 76
Canada 19, 37–8, 80–81, 109, 114, 134–43, 148–9, 171–3, 176, 185, 202, 231
cannabis 166–7
  see also marijuana
capitalism 23, 33, 61, 93, 210–11
caricatures 210
Casanova 199–202
Cassese 186
cathedrals 90, 96
Catholic 17, 21, 90–91, 97, 99, 102, 123, 126–7, 136, 139, 148, 153, 160, 220, 231
ceremonial deism 226
Chamberlain 135, 138
checks and balances 47, 65
Chen 57
children 1, 15, 50, 102, 117–8, 121, 132–3, 136–9, 144–7, 158, 167–8
Chile 126, 228
China 14, 34, 43, 55–6, 92–3, 104, 125, 133, 210, 219, 228

Choudhry 182
Christenson 17, 21
Christianity
  Christ 22, 95, 99, 174
  Christendom 125–6, 203–4
  Christian 1, 3, 9–10, 20–21, 75, 83, 92, 96–7, 99, 103–5, 112, 123, 125, 132–4, 138, 162, 165, 170, 172, 174, 200–201, 207, 209–10
church 9, 20–22, 67, 88, 91–2, 95–103, 110, 123, 126–7, 132, 153–4, 159–63, 168, 172–3, 198, 200, 203, 222, 224, 226
church and state 9, 20, 22, 25, 29, 91, 95, 99–101, 137, 159–60, 170, 198, 202, 205, 239
Cicero 10
circumcision 166, 168
citizenship 4, 12–14, 21, 30, 32, 39–40, 43–4, 55–6, 59, 62, 68–9, 77, 85, 88, 92–3, 99, 101, 105–6, 129, 131, 137, 144, 147–9, 154–7, 181–2, 187–90, 192–5, 205, 212, 225, 228–9, 236
civilization 1, 14, 53, 58, 87, 93, 125, 137, 198
Clarke 167
clothing 171–2, 176
  see also burkini, burqua, dress, headscarf, jewellery, religious dress
CODESA 197
Cohen 83, 184
Cold War 34, 62, 66, 156
Collins 1
colonialism 37, 51, 107, 209
Columbia 135
comity 78, 202
common law 13, 38, 78, 163, 167–8
communal 11, 18–9, 158, 165, 173
communism 37, 54, 57, 59–60, 67, 93, 104, 127, 210, 231
comparative constitutional law 34, 73
  see also constitutional comparison
Condorelli 186
Confucius 29, 59, 83, 125, 219

conscience 11, 15–16, 21, 94, 100–101, 109, 113, 116, 118, 122–3, 127, 134, 136–7, 140, 148–9, 157–9, 162–3, 193, 220, 230
conscientious objection 131, 155–7
Constantine 20
constitution-making 35–40, 42–3, 108, 184, 195–6, 199
constitutional
 agnosticism 177
 artefacts 107, 190–91, 194, 199, 214
 comparison 4, 31, 34, 36, 45, 85, 224
 law 4, 13, 19, 31–45, 49, 58, 70–71, 73, 77–8, 88, 92, 102, 107, 112, 122, 140, 161, 170, 177, 181–2, 185, 190–91, 199, 214, 224–7, 234, 236
 state 1–5, 48, 68, 76–9, 81, 83, 108–9, 167, 175, 179, 183, 187, 190, 198, 213, 216–9, 221, 225, 228–9, 236, 239–40
 value 107, 148, 163, 170, 177, 236
constitutionalization of international law 39–42, 52, 70, 72, 225
conviction 14–15, 18, 76, 143, 158, 174, 207, 218
convictions 7, 9–14, 17–18, 28, 48, 95, 99, 117–19, 136, 144, 147, 149, 154, 156, 159, 164, 171, 173, 176, 184, 204–5, 218, 221–22
Coptic 170
corporal punishment 15, 158
corruption 55, 60–61, 108
cosmopolitanism 34, 42, 46, 49, 189
counter-majoritarian dilemma 4, 38, 181, 183, 194, 197
Cox 188
creationists 224
creed 11, 14, 23, 43, 100, 103, 105, 135, 213, 230, 236
Croatia 154
Croxton 21, 103
crucifix 145, 147
culture 7, 10, 13, 18–20, 32–3, 44, 48, 51, 53, 57–9, 63, 73, 102, 105, 112, 115, 117, 119–20, 132–4, 136, 140, 147, 150–51, 155, 158, 160, 163–8, 170, 176, 178, 185, 188, 200–201, 208–9, 211, 214, 222, 234–5
Cumper 219–20

Dabestani 89
dagga 155
 see also cannabis, marijuana
Danchin 123, 225, 233
Dann 184
Daoism 219
Davies 204
Davis 23, 56–7
Dawkins 1, 143
days of rest 90, 100, 161, 163–5
De Been 208–9
De Búrca 41, 50
De Wet 73
death 13, 39, 105, 118, 192–3
decolonization 37, 43, 62, 127
defamation 124
democracy 2–3, 15, 19, 22–3, 26–7, 43, 46–7, 49–50, 55–62, 64–5, 67, 71–3, 78–9, 82, 88–90, 108, 116, 120, 122, 127, 144–5, 153, 157–9, 162, 164, 174, 181–3, 187, 189, 191–2, 194–5, 197–8, 201–3, 205–6, 208, 213–4, 216–8, 220, 225, 230–31, 234–5
 see also elections
demography 1–2, 85, 228
Denmark 63, 171
denomination 9, 13–14, 87, 90, 93, 96, 99–100, 115, 118, 125, 127, 143, 154, 173, 201, 220, 226, 230
Descartes 21–2
Deschamps 137–8, 140
despotism 65, 239
dialogue 20, 32, 127, 145, 210
Dicey 37–8
dictatorship 26, 43, 55, 59, 66, 79
Diggelmann 41
dignity 15, 22, 28, 63, 134, 155, 159, 163, 167, 207, 217, 229
diplomacy 111, 122, 227
discrimination 3, 43, 61, 81, 87, 100, 114–17, 123–4, 131, 134, 147, 154–5, 162–3, 201, 231

discriminatory 94, 119, 149, 152, 155, 165, 208, 221, 232
diversity 23, 25, 39, 42, 48–9, 102–3, 105, 137–9, 150, 167, 175, 188, 200–201, 204, 225, 230, 239
divorce 99–100, 166, 222
doctrinal 15, 41, 81–2, 125, 179, 182, 190, 199, 213, 225
doctrine 12, 15, 20–21, 25, 41, 43, 53, 76, 95, 103, 108, 113–14, 136, 158, 163, 186, 194, 211, 225–6, 232
Doehring 196
dogmatic 10, 15–18, 27, 48–9, 75, 81, 108, 119, 135, 172–4, 192–3, 222, 227
Dolnick 22
Donahue 33
Donnelly 24
Dooyeweerd 206
Dowdle 55–6
Dowell 147
Downs 70
dress 2, 106, 131, 146, 155, 169, 176, 200–201
    see also burkini, burqua, clothing, headscarf, jewellery, religious dress
dualism 183
Duijnstee 20
Dukes 161
Dworkin 27, 29, 207

East Asia 56–8
Eastern Europe 37, 56–60, 143, 200
Eastern Orthodox Church 95
Ebal 24
ecclesiastical 25, 95, 207
economics
    economic 22, 34–6, 43, 50, 53, 56–7, 59, 61, 63, 66, 73, 79, 102, 104–5, 107, 117, 119, 181, 188, 214–5, 228
    economism 73
    economy 61, 104, 187, 223, 228
Ecuador 228
Edict of Nantes 92

education 14, 18, 24, 93, 100, 106, 115, 117–20, 124, 131–9, 143–7, 153–4, 157–60, 172, 227
educational 92–3, 117, 119–20, 132–3, 139, 143–6, 170, 172, 223
Egypt 14, 54, 133, 209
Ehlers 100
elections 57, 62, 82, 93–4, 107, 183, 196–8, 214–15, 217–18
Ellis 195
emigration 21, 103, 199–200, 228
    see also migration
Enlightenment 10, 19, 22–3, 44, 90, 170, 211
environment 12, 18, 35, 59, 73–4, 78, 190, 223
epistemology 15, 19, 231
equality 15, 22, 44, 61, 68, 100, 109–10, 117, 130, 140, 142, 148, 157–8, 162–3, 187, 195, 202, 208, 233
establishment 23–5, 74, 77, 87–9, 91–2, 97–8, 105, 133–4, 161, 165, 185, 205, 224, 226, 228, 232–3, 236
ethics 9–10, 90, 93, 112, 136, 141, 147, 199, 210
ethnicity 114, 147, 163, 186
ethos 133, 182, 190, 206, 221
Europe 3, 9, 12–15, 21, 36, 20–21, 37, 40–41, 50–51, 53, 56, 59–61, 63, 67–9, 76, 91–2, 98–9, 101, 103, 106, 122, 126, 133, 143, 146–7, 149, 156–7, 161–2, 170–71, 174, 176, 189, 199–202, 204, 209–12, 219–20, 228, 232
Evangelical Lutheran Church 102, 123
Evangelische Kirche 161
Evans 146, 176
evolution 1, 56, 73, 120, 144, 224, 228, 233

fairness 2, 15, 19, 28, 76, 83, 215, 237
faith 9–12, 14–15, 17–18, 24, 94–7, 99, 101, 103, 112, 119, 134–5, 137–8, 150, 158, 165, 167, 171–4, 176–7, 192, 204, 208–9, 211, 213, 218–19, 221, 231–2

Falana 62
family 7, 59, 99, 121, 125, 135, 149, 164, 166–7, 186, 202
Fassbender 72
Fateh-Moghadam 168
Favoreu 32
Finnis 207
First Amendment *see* United States of America
Flores 29, 83
Fombad 63, 70
France 32, 36–8, 50, 56, 67, 87–92, 103, 109, 151, 156, 159–60, 165, 171, 182, 193, 200, 205, 209, 230
franchise 61, 187
Franck 37
freedom from religion 90, 93
freedom of religion 11–12, 45, 81, 92, 101–2, 109, 115–16, 121–2, 130, 137–40, 145, 148, 152–4, 156–7, 160, 162–3, 171, 173–4, 181, 204, 216, 231
Friedrich 67, 75–6
Frishman 47
fundamental rights 38, 45, 56, 63, 68–9, 78, 80, 82, 92, 108, 114, 117–8, 130–31, 157, 172, 216, 225, 236–7
fundamentalism 54, 127, 201, 210, 219, 233, 234–5
funding 24, 88, 131, 159

Gärditz 172
Gavison 165–6
gender 114, 132, 163, 201
Germany 13, 21, 27, 37–8, 50, 67–8, 76, 91, 100, 110, 119, 143–5, 151, 155, 160–61, 168–9, 171–2, 181, 184–5, 193, 196, 200, 209, 222, 231
  see also Grundgesetz
Ghai 60–62
Glenn 34, 40, 44, 102, 105, 182, 185, 188–9, 195–6
globalization 4, 31–5, 37, 39–47, 73–4, 78, 85, 102, 107, 120, 126, 133, 138, 156, 185–6, 189, 194, 199, 211, 224, 239

golden rule 28, 83, 176, 240
  see also reciprocity
good governance 2, 80, 107–8, 120, 235, 237
government 2–3, 19, 21–2, 24–6, 30, 40, 44, 47, 49–52, 54–8, 60–62, 64–9, 73, 76–8, 82–3, 92–3, 99, 102, 105–6, 108, 115, 124, 128, 138, 154, 156, 168, 171–2, 174, 182–5, 194–5, 197, 205, 215, 217, 220, 236–7
Gray 225
Greece 9, 29, 34, 67, 94–6, 112, 125, 132–3, 156, 207
Greek Orthodox Church 95
Greenawalt 205
Greenberg 79
Griffen 24, 65–6, 76
Grimm 71–2, 130
Groh 13
Gross 159
Grotius 16, 112
Grundgesetz 37–8, 100, 143, 145, 161, 196
  see also Germany
Gulf States 228
Gunn 11, 114–15
Guyana 228

Habermas 70, 184, 188, 209–11
Halberstam 50, 185–6
Hallaq 53
Harding 37
Hardt 35
Hassan 94
headscarf 91, 147, 169
  see also burkini, burqua, clothing, dress, jewellery, religious dress
Heckel 20
Heidegger 184
Henkin 47–8, 64–5
Henrard 208
Hepple 161
Herzog 196
Heyking 231–2
Hindu 147
history 3, 7, 9, 14–17, 20–22, 25, 29, 32–3, 35, 44, 46, 48–51, 53, 60,

63, 66–7, 76, 78, 88–93, 96–7, 100, 102, 111–12, 119–20, 127, 132, 136, 147, 150–51, 154, 160, 172, 175, 182, 184–5, 188–9, 192, 194, 198–9, 207, 209–10, 212, 214, 217, 221, 224, 228, 231, 234–6, 239
Hobbes 22, 193–4, 205
Höffe 73
Hoffman 26
Horwitz 177–8
hours of business 131, 163
  see also days of rest
House, H.W. 24
House of Commons 183
House of Lords 96–8, 147, 183
House of Representatives 183
Huber 44
human dignity 11, 13, 43, 68, 82–3, 144, 158, 206, 234, 236
  see also dignity
human rights 12–15, 22, 27, 43, 47, 57–8, 65, 67, 69, 76, 97–8, 101, 115–18, 121–2, 125, 128, 147, 149, 151, 153–4, 156–7, 161–2, 166, 176, 186, 201, 212–13, 227, 230
  see also fundamental rights
humanism 23, 170
humanistic 191–2, 236
Hungarian 60
Hunter 103, 206
Huster 204
hygiene 106, 150–51, 171

identity 7, 11, 15, 41, 46, 49, 53, 55, 89, 102, 138, 140, 142, 147–9, 157, 164, 167, 173, 184, 187–8, 190, 200–201, 215, 219, 235
ideology 19, 37, 47, 49, 54, 56, 64–6, 75, 80, 93, 108, 145, 170, 173, 125, 213
immigration 106, 148–50, 188, 200–202, 228
  see also migration
imprisonment 156, 174
Inca 14
India 34, 37, 103, 133, 209, 219

individual 3, 7, 10–13, 16, 18–19, 22–3, 30, 32, 38, 47, 51, 53, 55, 59, 63–5, 69, 72–3, 75–6, 82–3, 93–4, 98, 102, 107, 109, 113, 115, 120, 137–8, 140–42, 155–6, 158, 162, 165–6, 168, 172–3, 176, 187–8, 190–92, 195, 198, 201, 203, 205–7, 212–13, 216, 221–2, 225, 227–8, 230, 233, 235
indoctrination 135, 172
Indonesia 209, 219
inequality 61–2, 148, 195
  see also equality
injustice 3, 27, 45, 114, 120
  see also justice
intellectual 19, 21, 31, 53, 113, 223–4, 234
intelligent design 143
international law 2, 4, 12, 25, 36, 39–43, 52, 58, 70–72, 74, 85, 107, 111–15, 117, 119–23, 125, 127–8, 146, 150, 181–2, 184–7, 225–6, 236
international obligations 119–20, 146
internationalization of constitutional law 42, 45, 70, 225
internationalization of constitutionalism 69, 75
interpretation 16, 23, 25, 35, 45, 48, 64, 66, 71, 74, 78, 96, 105, 121–2, 159, 162, 164, 173, 177, 185, 194, 198, 215, 227, 237
intolerance 17, 92, 116–17, 123–4, 150, 192–3
Ipsen 198
Iran 1, 54, 87, 127
Iraq 149–50, 209
Ireland 99, 148
irrational 199, 222, 228
Isensee 196
Islam 3, 28, 43, 53–4, 59, 88, 92–4, 103–6, 123–4, 126–7, 132, 152, 168, 174, 182, 200–201, 204, 209, 219, 224
  see also Muslim, Shi'ite, Sunni
Islamic republic 93, 182
Islamic state 105
  see also Saudi Arabia
Israel 105, 148, 156, 163–4

Italy 93, 147, 209, 220

Jainism 103
Janis 111–13
Japan 14, 37, 39, 93, 143, 183
Jehovah's Witnesses 103, 123, 156
Jennings 38
jewellery 132, 169
Jewish 99, 151, 160, 164, 168, 173
  see also Israel, Judaism
Judaism 83, 103
judges 4, 14, 21, 43, 114, 119, 129, 131, 133, 135, 137–41, 143–5, 147, 149, 151, 153, 155, 157, 159, 161, 163, 165, 167, 169, 171, 173–7, 197, 216, 222, 224, 227, 232, 237–8
judiciary 19, 38–9, 56, 60, 64–5, 70, 77–9, 82, 108, 129, 181, 183, 198–9, 228–9, 231–2
justice 2, 9, 12, 15–16, 19, 22, 24, 26–9, 39, 46, 56, 68, 80, 101, 106, 110, 116, 119, 138, 148, 158, 164, 166, 176, 181, 192, 208, 213, 217, 222, 224, 226, 228–9, 232–3, 235–6, 238–40
  see also injustice

Kalman 164
Kant 28, 76, 196
Kellogg 55
Kelsen 184
Kennedy 112–13
Kenya 62
Kiiver 44
Kirchhof 196
Kistner 184
Kochenov 189
Kokott 100
Korea 88, 156, 219
kosher 151
Kötz 36
Krämer 210
Krisch 42
Kyriazopoulos 96

labour relations 131, 161, 163, 227
Ladeur 221, 231–2, 234–6

laicism 88, 90, 92, 159–60, 165, 170, 205, 220
Landau 217
language 10–11, 22, 25, 29, 37, 43, 45, 57–8, 60, 95, 105, 108, 117, 136, 163, 176
Latin 10, 57, 67, 126, 203–4, 207
Latin America 57, 126
Law, David 43
law and religion 4–5, 13–20, 25, 29–30, 85, 127, 159, 177, 212, 218, 224, 235, 237
Lawrence 132, 165
lawyer 19, 21, 35, 37–9, 112, 181, 191, 194, 222, 224
Laycock 24, 105
Lebanon 209
legality 57, 68, 82, 93, 216–17, 229, 234
legitimacy 19, 26, 30, 41, 47, 55, 71, 74–5, 82, 93, 117, 121, 126, 183, 186, 195, 198, 204, 214, 217–8, 232
Leibnitz 21
Lennox 1, 143
Levey 94, 202, 204
Leviathan 22
Levine 24–5
liberal democracy 27, 58, 72, 181, 191–2, 194, 206, 208, 213, 235
liberal paradox 147, 220
liberal secularism 175, 201, 204, 218
liberalism 19, 25, 27–9, 47, 50, 73, 127, 147–8, 166, 191, 201, 204, 206, 210–11, 213–14, 220, 228–9, 231–7
Libya 209
life 3, 11–12, 14–15, 22–3, 35–6, 51, 58–9, 63, 90–91, 93–4, 107, 109, 117–18, 132, 135, 140, 149, 157–8, 169, 187, 192, 196, 201, 203, 207–8, 210, 214, 223–4, 227–8, 232, 234–5
limitation 10, 29, 31, 53, 58, 61, 64–5, 68, 72, 77, 107, 115–18, 121–2, 139, 153, 162, 165–6, 171, 217, 222–3, 229, 236–7
Lindahl 184
Locke 22, 27, 36, 63, 76, 83, 195

Löhr 33, 35, 44
Loughlin 184, 191, 193
Lulic 218
Luther 23, 76
Lutheran 102, 123, 160

Machiavelli 22
Madeley 126–7
Madison 38
Maghreb 209
majoritarianism 4, 59, 96, 135, 181, 194, 197, 199, 217, 225
Malaysia 54, 56, 209, 219
Malaysians 228
Mancini 127
Maori 167
margin of appreciation 147, 162
marijuana 155
 see also cannabis
Maritain 207
marriage 13, 90, 97, 99, 154, 168–9, 188
Marshall 208
Marsilius 76
Martínez-Torrón 81, 87, 93, 95, 108–10
Marxist 55–6
Mauretania 209
McConnell 25
McIlwain 52, 65
medical 80, 154–6, 168
methodology 44, 51–2
Mexico 37
Meyerson 204–5, 230
migrants 104–5, 188, 228
migration 2, 33, 45, 73, 101, 103–4, 106, 115, 131, 147, 188–9, 199, 228
minaret 101, 106, 152
minority 79, 94, 101, 105, 120, 124, 134–5, 137–9, 141, 145, 152, 165–7, 171, 174, 217–9, 230
Mirabeau 193
Mirow 126
Mnyongani 150
mobility 45, 102, 104, 120, 138, 188–9
modern 12, 19, 23, 25, 29, 36, 38, 49, 63, 71, 87, 89, 97, 115, 125–6, 133, 156, 177, 182, 189, 191–4, 201–2, 204, 206–8, 219–20, 239
modernisation 201, 209, 211
modernism 22, 89
modernity 53, 209
Möllers 27
monarchy 59, 67, 97, 198
monism 40, 183
Montesquieu 22, 33
Moon, Richard 140, 142
morality 10, 16, 18, 26–9, 51, 74, 81, 89–90, 93, 99–100, 106–8, 112, 116–18, 122, 125, 128, 134–6, 141, 159, 187, 191–2, 205–7, 210–11, 216, 222, 225–6, 232–3, 237
Mormons 103, 123
Morocco 209
Moslems 54
 see also Islam, Muslim
multiculturalism 87, 133, 138, 147, 165, 189, 199, 201, 237
murder 83, 234
Muslim 27, 53, 89, 91, 93–4, 101, 104–6, 123–4, 126–7, 151, 168–71, 174, 200–201, 209–10, 219, 231
 see also Islam, Shi'ite, Sunni

Nafziger 113, 125–6
Namibia 62, 184
nation state 3, 35, 58, 71, 73, 102, 126, 133, 185, 187, 195, 239
national 2, 7, 33, 40–42, 44–7, 49, 52, 55–6, 59, 64–7, 69–71, 73–4, 89, 102–3, 111–12, 114–15, 124, 126–8, 133, 156, 162, 165, 185–90, 193, 195, 213, 225, 227
nationality 187–8, 228
nationhood 103, 185
naturalism 143, 224
Nergelius 63
Netherlands 68, 153, 171, 209
neutrality 2, 4, 13, 19, 28, 36, 46, 48, 61, 87–8, 91–2, 100–101, 105, 109–10, 112, 114, 123, 127, 133–4, 137–8, 140–43, 145–7,

154–5, 160, 165–6, 169–70, 172–3, 175–8, 204, 206–8, 212, 215–7, 222, 224, 226–32, 235–40
new atheism 177
New Zealand 114, 167–8, 185
Nigeria 62, 104
Nirenberg 90
nomocracy 53
non-establishment 23–5, 88–9, 91–2, 105, 165, 236
normative 2, 9, 16, 18–19, 31, 44, 48, 72–4, 79, 81–2, 108, 163, 175, 179, 187, 192, 224
Norway 63, 102

obedience 16, 18, 53
objectivity 12–13, 38, 48, 51, 75, 78, 108, 110, 136–8, 142, 145, 152, 154, 168, 170, 176–7, 208, 214, 216, 237–40
Ockham 76
offering 178
Oliva 98
ontological 16–17, 75, 177, 184, 215
Oppenheim 112, 125
Organization of Islamic Conference 124, 127

Pakistan 54, 93–9
Palestine 209
paradox of constitutionalism 72, 191, 193, 217
parent 14, 90, 117–9, 132, 135–9, 141, 144–7, 168, 190
parliament 94, 96, 183, 197
parliamentary sovereignty 77, 80
pastor 90
patriotism 93, 156, 188
Peté 150
Peters 41, 74
Phillips 210
philosophy 10, 14–15, 19–23, 29, 36, 48, 51, 83, 112, 119, 136–7, 140, 145, 147, 190, 193, 205–6, 211, 214, 234, 237
Pierard 20
plebiscite 196

pluralism 1–5, 13, 15, 23, 26, 29, 34, 36, 40, 45, 48, 50–51, 54, 61, 76, 80, 83, 88, 102–5, 109–10, 112, 114, 120, 144, 147, 157, 172, 175–6, 178, 181, 183, 185, 187, 189, 191, 193, 195, 197, 199–205, 207, 209, 211–12, 215–16, 220–21, 223–5, 227–31, 233–5, 237–9
Pohlmann 189
Poland 127, 147
political studies 181
politics 1, 3, 7, 12, 19, 22, 33–6, 43–4, 47–8, 50, 53–7, 61–2, 65–6, 68–9, 70–76, 78–80, 89, 91–9, 102–4, 108–9, 111, 116–17, 121–2, 125–6, 142, 145, 166, 175, 181, 183–5, 187, 190, 192–4, 196, 198, 201, 204–7, 209, 212, 214, 216, 218–20, 224, 227–8, 231, 234, 237
Pollis 51
polygamy 166
Pope 20, 97, 126, 210
popular sovereignty 54, 58, 64–5, 182, 184, 197
popular will 198
population 2–3, 30, 34, 45, 54, 102, 104–7, 126, 130, 174, 176, 181, 183, 185, 187–8, 190, 200, 209, 215, 221, 225, 231, 239
post-liberal 26, 235
post-secular 3, 26, 147, 149, 181, 209, 219, 223, 225, 227–9, 231, 233, 235, 237, 239
pouvoir constituant 181, 194–7, 225
praktische Konkordanz 145, 151, 173, 222
prayer 96, 105–6, 134, 143, 152–3, 157
preferentialism 2, 230–31, 233
prejudice 46, 208, 214, 221, 238, 240
priest 90, 153, 196
prison 23, 153–5
private 19, 21, 59, 97–8, 103, 109, 116, 122, 127, 139, 142, 158, 162, 170–71, 175, 187, 202, 204, 206, 219–20, 222, 228, 233
privatisation 201

procedure 16, 55, 60, 64, 68–9, 79, 81–3, 115, 122, 141, 151, 155–6, 168, 187–8, 192, 197, 235
proselytism 95, 123, 126, 225
Protestantism 21, 91, 154, 136, 204
Przeworski 62
public disturbance 131, 152, 157
public law 36, 38
public order 63, 82, 92–3, 95, 100, 116, 122, 228, 235
  see also social order
public school 136, 146, 149
  see also school
public sphere 97, 140, 164, 170, 217, 228, 231, 235

Quakers 103
Quebec 136–9, 142

rabbi 90
Raday 230
Ramcharan 47
Randall 101
Rastafarianism 104, 148, 155, 166
rational 16, 22,
rationalism 1, 10, 16, 19, 22, 24, 83, 158–9, 176, 191, 208, 214, 231–4
Rautenbach 150
Ravitch 143, 232, 236
Rawls 12, 27, 29, 193, 204–5, 207, 233
reason 10–17, 19, 26, 35, 52, 64, 71, 83, 93, 95, 105, 160, 171, 173, 175–6, 179, 181, 184, 190–91, 196, 202, 205–7, 210, 221, 224–5, 227–8, 230, 232, 239
reasonable 16, 52, 93, 148, 152, 154, 157, 166, 171, 199, 213, 225, 229–30
Rechtsstaat 68, 76–8, 81–2, 214
Rechtsstaatlichkeit 68
reciprocity 28–9, 83, 217, 226, 236, 240
Reder 211
referendum 101, 106, 196
Reformation 18, 20, 76, 97–8, 203–4
Reformed 160
refugees 104–5, 114, 149
Reisman 1, 54
relativism 136

religion
religiosity 1, 113, 201, 204, 207, 211, 216, 229, 231, 235, 237
religious affiliation 98, 168, 190
religious conviction 15, 18, 76, 143, 158, 207, 218
religious disputes 45, 127, 129, 131, 172, 174
religious dress 106, 131, 169, 200–201
  see also burkini, burqua, clothing, dress, headscarf, jewellery, religious dress
religious education 100, 133, 135, 143, 146, 154, 159–60
religious freedom 3, 10, 13, 18, 21, 94–5, 98, 100, 103, 106, 108–10, 115, 117, 129–31, 138, 140, 147–9, 152, 154, 158, 161–2, 166, 168, 177, 201, 218, 220, 222, 226–7, 231
religious persecution 114, 149
religious pluralism 1–5, 13, 26, 29, 34, 36, 45, 48, 50–51, 54, 76, 80, 83, 88, 103–5, 109–10, 112, 114, 120, 147, 175, 178, 181, 183, 185, 187, 189, 191, 193, 195, 197, 199–205, 207, 209, 211–12, 215–16, 220–21, 223, 225, 227–9, 231, 233–5, 237–9
religious symbols 2, 24, 101, 131–2, 146, 164, 169–71, 176, 188, 201, 208–9, 238
  see also crucifix, religious dress
reverence 99–100, 207
revolution 1, 20, 32, 36, 54, 67, 80, 90, 127, 156
rites 10, 94, 167
Ritsert 28
ritual
  ritual slaughtering 150–51
  rituals 10–11, 14, 18, 53, 104, 106, 113, 150–52, 166, 168
Roberts 42
Robinson 18, 119
Roman Catholic
  see Catholic

Rome 9–10, 14, 20, 34, 67, 97, 102, 133
Rommen 20
Rousseau 22, 192–3, 195
rule of law 29, 38, 48, 53–4, 55–7, 69, 75–8, 81–3, 89, 107–8, 148, 214, 240
Russia 104

Sabbath 157, 164
  see also Sunday
Sachs 14, 158
Sadurski 80
Sajó 59
Sallot 80
Samuel 24
Sarlet 67
Saudi Arabia 54, 105
Savez 154
Scepticism 9, 15, 71, 157, 207, 232
Scheinin 63
Schilder 153
Schilling 210
Schmidt 211
Schmitt 71, 184
scholarly 1, 15, 17, 21, 32–3, 36, 43, 48, 52, 56, 80, 101, 112–14, 125, 137, 175, 181, 189–90, 199, 223, 237
scholars 3, 41, 43, 50, 74, 191, 223
school 1, 15, 24, 32, 38, 47, 74–5, 90–91, 100, 132–7, 139, 143–7, 149, 154, 158–9, 161, 171–2
  see also public school
Schuller 210
Schwöbel 71–2
science 1, 7, 10, 12, 15, 17, 22, 31–2, 34–5, 73, 93, 110–11, 113, 120, 143, 169, 187, 190, 210, 215, 223–4
Scientology 168–9
Scotland 98
sectarian 134–5, 158, 231
secular
  secular neutrality 4, 36, 46, 140, 204, 216–17, 235, 237
  secular state 94, 109–10, 208, 220–21, 226, 239

secularism 3, 9, 12–14, 17, 19, 21–2, 24–8, 36, 39, 46, 48, 87–91, 94, 96, 104, 108–10, 119, 126, 134–41, 143, 145–50, 149, 158–60, 165, 169–70, 175–7, 181, 199, 201–4, 206–9, 211–12, 214–34, 237–9
secularity 28, 89–90, 92, 108–10, 126, 133, 136, 141, 201–3, 226, 237
secularization 25, 61, 103, 108, 133–4, 147, 200, 202–3, 207, 211
Segerdal 169
Sen 29
Senate 90, 183
separation of powers 44, 63, 65, 69, 78–9, 108
Seventh Day Adventist Church 157
sexual orientation 162–3
Shi'ite 54, 103
Shintoism 104
Sieyès 196
Sikh 103, 147
Sirkku 206
Slotte 12–13, 204, 212
Smit 150
Smith 38, 97–8, 105, 189
social contract 4, 22, 181–5, 192–5, 205, 214, 225
social order 13, 88, 109, 211, 213–15, 217
social peace 17, 115, 179, 239–40
Socialism 43, 59, 88, 93
socio-economic 61, 102
sociology 7, 20, 35, 91, 147, 190, 199, 219, 231
Solberg 165
South Africa 14, 37, 39, 62, 77–8, 80, 108, 119, 147, 150, 152, 154–5, 158, 162, 165–6, 181, 183, 197, 217, 228
sovereign 22, 113, 186, 192–3, 195
sovereign state 13, 25, 37, 40, 43, 49, 58, 73, 182, 185–7, 215
sovereigntists 41, 185
sovereignty 4, 17, 24, 35, 42, 44, 49, 54, 58–9, 64–5, 73, 77, 80, 82, 164,

181–2, 184–7, 193–4, 196–7, 206, 215, 225, 229
Soviet Union 56, 60
Spadijer 101
spiritual 20–22, 93, 96, 100, 132, 136, 140, 142, 144, 161, 168–9, 173, 202–3
spiritualism 104
spirituality 113, 219
Spiro 189
Sri Lanka 54
Staatskirchenrecht 100
Stark 193
state 1–5, 7, 9–11, 13–17, 19–30, 32–46, 48–50, 53–5, 57–61, 63–83, 85, 87–96, 98–115, 117–21, 124–50, 153–67, 169–83, 185–221, 224–34, 236–40
statehood 9, 39, 67, 71, 103, 133, 181–5, 187–91, 193, 195, 197, 199, 201, 203, 205, 207, 209, 211, 213, 226
statism 73
Stern 68–9
subjectivity 3, 10–11, 47, 114, 119, 141–2, 149, 187, 198–9, 215, 222, 227, 237–9
subvention 131, 159–60, 205
Sufi 126
Sumerians 133
Sunday 100, 134, 161, 164–5
  see also Sabbath
Sunni 54, 89, 94, 103
Sweden 63, 149–50
Switzerland 67, 101, 106, 156, 171
symbolism 146, 168, 227
syncretism 104
Syria 209

Taekema 208–9
Taiwan 219
Takemura 156
Talmudic 151
Tanzania 174
Taoism 104
Tardif 188, 202
Tawia 127

tax 93, 100, 115, 131, 159, 185
Taylor 123, 202–4, 207
teachers 119, 132, 144, 147, 162, 169–70
technology 1, 22, 34, 73, 209–10
teleological 192, 201
Temperman 20, 23, 121, 146–7, 212
Templeton 129
temporal 16, 20–22, 195, 203
terminology 9–10, 27, 77, 102, 127, 182, 190, 199
tertium comparationis 47, 51, 83
Teubner 187
theism 1, 76, 224, 143
theocracy 3, 27, 54, 109–10, 224, 226, 231
theological 15–17, 20, 53, 134, 172
Tiedemann 10–11
Tierney 9
time 20–22, 25, 34, 48, 51–2, 64–5, 67, 71, 76–7, 97, 103, 106, 126–8, 133, 142, 146, 152, 156, 170, 177, 188, 193, 198, 203, 207, 212, 215–16, 220, 225
tolerance 9, 11, 16–17, 20, 78, 91, 118, 123, 134, 143, 145, 163, 167, 170, 189, 193, 204, 231
Tom 188, 219
tradition 5, 32, 40, 63, 70, 72, 91–2, 95–6, 98, 104, 113, 115, 123, 134, 136, 139, 146, 151, 155, 164, 166, 186, 204, 211, 224
transcendental 11, 13, 16, 113, 203
transcultural 58
transnational 33, 49, 54, 73, 120, 126
Traub 209–10
travel 34, 210
Turkey 28, 89, 107, 156, 171
Turner 147–8, 219–20
two cities, two kingdoms, two swords 20, 25

Uganda 157
Ulpianus 28
Umkhosi ukweshwama 150
Unitarianism 104

United Kingdom
  Britain 37, 50, 67, 77, 97, 209
  British 37–8, 77, 98, 135, 148, 170, 183, 185, 200
  Church of England 96–8
  Crown 149, 183, 185
  England 38, 50, 96–8, 110, 143
  English 13, 15, 38, 52, 89, 92, 97–8, 102, 124, 151, 210
  labour relations 161–2
  marriages 168–9
  Queen 96, 148, 169
United Nations 79, 118, 124, 185, 188–9
United States of America
  American 31–2, 34, 50–52, 56, 58, 76, 79, 81, 104, 113, 151, 158, 165, 177, 200–202, 205, 209, 228
  First Amendment 23–5, 91, 105, 143, 171, 201, 236
  United States 20, 23–5, 32, 36, 38, 50, 64–7, 91, 114, 134, 143, 156, 169, 171, 183, 188, 199–201, 208, 210, 232
  USA 37, 51, 91–3, 105, 171, 181, 183, 219, 236
universal 13, 28, 36–7, 48–9, 51–2, 62, 65, 71–2, 76, 78, 80, 83, 87, 107, 116, 123, 125, 183–4, 186, 201, 213, 229, 232, 234, 236, 240
Universal Declaration of Human Rights (UDHR) 65, 116, 118
universalism 23, 73–4
universality 113, 149, 206
universalization 4, 44, 76, 177
university 20, 36, 91, 104, 157, 172
usage 11, 39, 95
USSR 37, 55, 67, 210

values 5, 11–12, 14, 16–17, 19, 22, 28, 37–9, 41, 49, 51, 58, 71–2, 75, 78, 89, 107–8, 111–12, 121, 134–6, 139, 141, 144–5, 148–9, 163–4, 167–8, 170, 177, 183, 186, 191, 201, 206–7, 209–10, 213, 218, 220–22, 225, 233, 236–7, 239

Van der Vyver 7, 12, 116, 121, 128
Van der Walt 184
Vattel 22, 112
Venice Commission 60
Venter 39, 52, 68, 76, 78, 83, 108, 132–3, 188–9
Ventura 220
Verfassungsstaatlichkeit 68
Vinx 70, 184–5
vocabulary 1, 10, 34, 48–9, 52, 79, 194, 224–5
Vorländer 49, 67
vote 101, 147
  see also democracy, elections, franchise
Voßkuhle 15

Walker 40, 184, 191, 193
war 3, 21, 34, 37, 43, 50–51, 57, 62, 66–7, 97, 107, 125–7, 133, 143, 146, 156, 160, 210, 219
Ward 133, 168
Wattles 28–9, 83
Webber 18
Weber 26
wedding 90
  see also marriage
Weiler 41, 50
Weltanschauung 75, 141, 145, 202
Wenzlhuemer 33, 35, 44
Western 21, 27, 29, 38, 50–51, 53–4, 57–9, 61, 63, 67, 75–6, 106, 112–3, 127, 132–3, 137, 151, 156, 170, 192, 198–200, 202–4, 208–9, 211, 213–14, 224–5, 228, 231, 234, 237
Westphalia 21–2, 40, 103
Wheaton 112
Whitlocke 50
Whitman 91–2
Wiener 74
Wieser 36
Willems 175
Wilson 148
Witte 11, 22
Witten 19, 176, 231–2
World Trade Organization 74, 185
World War II 37, 50–51, 66–7, 143

worldview 140, 211
   see also Weltanschauung
worship 9–11, 21, 94–5, 99–100, 103–4, 116, 121–2, 142, 163, 169, 173

Zafirovski 22–3
Zionism 164
Zoroastrianism 104
Zweigert 36